The India-China Opium Trade
in the Nineteenth Century

ALSO BY HUNT JANIN AND
FROM MCFARLAND

Mercenaries in Medieval and Renaissance Europe
(coauthor, with Ursula Carlson 2013)

Rising Sea Levels: An Introduction to Cause and Impact
(coauthor, and Scott A. Mandia 2012)

*Trails of Historic New Mexico: Routes Used by Indian, Spanish and
American Travelers through 1886* (coauthor, and Ursula Carlson 2010)

*Medieval Justice: Cases and Laws in France, England and
Germany, 500–1500* (2004; paperback 2009)

The University in Medieval Life, 1179–1499 (2008)

*Islamic Law: The Sharia from Muhammad's Time to
the Present* (coauthor, and André Kahlmeyer 2007)

*The Pursuit of Learning in the Islamic World,
610–2003* (2005; paperback 2006)

*Four Paths to Jerusalem: Jewish, Christian, Muslim, and Secular
Pilgrimages, 1000 BCE to 2001 CE* (2002; paperback 2006)

*Fort Bridger, Wyoming: Trading Post for Indians, Mountain
Men and Westward Migrants* (2001; paperback 2006)

*Claiming the American Wilderness: International Rivalry in
the Trans-Mississippi West, 1528–1803* (2006)

The India-China Opium Trade in the Nineteenth Century

Hunt Janin

McFarland & Company, Inc., Publishers
Jefferson, North Carolina

The present work is a reprint of the library bound edition of
The India-China Opium Trade in the Nineteenth Century,
first published in 1999 by McFarland.

LIBRARY OF CONGRESS CATALOGUING-IN-PUBLICATION DATA

Janin, Hunt, 1940–
    The India-China opium trade in the nineteenth century / Hunt Janin.
       p.   cm.
    Includes bibliographical references and index.

    ISBN 978-0-7864-9357-9
    softcover : acid free paper ∞

    1. Opium trade — India — History — 19th century.
    2. Opium trade — China — History — 19th century.
    3. India — Economic conditions — 19th century.
    4. China — Economic conditions — 19th century.
    5. China — History — Opium War, 1840–1842.   I. Title.
II. Title: India-China opium trade in the 19th century.
HV5816.J357   2014
382'.41375 — dc21   99-40906

BRITISH LIBRARY CATALOGUING DATA ARE AVAILABLE

© 1999 Hunt Janin. All rights reserved

No part of this book may be reproduced or transmitted in any form or by any means, electronic or mechanical, including photocopying or recording, or by any information storage and retrieval system, without permission in writing from the publisher.

On the cover: illustration of two 19th century Chinese opium smokers (Dorling Kindersley RF/Thinkstock)

Manufactured in the United States of America

McFarland & Company, Inc., Publishers
  Box 611, Jefferson, North Carolina 28640
    www.mcfarlandpub.com

Contents

Preface		1
Introduction: Clearing the Decks		5
1	Running Great Risks for Great Rewards	21
2	A Stream of Wealth: Opium, India and China	31
3	The Rise of the Great Trading Houses	57
4	Ships of the Opium Trade	75
5	The Opium Wars	99
6	The Heat of Battle	119
7	Pirates of the South China Sea	131
8	Typhoons, Monsoons and Hazards to Navigation	151
9	The Twilight of the Opium Trade	169
10	Legacies of the Opium Trade	185
Appendix I: A Modern Recipe for "Country Captain"		197
Appendix II: Falcon *and Her Crew*		199
Appendix III: Antelope *and Her Crew*		205

Appendix IV: Excerpts from "The Opium War"	207
Appendix V: Selected Wade-Giles/Hanyu Pinyin Equivalents	209
Bibliography	211
Index	221

The profit upon Opium is at this time so immense,
that people are tempted to continue smuggling it,
although at a very great risk of life.

A letter of 6 August 1839 from "a Gentleman at Macao to his Friend in London," cited by Major-General R. Alexander in *The Rise and Progress of British Opium Smuggling* (1856), p. 27.

Preface

In 1857, during the early days of the second Opium War, Donald Matheson, a nephew of the cofounder of the great trading house of Jardine Matheson, described the opium trade as it was then being practiced:

> The merchants in India purchase the opium either on their own account or for the mercantile houses in China or elsewhere, and it is then shipped in fast-sailing vessels capable of carrying from 500 to 1000 chests.... On arrival in China, say, at Hong Kong, the opium is usually transferred to large receiving ships stationary in the harbor.... From these receiving ships, supplies [of opium] are forwarded in small schooners and other fast sailing craft to different points on the coast according to demand. At these coast stations there is no other trade carried on but that in opium. The drug is transferred from the small schooners to ships permanently anchored there, and the local Chinese Government makes no attempt whatever to interfere, as it is enriched by the bribes or fees of the native dealers. These dealers come off in boats to purchase the opium, bringing silver in payment; but if the station be in the outer anchorage of one of the free ports [the treaty ports established after the first Opium War] ... the sale is usually made on shore, in exchange for silver or Chinese produce, and an order given on the ship for the delivery of the quantity sold.[1]

The book you have in your hands is a primer on ships and men of the opium trade and on the hazards associated with this business. If you

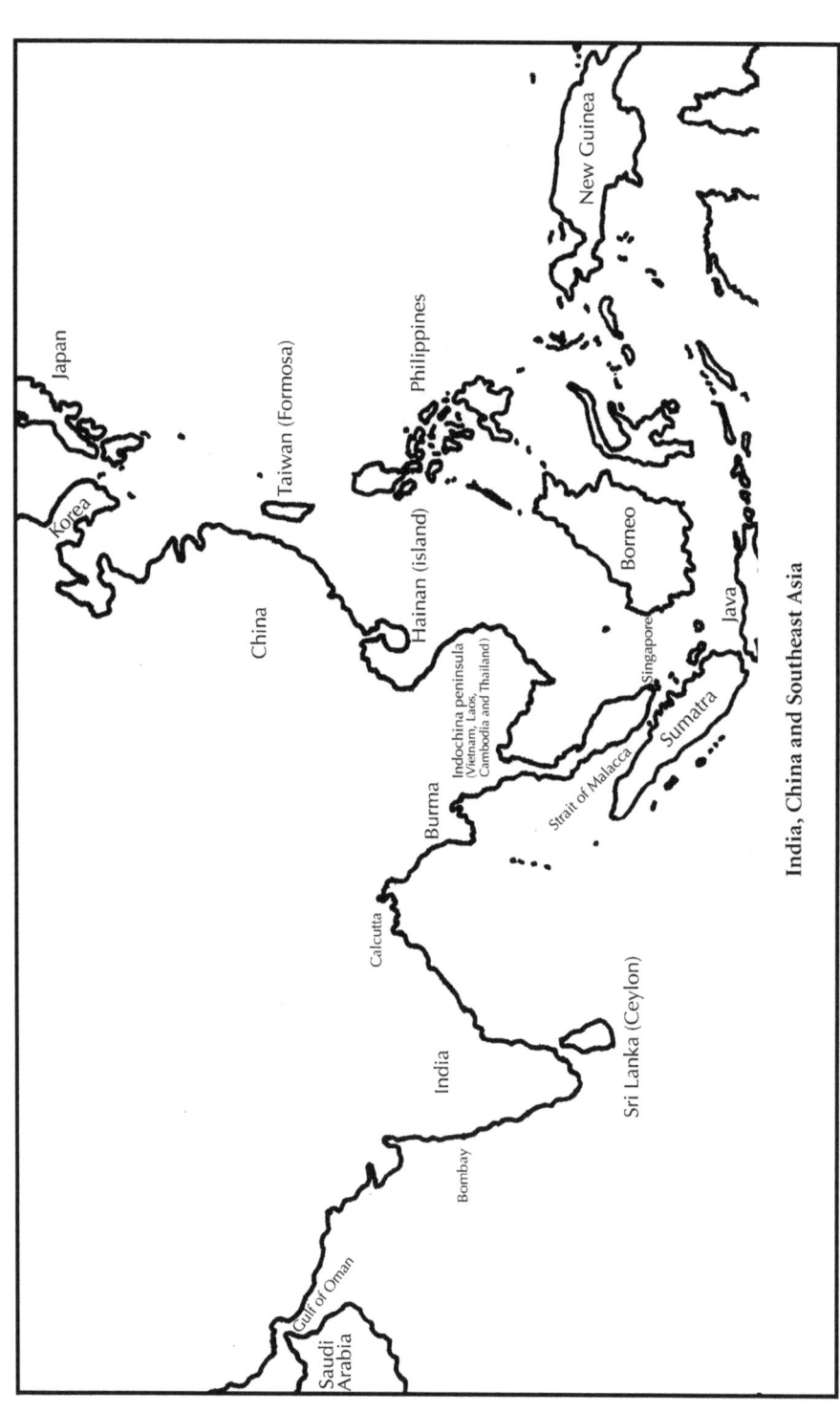

had lived in the nineteenth century and wanted to run opium from Bombay or Calcutta through the Strait of Malacca up to the Canton estuary, or if you decided to carry it north from Canton to one of the small ports along the east coast of China, much of the information presented here would have been useful indeed. This book is, I believe, the broadest general survey of the opium trade undertaken since 1933, when the British mariner Basil Lubbock (1876–1944), the most prolific writer about the latter days of sail, published *The Opium Clippers*, which is still in print.[2]

The present work, however, tries to go beyond Lubbock. It sets the opium trade in a broader nautical and historical context. It discusses political and economic matters in India and China that Lubbock touched on only in passing or not at all. It uses original sources, such as the Jardine Matheson archives, that were not available to Lubbock. And finally, it looks at the historical consequences of the opium trade and at its political legacies for the twenty-first century.

At the same time, this book is supposed to be what nineteenth century ships' officers would have called *a rattlin' good yarn*. It is a work for the general reader rather than for the scholar or naval historian. If a more academic discussion is needed, the reader should consult the books of Hosea Ballou Morse, the British Commissioner of Customs and Statistical Secretary who spent 33 years in China. His works include *The Trade and Administrative Structure of the Chinese Empire* (1908); the two-volume *International Relations of the Chinese Empire* (1910); and the five-volume *Chronicles of the East India Company Trading to China, 1635–1834* (1926). A more concise and equally scholarly account is David Edward Owen's *British Opium Policy in China and India* (1934).

Relying on Firsthand Accounts

I have tried to recapture the danger, adventure and romance of the opium trade by letting the historical participants speak for themselves. This is the reason for the unusual number of long, direct quotes in this book. It would have been easy enough to paraphrase them, but in their original form they convey the full flavor of their times much better than any modern paraphrase possibly could. These quotes are also useful because most of the nineteenth-century sources from which they are taken are long out of print now or were never published at all. Many of these primary and secondary sources are available only at such specialized institutions in the United Kingdom as the British Library in London, the National Maritime Museum in Greenwich and the Jardine Matheson archives at Cambridge University. Using direct quotes seemed the best way to introduce readers to these remarkable but relatively inaccessible documents.

Thanks and Responsibility

I owe a great deal of thanks to British historian Nicki Faircloth, who had the initial idea for this book and who wrote some of the text. Through her it was possible to get access to the Jardine Matheson archives, where the staff of the Cambridge University Library, especially John Wells in the Department of Manuscripts, was exceptionally knowledgeable and helpful. I would also like to thank Jeremy Brown, Director of Matheson & Co. in London, for permission to use the archives and for helping me obtain the illustrations in this book.

Professor Thomas N. Layton, author of *The Voyage of the "Frolic": New England Merchants and the Opium Trade*, read an early draft of this book and offered trenchant criticisms, as did Dr. Jacques M. Downs, author of *The Golden Ghetto: The American Commercial Community at Canton and the Shaping of American China Policy, 1784–1844*. Some of the Wade-Giles/Hanyu pinyin equivalents listed in Appendix V have been taken from Downs's book. Others were kindly provided by a scholar in China, Dr. Ching May-bo. I must also thank Nanda Purcell for her research into original documents on the tea trade and Petronella van Gorkom for her editorial suggestions. Any factual errors or misjudgments remaining in this book are my responsibility alone.

Hunt Janin
St. Urcisse, France
1999

Notes

1. Donald Matheson, *What Is the Opium Trade*, pp. 7–8.
2. *The Opium Clippers* and 13 other books by Basil Lubbock are still published by the venerable Scottish firm of Brown, Son and Ferguson in Glasgow.

Introduction: Clearing the Decks

When a ship was preparing for combat or some other demanding activity, the captain's first job was to clear the decks of anything that might get in the way of the work ahead. This is a good approach for us to adopt here, so a few comments on the legality and morality of the opium trade, on nautical matters, on silver currencies and on the spelling of Chinese words may be useful.

Was the Opium Trade Illegal or Immoral?

This question is best answered in the light of legal and moral standards prevailing at the time. In the mid-nineteenth century the answers depended on one's point of view. From the Chinese government's point of view, the trade was illegal for 129 years—from 1729, when the first Imperial antiopium edict was issued, until 1858, when during negotiations with the British in the course of the second Opium War the Chinese agreed to a tariff on imported opium and thus quietly legalized the trade.

This tariff was imposed for good reasons. China had lost the first Opium War with the British and in 1858 was in the process of losing a second war. The ruling dynasty had been unable to resist the tide of

Western encroachments, of which the opium trade was the most dramatic example. The British themselves wanted to put the opium trade on a legal basis. The Chinese government, unable to stop it, decided to use it to generate income, which was needed because China's revenues had fallen off sharply due to the Taiping Rebellion of 1850–1864, which will be discussed later. Thus a modest tariff on imported opium was an attractive proposition to both the British and the Chinese. This measure worked well: after it had been legalized, the trade flourished, making money for Chinese and foreigners alike until finally peaking in the 1870s and going into a slow decline thereafter.[1]

Long before the trade was legalized, however, because of the great amount of money they could make from it by *cumshaw* (literally, "gold sand," i.e., a present, a tip or a bribe) or by fees, commissions and the sale of opium itself, Chinese officials of all ranks openly aided and abetted the foreign traders. A contemporary British writer tells us that before Imperial Commissioner Lin's seizure of British opium in 1839, "boats belonging to the [Chinese government's] Custom House engaged in the traffic. The governor of Canton himself, Tang by name, employed his own boat to fetch it; and so publicly and undisguisedly was the traffic carried on, that a stipulated sum was paid to the [customs] officers for every chest landed, precisely as if it had been a bale of cotton or a box of glass."[2]

Few of the Chinese working in the opium trade questioned the morality of their own actions, chiefly because the trade was so lucrative but also because they were the products of a Confucian culture, which was based on different criteria from the Judeo-Christian culture of the West. In 1836 and 1837, for example, the governor-general in Canton mounted a token campaign against opium only as a duty and as a gesture to please the emperor, not as a crusade based on any moral principles.[3]

At the same time, very few of the Western traders in China were prepared to agree, publicly, with the proposition that the opium trade was illegal or immoral.[4] They were aware of the Chinese government's point of view, but as one British observer pointed out in 1836, "The laws of the empire prohibit the introduction or sale of opium; *yet this forms the principal part of Imports, and to an extent which can scarcely be matched in any one article of consumption in any other part of the world.*"[5]

Because the trade did not violate any of their own national laws, most Westerners felt free to engage in it. Indeed, for 144 years (from 1773 to 1917) it was the official policy of the British government to grow opium in India for sale in China but to disavow and abstain from the trade itself. The traders saw that all the Chinese men and women directly or indirectly involved in this business wanted it to continue — the mandarins, lesser officials, linguists (translators), merchants, money changers, pilots, seamen, smugglers, opium smokers, waterborne prostitutes and even the pirates (always ready to attack a weakly manned opium clipper).[6] Opportunistic Westerners also discovered that because of the weakness and corruption of the Chinese government they could usually ignore its antiopium edicts with impunity.

The Westerners justified their trade on religious grounds as well. A Prussian missionary, the Reverend Karl Gützlaff, was remarkably fluent in Chinese coastal dialects. He acted as an interpreter for the opium traders in return for the opportunity to distribute his religious tracts, in Chinese, along the coast. By the same token, James Innes, variously described as "a devout, Bible-trading Scot" or as a pious fraud, sold opium and distributed tracts, too.[7] An anonymous British author in 1840 called his readers' attention not only to "the advantages derived to the Indian Government in the shape of a revenue [from the sale of opium] amounting to between one and two millions sterling" but also to "the great benefit accruing to myriads of human beings [in India] as a consequence of the firm administration of a Christian [British] Government in the East, which might be greatly weakened were this source of wealth cut off or diminished."[8]

Prior to the beginning of the first Opium War in 1839, only one of the three or four major American companies doing business in Canton believed the opium trade was morally wrong and refused to have anything to do with it. This was Olyphant and Co. Its righteous attitude, coupled with its friendliness to missionaries, soon won it the nickname of "Zion's Corner." The famous American opium captain Robert Bennet Forbes would joke in 1839 that the head of Olyphant and Co. was "the only Godly man in China."[9] However, a second American firm, Wetmore and Co., did abandon the trade during the first Opium War and never resumed it.

A Few Nautical Explanations

Because opium could be carried only under sail until the advent of the steamers in the 1850s, it is important to be familiar with some nineteenth-century nautical terminology and with the hardships and dangers of life aboard square-riggers and other ships.

SAILS AND SAILING VESSELS[10]

Square-rigged sails, such as courses and topsails, hung down from the yards (horizontal spars, or poles, hung from the masts) with their foot across the line of the ship's keel. The foot is the lower edge of a sail; the head is its upper edge. To reef these sails (that is, reduce their area by taking in their head), seamen had to work high aloft in the rigging, standing on slippery footropes and leaning out over equally slippery yards.[11] The old adage "One hand for the ship and one hand for yourself" did not prevent many men from toppling out of the rigging onto the deck or into the sea. Either accident was likely to be fatal, the latter especially so in a storm because a ship's boat could not be lowered when the sea was high and the ship herself could not come about quickly enough to pick up a man before he drowned.

Fore-and-aft sails, such as jibs and spankers, were set on gaffs (spars rising aft from the mast to support the head, or top, of the sail) or on stays (strong ropes or wires), their foot running along the line of the keel. The foot was often attached to a long horizontal spar known as a boom. Fore-and-aft sails were reefed by taking in their foot. Because they had no yards these sails could be worked more easily from the deck.

Studding sails were light sails set outside the square sails on booms rigged for that purpose.

Under ideal conditions, a full-rigged ship (see the definitions below) could, if it were big enough, set as many as 36 different sails at the same time. Such a cloud of canvas (over 65,000 square feet in the biggest and last of the square-riggers in the 1890s) was in practice rarely used. When it was, the ship would be entirely covered above its decks by the sails, from the end of the bowsprit, where a jib-o'-jib could be set outside the flying jib, to the top of the mainmast, where a small square-rigged sail known as a moonsail could be set above the royal sail when the ship was ghosting along (barely making headway) under light airs (gentle breezes). At the same time, studding sails would be rigged and a big fore-and-aft spanker would almost overhang the sternpost. Each sail and each bit of rigging had its own name (e.g., fore topgallant studding sail or upper fore topsail buntlines), and each crewman literally had to learn the ropes so he could instantly help raise, trim (adjust), reef or lower the sails day or night and in all weathers.[12]

A ship was a vessel with at least three masts, all square-rigged. A bark (also spelled *barque*) was a three-masted vessel with the mizzenmast (rear mast) rigged fore and aft and the fore and mainmasts square-rigged. Although there was at least one full-rigged ship in the opium trade in the 1830s, most of the vessels were small brigs or schooners. A brig was a vessel with two masts, both square-rigged. A variation on this theme was the brigantine, whose mainmast also carried small square sails aloft. A schooner had at least two masts, one or both of which consisted of a short topmast fitted to a thicker and longer lower mast. Both these masts were gaff-rigged fore and aft.

In the mid-nineteenth century there were many kinds of schooners afloat. Some of the fastest vessels in the opium trade were the two-masted pilot boat schooners developed in New York and other east coast ports of the United States in the 1830s. These were modeled after the American privateers that attacked British merchantmen during the war between the United States and Britain from 1812 to 1815. Pilot boat schooners had big jibs and topmasts on their aft but not on their foremasts. Their hulls were usually painted black and were sheathed with copper to protect them from marine growth. In a gale these handy vessels could lie to (that is, remain more or less in the same spot at sea) under a close-reefed foresail alone. The racing schooner *America*, winner in 1851 of the yachting cup later named after it, was built along pilot boat lines.

On a topsail schooner the foremast was square-rigged on top with a fore-and-aft foresail below; the mainmast was rigged fore and aft. A fore-and-aft schooner was rigged fore and aft throughout. A clipper (this a journalist's description rather than a naval architect's term) was primarily built for speed, not for carrying capacity or economy. As one writer noted in 1853, "The ships used for transporting the opium from the ports of India to China are built and fitted up expressly for this business, and are said to be among the finest vessels anywhere to be found. Most of them are constructed in the form of schooners or brigantines, with low hulls, and being adapted to cut the waves with remarkable speed, are called 'clippers,' or 'runners.'"[13]

A clipper had sharp (i.e., narrow) forward-raking bows, with its masts and stern post raked aft. As early as 1834, the *Canton Register*, a shipping journal published in China, referred to the remarkable "deeds of speed" accomplished by the opium clippers, which were some of the loveliest ships ever built.[14] As mentioned above, these clippers were generally small brigs and schooners, perhaps 54 to 114 feet long, not big ships like the later China tea clippers. American opium schooners combined elements of the designs of the extreme Baltimore clippers of the 1830s and the east coast pilot boats.[15] Many of them had long, low hulls and the handsome "Baltimore clipper bow"—a raked and overhanging bow that provided a sharp entry into the water.

A cutter was a small, fast vessel up to 32 feet long, manned by as many as 20 men and equipped with oars, one or two masts and sometimes armed with swivel guns and cannonades. Cutters were used to ferry passengers and supplies from one ship to another or ashore, to tend a ship's anchors, to explore shallow waters or, more rarely, to run opium.

A sloop was a vessel, usually a small one, with only one mast, always rigged fore and aft. A lorcha was a light sailing vessel that was something of a cross between East and West: Chinese rigging made it an easy vessel for Chinese crews to handle, and a European hull made it fast and maneuverable. A hulk was an old ship, often dismasted, that could be used to store opium on the China coast, where it was known as a receiving ship.

HMS means His or Her Majesty's Ship. *HM* refers to a British naval vessel that was smaller than a full-rigged ship, such as HM cutter *Louisa*. *RN* stands for the Royal Navy. Ships' tonnages cited in this book may not be comparable because three different tonnage measurements were used by the British between 1775 and 1875: "Old Measurement" until 1835, "New Measurement" until 1854 and after that the system specified by the Merchant Shipping Act of 1854. See the endnotes for other nautical explanations.

The Crew

Landsmen, often referred to as boys no matter what their age, were green (inexperienced) hands and did the less-demanding work on a sailing vessel. If they applied themselves they could become ordinary seamen and would learn how to maintain the running rigging (ropes that were pulled through blocks, such as braces and halyards) and the standing rigging (which was made fast and did not move, such as stays and shrouds) and how to work aloft safely.

The next step up the nautical ladder was the able seaman (also called an able-bodied seaman or simply A.B.), who was a man who could hand, reef, steer and heave the lead. This meant he could gather a sail into a compact roll and bind it securely to a spar (hand it); reduce the area of a sail (reef it); keep the vessel on course by moving her rudder by means of a spoked wooden wheel (steer her); and throw overboard (heave) a lead weight attached to a line marked to indicate the depth of the water immediately under the ship. This depth was known as a sounding. The lead weight sometimes had a wax base that would pick up a small sample of the bottom (mud, sand, etc.), which would give clues to the ship's location.[16]

THE VOICE FROM THE FO'C'SLE

Before the middle of the nineteenth century, most of the writing about the sea was produced by or for captains, merchant or naval officers, or rich passengers. Almost nothing was written about the nameless and often illiterate men of many nationalities who shipped "before the mast" as common seamen, working under appalling conditions and living in the dark, cramped, forward area of the vessel under the deck known as the fo'c'sle (forecastle).

One of the first writers to try to correct this imbalance was Richard Henry Dana, whose experiences in the brig *Pilgrim* and the ship *Alert* are reflected in his famous *Two Years Before the Mast* (1840). Another author with hands-on experience afloat was Herman Melville, who had been a merchant seaman in *St. Lawrence*, a whaler aboard *Acushnet* and an ordinary seaman in the man-of-war frigate *United States*. Melville acknowledged his literary debt to Dana but went on to surpass him in *Moby Dick* (1851), which invests the tedious and bloody business of hunting whales with heroic and mythic overtones.

Toward the end of the nineteenth century, Joseph Conrad, who had first sailed to England as a common seaman in 1878 and later earned a Master Mariner's (captain's) Certificate in 1886, wrote eloquently about the lot of merchant seamen. In *The Sea-Wolf* (1904), Jack London, who had been an oyster pirate, sealer and a participant in the Klondike gold rush, showed what life afloat could be like under a demonic captain.

A few square-rigged three-masted ships from other nineteenth century maritime trades have survived as floating museums and can still be seen today. The 314-ton American whaler *Charles W. Morgan*, which was launched in 1841 and continued whaling until 1924, is now on display at Mystic Seaport in Connecticut. The 963-ton British tea clipper *Cutty*

Sark, built in 1869, made its last commercial voyage in 1935 and is now preserved at the National Maritime Museum in Greenwich, United Kingdom. The big 1862-ton Pacific Coast salmon carrier *Balclutha*, built in 1886, was retired from service in 1932 and is now berthed near the Maritime Museum in San Francisco, California. But, sadly, there are no opium clippers left anywhere in the world today, and the opium trade itself never had a Dana, a Melville, a Conrad or a London.

Some of the few "I-was-there" accounts of the opium trade that still survive are cited in this book. In his *China Clippers* (1919), Basil Lubbock also quoted from two nineteenth-century sources that discussed, albeit briefly, the *men* as well as the officers of opium clippers; these citations are reproduced here in Appendices II and III. However, it is only by drawing on contemporary accounts of *other kinds of shipping* in the mid-nineteenth century that we can make some educated guesses about the men in the opium trade, who must have been, in Conrad's words, "hard to manage, but easy to inspire; voiceless men … as good a crowd as ever fisted with wild cries the beating canvas of a heavy foresail; or tossing aloft, invisible in the night, gave back yell for yell to a westerly gale."[17]

The first guess is that when contrasted with other kinds of merchant shipping around the world, which employed large numbers of seamen, relatively few men served in the opium ships. It is true that when opium clippers were in waters where pirates were a threat they could be strongly manned despite their small size. The American-built clipper *Ariel* carried as many as 12 officers and a crew of 42 seamen; in addition it also had petty officers (boatswains), boatswains' mates, stewards and cooks.[18] The 12-gun opium clipper *Lady Grant*, which carried 77 chests of opium from Singapore to China in 1839, had 55 men aboard.[19] And a little Boston-built opium runner, the pilot boat schooner *Gazelle*, had a crew of 80 men and officers.[20] Vessels of the British Navy were well manned, too: the 80-foot HM schooner *Spider*, for example, carried up to 50 men.[21]

So many hands were not needed simply to work a small ship: the clipper-brig *Antelope* had a complement of only 17 seamen, not counting the captain and one or two mates, and Dana's brig *Pilgrim* got along with 15 men, four of whom were landsmen or boys.[22] On its last, ill-starred voyage, from Hong Kong to San Francisco, the former opium clipper *Frolic* carried a total of 26 officers and men. Another vessel in the China trade, *Ewan*, also carried 26 men.[23]

If we therefore take the American vessel *Citizen* as an example of a ship bringing a valuable cargo to China — with a crew of 32 men and boys, two officers and her captain, it carried 350,000 Spanish silver dollars to the opium-trading island of Lintin in the Canton estuary[24] — it would seem that 35 men would have been enough to handle a ship and at the same time be ready to beat off pirate attacks. In his Register of the Opium Fleet, Basil Lubbock estimated that during the peak years of carrying opium under sail (1830–1850) the fleet never consisted of more than 100 vessels.[25] This figure suggests that given a theoretical complement of 35 men per ship and making the unrealistic assumption that every ship was always fully manned and was always engaged in carrying opium or other cargoes, a maximum of about 3,500 men were probably on active duty in the opium fleet at one time.[26]

A second guess is that ships in the opium trade had multinational or multiethnic crews. In 1848 the American opium clipper *Frolic* carried two American or English officers, a carpenter and a cook (the latter might be a Westerner or a Chinese), a Chinese servant to look after the needs of the officers, and 14 to 16 native seamen.[27] Most of the officers in the opium trade were Englishmen or Americans, but there were European officers as well. In 1830 the Portuguese ships *Don Manuel* and *Letitia*, the Danish brig *Dansborg* and the French vessel *La Rose* all called at Lintin.[28] The Spanish receiving ship *General Quiroga* was moored there and another Spanish ship brought goodly amounts of silver — the proceeds of opium sales — down the China coast.

Seamen in the Pacific trades could be of any nationality or race. The member of *Gazelle*'s crew who was killed in a fight with pirates was an Italian. In Melville's whaler *Pequod* the most valuable and the best-paid men (after the captain and the mates) were the three harpooners: Queequeg, from Polynesia; Tashtego, an American Indian; and Daggoo, an African. The crews of East Indiamen and opium ships included sailors from the west coast of India known as lascars, as well as Portuguese-speaking seamen from Goa, Bombay or Macao (known as Manilamen or seacunnies). These seacunnies were prized because they were good at "cunning" (i.e., conning, or steering) a ship and at heaving the lead.

A third guess is that men did not go into the opium trade for the sake of adventure but because it was a good way to make money. Melville put it whimsically in *Moby Dick* but his point was as valid for the opium trade as it was for whaling: "Having little or no money in my purse, and nothing particular to interest me on shore, I thought I would sail about a little and see the watery part of the world ... when I go to sea, I go as a simple sailor, right before the mast, plumb down into the forecastle, aloft there to the royal mast-head.[29]

Going to sea may have seemed romantic to landsmen, but sailors felt differently. In *The Sea-Farmer* Jack London tells us that his fictional Captain MacElrath did not like the sea and never had:

> He wrung his livelihood from it, and that was all the sea was, the place where he worked, as the mill, the shop, and the counting-house were the places where other men worked. Romance never sang to him her siren song, and Adventure had never shouted in his sluggish blood.... Tornadoes, hurricanes, waterspouts, and tidal waves were so many obstacles in the way of a ship on the sea or a master on the bridge — they were that to him, and nothing more.[30]

The fourth guess is that because of its physical demands and dangers, the opium trade was a job for young men. When Dana joined the crew of the brig *Pilgrim*, the oldest and best sailor on the ship was a 27-year-old Swede; the youngest boy was only 12. The officers themselves were not gray-haired elders, either: the captain was 30, the first mate 28 and the second mate 23 years old. Dana himself was 19.[31]

Finally, it is also safe to guess that the officers kept the men very busy. As Dana puts it, "Six days shalt thou labor and do all thou art able / And on the seventh — holystone (sand) the decks and scrape the cable (remove rust from the chain cable, which was attached to the anchor)."[32] Although the amount of spit and polish needed afloat varied with each opium captain, most took pride in having a well-maintained vessel that was kept "shipshape and Bristol fashion." This goal was achievable because shipboard discipline demanded that when a man was on deck (except on Sunday), he had to be working at something — at scraping the cable or picking oakum (made from old ropes and used for recaulking the planks of the ship) if there was nothing else to be done.

In fact there rarely was a shortage of chores because nineteenth-century seamen had to

> — steer the ship, day and night, keeping her under control even during typhoons. This was a job only for A.B.s or seacunnies because careless steering in heavy seas could easily result in a vessel being caught aback (that is, with the wind pressing the square-rigged sails against the mast rather than filling them from behind; this tended to drive the ship

backward) or, even worse, broaching-to (falling off into the trough of a sea, where the ship was temporarily unmanageable).
— go aloft in the rigging in all weathers to fist (handle quickly) the heavy square-rigged sails, which had to be bent (attached to a yard), reefed or furled (rolled up).
— stand watches and be ready to turn out in the middle of the night if all hands were called on deck because a storm was coming up.³³
— adjust and maintain all the rigging. This involved coiling the running rigging and setting up (tightening) the standing rigging; taking off, putting on and repairing the chafing gear (twine or cord wrapped around rigging or spars to prevent excessive wear) and making the chafing gear itself by picking apart old ropes and twisting their yarns together.
— keep the rest of the ship in good order by tarring the rigging, slushing down (greasing) the masts and sheets (the ropes used to set the sails); cleaning and polishing the guns (the ship's cannons); holystoning, scrubbing and swabbing (mopping) the decks; and oiling, varnishing or painting other parts of the ship as required.
— wash, mend and sometimes make their own clothing.

THE FIRST MATE

An ambitious A.B. could aspire to become a *boatswain* (abbreviated to bo's'n) or even a *mate* (an officer). Because the captain often held himself aloof from the crew to preserve the dignity of his command, he relied on the first, or chief, mate (the senior mate, often known simply as *the mate*) to carry out his orders. This man was a key figure in every ship. Seeing that the crew were fully employed was part of his job. The chief mate of an American clipper ship once joked that his job required him to be "the general manager, sailing master, official log-keeper, work-creator and sleep-destroyer."³⁴ Most sailors liked to work under a fair but firm mate rather than under an affable weakling. Conrad's fictional mate, Mr. Baker, was popular with the crew of the *Narcissus* because he did his own job well and kept others at their jobs, too. Mr. Baker never shied away from using abusive language if the need arose: the men relished the fact that "on a fitting occasion the mate could 'jump down a fellow's throat in a reg'lar Western [Pacific] Ocean style.'"³⁵

American humorist Mark Twain was a pilot on a Mississippi River steamboat from 1857 to 1861 and wrote an exaggerated account of how a mate would order his men about. If the mate wanted the gangplank on a ship moved forward a bit, he would not ask politely, "James or William, one of you push that plank forward, please," but would bellow out:

Here, now, start that gang-plank for'ard! Lively, now! *What* 're you about. Snatch it! *snatch* it! There! there! Aft again! aft again! Don't you hear me? Dash it to dash! are you going to *sleep* over it? *'Vast* [avast, i.e., stop] heaving. 'Vast heaving, I tell you! Going to heave it clear astern? WHERE're you going with that barrel! *for'ard* with it 'fore I make you swallow it, you dash-dash-dash-*dashed* split between a tired mud-turtle and a crippled hearse-horse![36]

Dana makes the same point in more restrained language. "With a voice like a young lion," the chief mate of the clipper *Alert* was "hallooing and bawling, in all directions, making everything fly, and at the same time, doing everything well."[37] Not surprisingly, a good first mate was usually promoted to captain.

A Note on Silver Currencies

In addition to *specie* (silver coins and silver or gold ingots), several different kinds of silver dollars were in circulation in China during the nineteenth century: the Carolus dollar, which was minted in Spain and Mexico from 1759 to 1808 and was in widespread use in China before 1848; the Mexican dollar, introduced shortly after Mexican independence in 1821; and the special American "trade dollar," which was not introduced until about 1878, although American ships were bringing silver dollars from North and South America long before that.[38] The Mexican dollar was readily accepted in Canton, but the Carolus dollar remained the sole currency in Shanghai and the Yangtze valley, as well as for foreign banks and merchants, imports and exports and exchange rates quotations. It was also the preferred currency in Canton itself, commanding a 10 to 15 percent premium above its silver content.

In the nineteenth-century sources it is rarely clear what kind of "dollar" is being discussed; the relative values of all these dollars also fluctuated over time. To get a rough idea of what a "dollar" was worth in the first half of the nineteenth century, we can note that

— in 1823 a member of a flatboat crew on the Mississippi River earned about $1.25 per day, plus room and board.
— a common seaman in the California hide-and-tallow trade in 1834 was making $12 a month, out of which he had to clothe himself.

- in 1841 a dollar would buy three to four "good fowls" near the Shanghai estuary and three dollars would buy a goat.
- in 1844 a fast opium clipper such as *Frolic* could be built and readied for sea for $20,000 at a shipyard in Baltimore, Maryland, where unskilled itinerant workers (or sometimes slaves) were earning $.60 a day.
- in 1846, excluding whatever personal profit he might make by trading on his own account or by partial ownership of the ships he commanded, a captain of an opium clipper drew a salary of about $150 per month plus an additional $50 for his food.[39] In contrast, a captain carrying cargo other than opium earned only about $50 a month.
- on big inland waterways such as the Mississippi River, a steamboat pilot such as Mark Twain earned between $150 and $200 a month.
- during the 1830s, the profits (from opium and other sales) of Jardine, Matheson & Co., the greatest merchant house on the China coast, may have amounted to 15 million American dollars.[40]

The Chinese frequently melted down their battered or clipped silver dollars and added some of their domestic silver to produce a valuable bullion known as *sycee* silver, which they also used, by weight, to buy opium. The Cantonese called pure silver "sycee" because in their dialect this sounded like the words for "pure silk"; if pure, the silver could be drawn out into fine threads. The *Chinese Commercial Guide* of 1856 explains:

> Treasure ... is exported from China almost entirely in the form of sycee.... The ingots are shaped like a Chinese shoe and vary in size from 50 taels' weight down to three mace, and are always stamped with the seals of the assayer and banker in evidence of their purity. The foreign coins which are brought to China gradually become reduced to small bits by stamping and clipping, which in that state finds its way to other countries, undistinguished from the native production; the export of sycee silver is almost wholly to India in exchange for opium, where it is recoined into rupees.[41]

Wherever primary or secondary sources have expressed values in terms of British pounds, Indian rupees or Chinese taels, I have let these figures stand rather than trying to convert them into "dollars." A picul was a Chinese unit of weight equal to 133⅓ pounds. Because opium balls were usually packed in chests weighing about 140 pounds (of which 120 pounds were smokable opium), piculs and chests may be considered for our purposes as being roughly equal.

The Spelling of Chinese Words

The Chinese language has characters but no Roman spelling. There are several ways, the Wade-Giles and Hanyu pinyin transcriptions among them, to represent by means of the Roman alphabet the sounds and concepts of Chinese characters. Hanyu pinyin is now the international standard but was introduced only at the end of the 1970s; before that, Wade-Giles or other systems were the norm.

This means that almost none of the references cited in the bibliography use Hanyu pinyin spelling. Indeed, Wade-Giles is the spelling still familiar to most readers today: "Canton" rather than "Guangzhou," "Peking" rather than "Beijing," "Hong Kong" rather than "Xianggang" and "Ch'ing dynasty" rather than "Qing dynasty." For this reason, in many cases the Wade-Giles spelling will be retained. From this point on, however, the first time that selected Chinese names or place-names appear in the text, both the Wade-Giles and Hanyu pinyin versions will be given—Wade-Giles first and Hanyu pinyin in brackets. An example: Empress Dowager Tzu-hsi [Ci Xi] ruled China with an iron hand. For ease of reference, these equivalents are also listed in Appendix V.

Notes

1. Hao, *Commercial Revolution*, pp. 113, 132.
2. Bernard, *Nemesis*, p. 185.
3. Downs, *Golden Ghetto*, p. 132.
4. What Western opium traders said publicly about their business may have been only a rationalization: they must have been aware that opium abuse could be fatal. The income from the trade, however, far outweighed any moral scruples they may have felt privately. (Private communication from Dr. Jacques M. Downs of 21 May 1998; see also Downs, "Fair Game," pp. 144–146.)
5. Phipps, *Treatise*, p. viii. Emphasis added.
6. No reliable estimate can be made of the numbers of Chinese directly involved in the physical handling of opium, but the American opium captain Robert Bennet Forbes reported that after the drug was off-loaded in the Canton estuary it was distributed there by a network of about 40 Chinese opium brokers. We may assume that each of these men had others working for him and that the ports north of Canton must have had their own brokers and staffs, too. Regarding prostitution, according to an Englishman who was in China in 1769, waterborne prostitutes were even then offering their services to seamen at Whampoa, the port serving Canton. See Downs, *Golden Ghetto*, pp. 389, 407.
7. Cited by Beeching, *Chinese Opium Wars*, p. 68.

8. *Some Pros and Cons*, p. 42.
9. Kerr, *Letters*, p. 116.
10. After Gardiner, *Sail's*, p. 113; Svensson, *Sails*, pp. 51, 76, 115; Lubbock, *China Clippers*, pp. 3–4, and *Opium Clippers*, pp. 13–15; Dana, *Two Years* and *Seaman's Friend*, plate IV; and Smyth, *Sailor's Word-Book*.
11. For superb photographs of men aloft in the big square-riggers, see Villiers, *Voyaging with the Wind*.
12. Paasch, *Encyclopedia*, plates 75, 80; and Villiers, *Voyaging*, p. 18.
13. Allen, *Opium Trade*, p. 18.
14. Cited by MacGregor, *Fast Sailing Ships*, p. 102.
15. Chapelle, *Baltimore Clipper*, p. 146.
16. The wax base gave good results: Dana reported, "The soundings on the American coast are so regular that a navigator knows as well where he has made land, by the soundings, as he would by seeing the land. Black mud is the soundings of Block Island. As you go toward Nantucket, it changes to a dark sand; then, sand and white shells; and on George's Banks, white sand; and so on." Dana, *Two Years*, pp. 452–453.
17. Conrad, *Narcissus*, pp. 25, 173.
18. Owen, *British Opium Policy*, p. 202.
19. Alexander, *Rise and Progress*, p. 29.
20. Davis, *Recollections*, p. 249; and Downing, *Fan-Qui*, pp. 4–5.
21. Chapelle, *Baltimore Clipper*, p. 116.
22. Even very big sailing ships did not need many men to handle them. In the 1890s, for example, the five-masted bark *Potosi* had a crew of 44 all told, of which only 20 were A.B.s. See Villiers, *Voyaging*, p. 44.
23. H.W.C., *Fan-Kwae*, p. 65.
24. H.W.C., *Fan-Kwae*, pp. 1–2.
25. Lubbock, *Opium Clippers*, p. 383.
26. After the heyday of the opium clippers, opium was carried by steamers, but these required even smaller crews than sailing ships of comparable size. For example, in Conrad's story *Typhoon*, the fictional steamship *Nan-Shang*, carrying Chinese coolies back to their native Fukien province in about 1887, had a complement of less than 20 men — the captain, two mates, three engineers, a boatswain, a carpenter, a few crewmen who stoked the ship's boilers with coal, a handful of seamen and a steward and a cook.
27. Layton, *Frolic*, p. 114.
28. Hao, *Commercial Revolution*, p. 116.
29. Melville, *Moby Dick*, p. 21, 24.
30. London, "The Sea-Farmer," in *The Sea-Wolf and Other Stories*, pp. 279–280.
31. Dana, *Two Years*, Introduction by Thomas Philbrick, pp. 11–12.
32. Dana, *Two Years*, p. 56. Most of the definitions are taken from *Two Years* or from Dana's *Seaman's Friend* (1841).
33. The crew was divided into two equal *watches*, known as the larboard watch (commanded by the first mate) and the starboard watch (commanded by the second mate). In bad weather or in dangerous waters, each watch was on

duty for four hours and then off duty for four hours. Two-hour watches known as *dog watches* were used to shift the watches each night so that the same watch would not always be on deck at the same time. See Dana, *Two Years*, pp. 52–53.

34. Perry, *Fair Winds*, p. 17.

35. Conrad, *Narcissus*, p. 21.

36. Twain, *Life on the Mississippi*, p. 70.

37. Dana, *Two Years*, p. 254.

38. To further complicate the currency situation, there were two kinds of Carolus dollars: "old heads," bearing the likeness of Charles III or IV, and "new heads," with the image of Ferdinand VII on them.

39. See Morse, *Trade*, pp. 163–165; Layton, *Frolic*, pp. 106, 189, 206; and Downing, *Fan-Qui*, vol. 3, p. 183.

40. This figure comes from Hao, *Commercial Revolution*, p. 268: "Andrew Jardine [a nephew who was a partner of the firm c. 1839–1843] ... is said to have divided with his partners the immense sum of £3,000,000 (about $15,000,000) of profits, much of which had been accumulated from the opium trade during the previous decade."

41. Williams, *Guide*, p. 198.

1

Running Great Risks for Great Rewards

For Lindsay Anderson, a young British seaman, 1859 was a good year. First, he found a well-paid if dangerous job as third mate aboard *Eamont*, a smart topsail schooner running opium in the South China Sea. Later that year he and his shipmates repelled an attack by pirates, when *Eamont* demonstrated the superb sailing qualities built into it by White's, a British shipyard on the Isle of Wight. On this point Anderson can speak for himself:

> The *Eamont* is surging along like a mad thing, close hauled on a bowline, with every rag spread upon her, going along eleven and twelve knots across the north-east monsoon. The guns are all well covered up, as they had need to be, for the *Eamont* leaves no dry spot about her when she is thus driven through the water … there is no taking in sail here so long as she would stand up to it. You might be seen at sea with a broken spar, but would not need to be seen at any time under shortened sail.[1]

Finally, he was lucky to escape with his life when *Eamont* was knocked down in a typhoon. "The squalls," he reports, "were now upon us in fierce and rapid succession, seemingly one long, dismal howl. About eleven [A.M.] it seemed to culminate in one wild burst, as if all the windows of Heaven were opened. Over went the *Eamont* with her cross-trees in the water, flat on her broadside.[2]

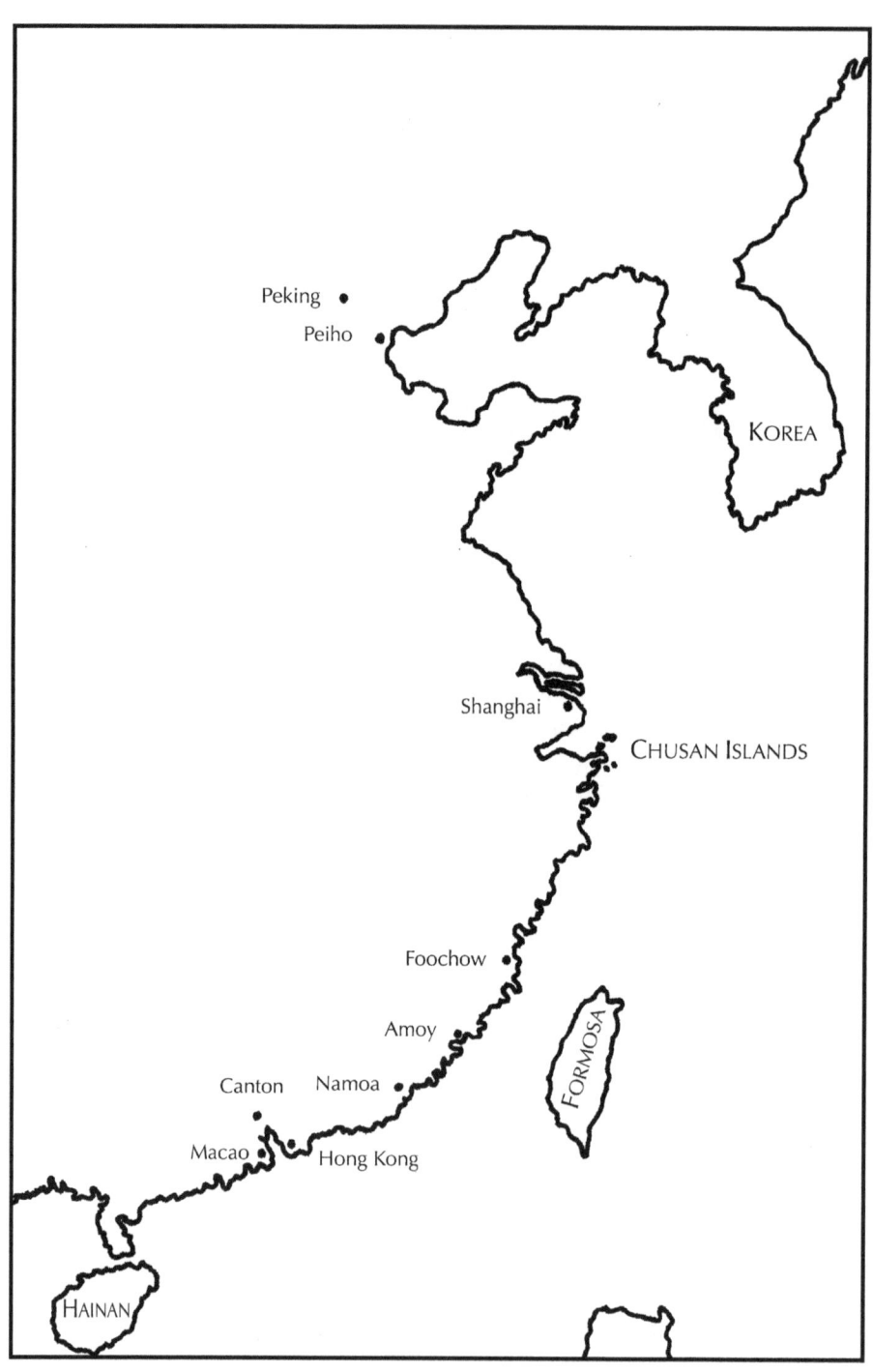

The coast of China in the nineteenth century

Such adventures befell Anderson, who was one of the few men to write about his own experiences, because he was part of a far-flung army of Westerners, Chinese and Indians engaged in the nineteenth-century opium trade. By the 1830s opium was the single most valuable commodity being traded in the entire world, and personal fortunes were being made from it. According to a contemporary account, opium sales in China in 1833 — well before the trade reached its zenith in the 1870s — were equal in value to the total amount then being paid by the British and Americans for Chinese tea, namely, about $14 million.³ That same year the English schooner *Jamesina* sold £330,000 worth of opium at Foochow [Fuzhou], Amoy [Xiamen], Ningpo [Ningbo] and other Chinese coastal ports.⁴ By 1836 opium imports were running at about $18 million annually; this amounted to roughly 1,820 tons of the drug each year, smoked by about 12.5 million Chinese.⁵

Even though the trade was illegal — the Chinese government had repeatedly tried to ban the import and sale of the drug — dealing in opium was so profitable that despite the dangers posed by pirates, typhoons and currents along poorly charted coasts, merchants and seamen alike fought to get into the trade. The average annual rate of profit for foreign merchants in the opium trade on the China coast was around 30 percent.⁶ If they survived the rigors and diseases of their calling (typhoid fever, dysentery, malaria), the captains of opium clippers — men described by an experienced observer in 1843 as being "remarkable for their seamanship and not infrequently for their kind and generous conduct"⁷ — could look forward to an early and comfortable retirement.

Captain Robert Bennet Forbes, at one point the commander of *Lintin*, Russell and Co.'s receiving ship, and later the head of the American opium-trading firm Russell and Co., is said to have made a fortune in only three years by wise investments in opium, not from his modest salary. Forbes went back to China twice to replenish his fortune. For their part, the crews of opium clippers were well paid, too, but as soon as they fetched up at the fleshpots of the China coast many of them spent their money like the drunken sailors they were and soon had nothing left. When their ship sailed, however, they were ready to hand, reef, steer and heave the lead again to earn enough for another wild carouse ashore.

Opium clippers were fast, well-armed craft specially designed for this business. *Eamont*, built in 1853 of nearly solid mahogany, was among the best, but she was merely following in the wake of earlier clippers, such as the American brig *Eagle*. An American seaman who signed on aboard

Eagle, which had been launched at New York in 1835 and was being fitted out for a voyage to China, remembered that it was a splendid example of an American clipper: strongly manned, well armed and heavily sparred and carrying an extraordinary spread of canvas, amounting to 40,000 square feet.[8] These fine-lined, heavily canvassed ships were more like yachts than cargo vessels and had one great virtue — they could beat to windward (i.e., sail into the wind by making zigzag tacks) against the prevailing monsoons, thus making possible several India-China voyages each year rather than the one annual voyage possible for the heavy East Indiamen.

Opium itself had a long tradition of medicinal use in India and China. After the British, under General Robert Clive of India (who was later to die of an opium overdose himself at the age of 49), gained control of Bengal at the Battle of Plessey in 1757, the British East India Company gradually expanded the existing opium cultivation there. By the nineteenth century the export and shipping of opium was in the hands of private traders such as the British firm of Jardine, Matheson and Co. and the American firm of Russell and Co., which owned or chartered fast opium clippers to carry the drug from Bombay or Calcutta to China — first to Whampoa [Huangpu], a port 12 miles below Canton [Guangzhou], and then, after 1821 when the trade was halted there, to Lintin [Lingding] island and other anchorages in the Canton estuary.

In Western countries opium was a widely available painkiller and was socially acceptable as well. The first recorded shipment of Indian opium to England was in 1609, when on its sixth voyage the East India Company brought in 500 pounds for the London market.[9] The drug was soon being used to such an extent that in 1797 the British Royal Society for the Encouragement of Arts, Manufactures and Commerce could offer a 50-guinea award to anyone who could produce "not less than 20 pounds of Opium, from Poppies grown in Great Britain, and equal in quality to the best foreign Opium." In announcing its competition, the society explained, "When the great importance of this drug in medicine, and the abominable adulterations it is liable to, are considered, it will appear to every judicious observer, that a more proper object of attention and encouragement of the Society can hardly be found."[10] The 50 guineas were eventually won by a John Ball of Somerset, but opium growing never caught on in Britain. The weather was too cold and variable and collecting poppy juice by hand proved to be too expensive, even though some enthusiasts tried to overcome this latter problem by sending children out into the fields.

The Canton Estuary

By the early nineteenth century, opium mixed with alcohol — a mixture known as *laudanum*— was cheaper than wine or beer and was easy to buy from every pharmacy: a bottle of this compound could be found in most homes. *The Prairie Traveler*, the most reliable handbook for nineteenth-century pioneers crossing the United States in covered wagons en route to the Pacific coast, listed opium "put up in doses for adults" as one of the absolute necessities of the medicine chest. It also recommended a laudanum-and-brandy mixture as a surefire remedy for colic in animals. The incidence of opium dependence steadily increased in England, the United States and Europe during the first half of the nineteenth century. In England in 1839, opium and its preparations were responsible for more premature deaths than any other chemical agent: opiates accounted for 186 of 543 poisonings, including 72 among children.[11]

Opium's addictive properties were not yet fully understood. As Thomas de Quincey, an arch-apologist for opium, wrote in his *Confessions of an Opium Eater* (1821), a work that did much to bring opium into public notice: "Three respectable London druggists, in widely remote quarters of London, from which I happened to be purchasing small quantities of opium, assured me that the numbers of *amateur* opium-eaters (as I may term them) was at this time immense" (p. 180). De Quincey was not alone in this belief. Even up to the early years of the twentieth century it was a common belief among Westerners living in China that an occasional indulgence in opium was no more harmful than smoking a pipe or a cigar.

However, once a person began to smoke opium it was very difficult to break free from it; indeed, the withdrawal process was considered worse than the addiction. Opium affected all levels of society. For the poor in Britain, opium was used to silence crying, hungry children and to help adults forget the miseries of their newly industrialized world. To cite de Quincey again:

> Some years ago, on passing through Manchester, I was informed by several cotton manufacturers, that their work-people were rapidly getting into the practice of opium-eating; so much so, that on a Saturday afternoon the counters of the druggists were strewn with pills of one, two, or three grains, in preparation for the known demand of the evening. The immediate occasion of this practice was the lowness of wages, which at that time would not allow them to indulge in ale or spirits [p.181].[12]

Later in the nineteenth century opium addiction was to become a constituent part of the literary world, and such well-known figures as Samuel Taylor Coleridge, Elizabeth Barrett Browning, Charles Pierre Baudelaire, Edgar Allan Poe and Sir Walter Scott all took opium at some stage in their literary lives. Charles Dickens may not have used opium himself, but he knew enough about it to give a convincing account of an opium den in *Edwin Drood*—a sure sign that opium was part of British life. In the eighteenth century the father of Jane Austen, the doyenne of English literature, was involved as an agent in the trade, selling opium in England for Warren Hastings, then the governor of the East India Company. As a young man, William Wilberforce, better known for bringing an end to the British slave trade, was prescribed opium for pain relief and never broke the habit, taking opium on a daily basis for the last 45 years of his life. Hector Berlioz's *Symphonie Fantastique* was an attempt to convey in musical terms the obsession of the opium addict.

In a world emerging from the evils of gin—"drunk for a penny, dead drunk for twopence" as a popular saying had it—opium was regarded as less harmful than alcohol. As James Matheson wrote to John Abel Smith, a member of Parliament, on 29 September 1839:

> During the 21 years that I have passed almost entirely in China I can conscientiously declare that I have never seen a nature in the least bestialized by opium smoking, like drunkards in Europe, nor any Chinese with his faculties more impaired from excessive indulgence in the habit, nor indeed so much as Gluttons and Topers in our own Country, while of this the influence are far from Common, and much of the Opium smoked used to be on convivial occasions of the upper class as in England Champagne and costly wines [sic]. Forgive this little digression.[13]

In their occasional apologias for the opium trade, Western merchants claimed that it flourished only because of Chinese complicity. As H. Piddington, a Calcutta-based business associate of James Matheson, put it sarcastically in 1839:

> I think what is to be wondered at is, that [opium clippers] have ever been able to trade at all. A European-rigged vessel gives the alarm against herself whenever she appears, and lodges an information in the hands of every individual who may have a spite at the authorities. Only think of the Chinese going to smuggle tea on the coast of England in a junk! and a number of those anchored at the spot, at the mouth of the Thames or the Severn![14]

In the same spirit James Matheson wrote to the governor of Ceylon in 1839: "The introduction of Opium into the country is a point of contention at issue and however much philanthropists may justly lament the immoderate and hurtful influence of the Drug in China, as of Gin in England and America, it is clearly the exclusive province of the Chinese Government alone to enforce its prohibitory laws on the subject."[15]

Once off-loaded in the Canton area, opium was stored in receiving ships. With the active connivance of Chinese officials, it was then carried to ports along the coast by shallow-draft Western ships known as coasters and by Chinese smugglers in small boats variously known from the number of their oars as centipedes, scrambling dragons or fast crabs. The Chinese paid for the opium with silver dollars or ingots, which Western traders used not only to enrich themselves and to buy more opium in India but — and in balance of payment terms this was an important benefit — also to pay for Chinese tea, which was in demand in Britain and the United States. It was Indian opium, in short, that financed the China tea trade.

In an ill-fated effort in 1839 to suppress the opium trade, Imperial Commissioner Lin Tse-hsü [Lin Zexu] destroyed more than 20,000 chests of opium owned by Western traders. This triggered the first Opium War (1839–1842) and, indirectly, another armed conflict with the West — the second Opium War (1856–1860). China lost both of these wars (which are discussed in later chapters). As a result, Hong Kong [Xianggang] was ceded to Britain, five coastal "Treaty Ports" were opened up to free trade with the West and the importation of opium was legalized. So many Westerners poured into China after 1860 that even the most conservative Chinese scholar-official could see that a cultural watershed was being crossed. The expansion of contacts between a tradition-bound China and an expanding, entrepreneurial West was a change greater than any that had occurred in China within a thousand years.

This clash of cultures was recognized in the West as well. John Quincy Adams, then chairman of the Senate Foreign Affairs Committee, was eloquent on the subject:

> It is a general but I believe altogether mistaken opinion that [the Opium War] is merely for certain chests of opium imported by British merchants into China, and seized by the Chinese government for having been imported contrary to law. This is a mere incident to the dispute; no more the cause of war than the throwing overboard of the tea in the Boston Harbor was the cause of the North American revolution.

> The cause of the war is the kow-tow! [i.e., the obligatory way of showing respect to the emperor by kneeling before him and knocking one's forehead against the ground]—the arrogant and insupportable pretensions of China, that she will hold commercial intercourse with mankind not upon terms of equal reciprocity, but upon insulting and degrading forms of relation between lord and vassal.[16]

At this point, we may reasonably ask: *Why should anyone today care about all this?* The answer is that this clash of cultures is still going on. Although the Chinese Communist Party has been in power since 1949, opium (or more accurately its derivative, heroin) still remains a problem in China despite repeated claims by the government that the drug's hold over the country has finally been broken. More important, however, China's uneven political relations with the West since 1949 ultimately have their roots in the great cultural divide symbolized by the opium trade. The legacies of the opium trade may affect the fortunes of the Chinese Communist Party itself in the twenty-first century. For this reason alone, if for no other, the nineteenth century opium trade is worth studying.

Notes

1. Anderson, *Among Typhoons*, p. 38.
2. Anderson, *Cruise*, p. 50.
3. Phipps, *Treatise*, p. viii.
4. Clark, *Clipper Ship*, p. 58.
5. Wakeman, "Canton Trade," p. 178.
6. Hao, *Commercial Revolution*, p. 276.
7. Lay, *Chinese As They Are*, p. 109.
8. Davis, *Recollections*, p. 241.
9. Owen, *British Opium Policy*, p. 81.
10. Seidmann, "Opium," pp. 147–148.
11. U.S. Department of Health, Education and Welfare, "Opium in China," pp. 134–140.
12. Both the de Quincey quotes come from his *Confessions*.
13. This and other James Matheson quotes come from his Private Letter Book. Jardine Matheson archives.
14. Piddington-Matheson letter, 1839. Jardine Matheson archives.
15. Letter from Matheson to the governor of Ceylon. Jardine Matheson archives.
16. Cited by Inglis in *The Opium War*. Adams made these remarks in 1841 when addressing the Massachusetts Historical Society.

2

A Stream of Wealth: Opium, India and China

To understand where the stream of wealth generated by the opium trade came from and where it went, let us first look at the properties and effects of opium. We will then turn to the state of affairs in India and, in somewhat greater detail, in China itself. There we will find that an apparently unrelated factor — the civil service examination system, which was based on the teachings of Confucius — had a profound impact on the conduct of the Opium Wars and on China's long term relationship with the West.

Opium: A Complex Substance

The 40 balls of Bengal opium (the drug produced in east India) that were packed into a chest and ready for shipment to China were not impressive if judged by their physical appearance alone. Inside each ball, which weighed a little over three pounds, there was only the thick, heavy juice of crude (partially processed) opium. An inch-thick protective shell, plastered together from poppy leaves and an inferior grade of juice, formed the outside of the ball. Fully packed and ready for shipment, a chest of Bengal opium weighed about 133 pounds (that is, a picul) and contained about 120 pounds of semiprocessed opium. An average cargo for an opium clipper loading in India was about 1,000 chests (i.e., 40,000 balls), which could be delivered from Calcutta to the Canton estuary in as little as 25 days with a fast ship and good weather.[1]

Opium passed through many hands on its journey from poppy to pipe. A chest could easily be tampered with, so dealers had to be on guard. In 1863, for example, an English opium trader in Foochow reported to Jardine Matheson that "On opening the chest [I] found it to contain nine stones of about the weight of nine balls of Opium and thirty balls of made-up stuff resembling Opium, but I found them to contain no drug whatever."[2]

The apparent simplicity of balls of opium masked the chemical complexity of opium itself, which is produced from the poppy *Papaver somniferum*. Opium is not a single compound but a combination of sugars, proteins, ammonia, latex, gums, plant wax, fats, sulfuric and lactic acids, water, meconic acid and alkaloids. From the opium user's point of view, the most important of these substances were the alkaloids; the most important alkaloid was morphine. This was the active ingredient responsible for both the positive and negative effects of opium and the substance from which heroin can be made.[3]

In the early nineteenth century, the Cantonese underworld slang for

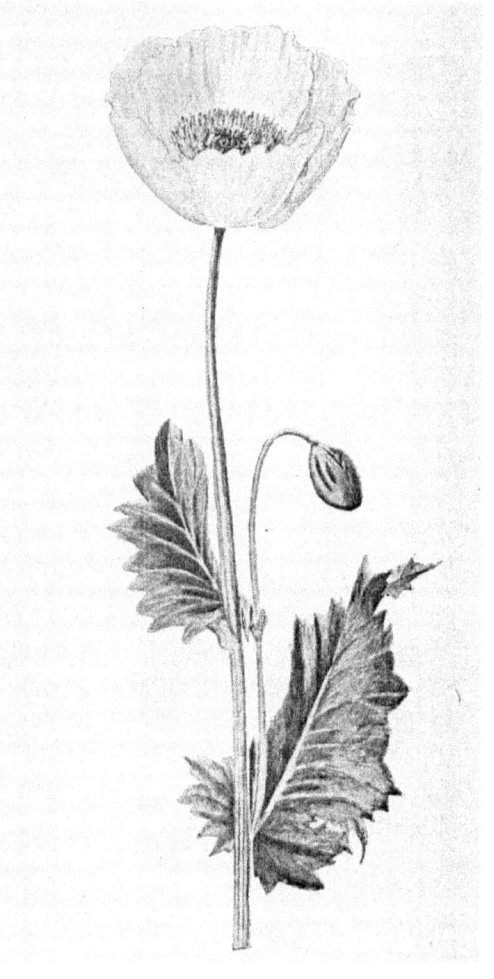

The opium poppy, *Papaver somniferum* (private collection)

opium smoking was "chasing the dragon," which meant the futile pursuit of the imaginary and the unattainable.[4] Yet opium really worked: that is, it dispelled entirely the cares and concerns of this world and even gave the smoker the delusion of weightlessness. Reclining on his side in an opium den, after several pipes a smoker was talkative at first but gradually became listless and drifted off into an unrefreshing sleep.[5]

The appeal of opium was not confined to the Chinese alone. As we have already mentioned, Europeans were fond of the drug, too. The English addict Thomas de Quincey enthused,

> Here was a panacea ... for all human woes; here was the secret of happiness, about which philosophers had disputed for so many ages, at once discovered; happiness might now be bought for a penny, and carried in the waist-coat pocket; portable ecstasies might be corked up in a pint-bottle; and peace of mind could be sent down by the mail ... [Opium produces] the most exquisite order, legislation, and harmony ... [it] communicates serenity and equipoise to all the faculties...[6]

In the long run, of course, these pleasant effects were overshadowed by the dangers of opium abuse. The gravest of these was addiction, which occurred when an addict's body became physiologically dependent on the drug and his of her body chemistry could not function without it. Other maladies associated with smoking opium included inflammation of the mouth and throat, gastric illnesses, circulatory disorders, emaciation resulting from loss of appetite, hoarse voice, constipation, impaired memory, hallucinations or nightmares, and the risk of premature death.[7]

Breaking the opium habit was extremely difficult, requiring either a physical separation from opium itself (as in a hospital or a prison) or the strongest possible willpower. Without a regular dose, an addict would be subject to perspiration, dilation of the pupils, nasal discharge, abdominal cramps, tearing (tears would flow from the eyes) and a high fever.[8] These symptoms were well known to the Chinese. A memorial (an official report) to the emperor commented that when opium smokers could not get their daily dose of the drug,

> their limbs become debilitated, a discharge of rheum takes place from the eyes and nose, and they are altogether unequal to any exertion; but, with a few whiffs [from an opium pipe], their spirits and strength are immediately restored in a surprising manner. Thus opium becomes, to opium smokers, their very life;

and, when they are seized and brought before magistrates, they will sooner suffer a severe chastisement than inform against those who sell it.⁹

Despite Western claims that smoking opium was an innocuous pastime, the physical, moral and social decline of Chinese addicts was evident to the British and other foreigners as well. An English missionary reported that

> It is doubtful if the drug can be taken in moderation, though some affirm this. The habit is liable to grow till it becomes overmastering. The victim is, however, the reverse of violent, and should he be rich, does not seem much the worse. But should he be poor, his family are deprived of the necessaries of life, and perhaps sold as slaves. To stay his craving, he then resorts to smoking the ashes and refuse of others' pipes, till want of food hastens his own wretched end.¹⁰

Lindsay Anderson of the opium clipper *Eamont* noticed that "some of the loungers [in an opium den] are young and still ruddy with the hue of lusty health; but the elder ones, what a spectacle of humanity they represent, their whole bodies shriveled up like boiled parchment after it has dried!"¹¹ Anderson admitted that "a thinking man has only to see the shriveled and shrunken carcasses of the inveterate opium smokers to give him an everlasting disgust against the use of this pernicious drug in any form," but he did not apologize for his own involvement in the trade. He offered instead a familiar justification: "if we don't do it, others will." The Chinese were not compelled, he declared, to buy opium from the foreigners, but "they were as eager for it as our owners were to supply it. If our countrymen had stopped the supply, the adventurous merchants of another nation would soon have entered the gap, and perhaps carried on the trade in a less scrupulous manner."¹²

The State of Affairs in India

Traditional Use of Opium

Opium was first mentioned in Sanskrit medical works when Arab armies conquered part of India in the eighth century, but it was not then being produced in India itself. Small quantities were imported from Egypt, but it was not until late in the sixteenth century that a Dutch traveler reported that the Indians along the Malabar coast were consuming large quantities of opium (probably by drinking a beverage containing poppy seeds) and that during the reign of the Moghul emperor Akbar (1556–1605) the fields producing poppies were a good source of income for his government.[13]

In about 1667 an Indian ally of the Dutch East India Company, the Ali Raja of Cannanore, was allowed by the company to import opium for his own use, but he was forbidden to sell it to other Indian rulers.[14] Although there was some local production of Bengal opium in east India and of Malwa opium in the nominally independent princely states in western and central India, the drug was not widely grown in the subcontinent until Western traders discovered the bottomless market they created for it in China. Writing in 1858, a surgeon in the British Army stated categorically that "Ninety years ago [c. 1768] no regular trade in it existed" in India itself.[15]

The East India Company

How did Britain, which was only one-seventeenth the size of preindependence India, manage to dominate this huge subcontinent and turn parts of Bengal and western and central India into opium plantations for the China trade? The answer seems to be twofold:

(1) The British were more interested in trading with India than in conquering it, but their flag, as it were, followed their trade. The subcontinent was not united when they first arrived there in the early seventeenth century. Indeed, the idea of "India" as a single entity, bound together by a centralized administration and by a common language for all educated people, was a foreign (that is, British) notion. Because the subcontinent was fragmented politically, the well-disciplined and highly centralized British were able to dominate it at the cost of relatively little blood and treasure. They maintained their hegemony until India finally became independent in 1947.

(2) The export trade in Indian opium was largely the handiwork of the British East India Company, also known as the Honourable Company or, less formally, as John Company, after the British caricature figure of John Bull. This company had been granted a charter by Queen Elizabeth in 1600 and was much more than a commercial concern.[16] For years it was also the de facto government of India and was explicitly responsible for

carrying out the policies of the British Crown, such as growing opium for export to China.

When the Mogul Emperor Jahangir gave the East India Company permission in 1613 to set up a small trading post at Surat, north of Bombay, he could not have foreseen that this would slowly lead to British domination of the whole of India. In 1615 the English ship *Hope* was the first vessel to sail from India with a cargo for London; that same year the first English ambassador arrived at Jahangir's court. By 1619 the East India Company had established other trading posts; Bombay later replaced Surat as the company's headquarters on the west coast of India. Its headquarters on the east coast were at Fort St. George, built near Madras in 1640. By 1651 the company had also established a "factory" (fortified trading post) in Bengal. Another post, Fort William, was built in 1696 and grew into the Calcutta of today. In these years the East India Company was getting a foothold in China, too, setting up a "factory" in Canton in 1685 and beginning annual trading operations there in 1699.

While the East India Company was expanding its operations in India, the Moghul empire itself was slipping into a downward spiral. The political and religious intolerance of Jahangir's son Aurangzeb, who assumed the throne in 1658 after defeating his brother in battle and imprisoning his own father, alienated the Hindu majority of his realm and led to an economic decline. Problems multiplied: Aurangzeb's successors were inept, northern India was invaded by Nadir Shah of Persia (who made off with the famous Peacock Throne and the fabulous 106-carat Koh-i-noor diamond, which later became part of the British crown jewels), civil wars racked the land and *nawabs* (local rulers) paid no heed to the dictates of the central government.

Matters came to a head in 1756 as far as the British were concerned. The forces of a Bengal *nawab* attacked and captured the English settlement of Calcutta, imprisoning 146 Englishmen one night in a tiny prison known as the Black Hole, from which only 23 men emerged alive the next morning. To avenge this atrocity, British forces, acting on behalf of the Honorable Company and led by Robert Clive and Admiral Charles Watson, sailed north from Madras and recaptured Calcutta in 1756. The next year, Clive defeated the *nawab*'s forces at the Battle of Plessey, a victory that marked the beginning of the Raj (British rule) in India.

Clive's success permitted the Honorable Company to acquire the revenue rights for Bengal in 1765. In 1773 the British declared a monopoly over the nascent Indian opium industry in Bengal and began to produce the drug on a large scale for the Chinese market. They did this by advancing money to local growers to encourage them to produce better opium than the Malwa opium then being produced in western and central India for Portuguese traders. John Company held monopolies on all British trade with India until 1813 and with China until 1834, but opium was only one of the many commodities it handled. For example, on its maiden voyage in 1787 the company's ship *Hartwell*, bound for China via India, was carrying British watches, microscopes, telescopes, vanity cases and more than 100,000 silver dollars when she was wrecked on the rocks of the Cape Verde Islands.

The East India Company was inextricably involved in the opium trade with China from the earliest days of large-scale cultivation. Duties from the export of the drug made up about 15 percent of the Honorable Company's total revenues. A former missionary to China, who later became the secretary of the Anglo-Oriental Society for the Suppression of the Opium Trade, complained that the company's policy was "to discourage opium-eating among its own subjects [in India], and at the same time to acquire the maximum of revenue by the exportation of the opium [to China]."[17]

Opium could be grown in India only with the Honorable Company's permission. Its secret Department of Inspection stated on 9 April 1785,

> It is well known how fond the Chinese are of Opium & what risks they run to come at it.... The contract for providing the Ophium [sic] expires on the 1st of next September ... To keep the preparation of the Opium perfect & uniform for public sale the whole Provision of it must be given by Agency or Contract to Special Managers or to a Society of Merchants contracting the whole. To such a society the contract may be made out for five years on condition that they supply the Company's Cash at China annually to a certain amount with the proceeds of the Opium.... The Company's own ship Admiral Hughes would answer the purpose of a floating Factory [receiving ship] extremely well...[18]

In an entry of 27 March 1787 the Department added, "Thus far we have considered Ophium [sic] as an article of *Internal Revenue*. We shall now view it as an Article of *Foreign Commerce* and we know not how it can be so beneficially applied as in the Aid of our China Trade ... you have our full permission to apply the proceeds of the Ophium Manufactory [sic] ... to the exclusive benefit of that Trade."[19]

How Opium Was Produced in India

The opium produced in Bengal under the control of the East India Company was of excellent quality and was easily recognized. Each chest of opium had the company's mark on it; inside was a receipt showing where it had been packed and how much it weighed. Because of the black outer shells of these opium balls, the Chinese often called them "black earth," but opium was also called "black smoke" or "foreign mud." The city of Patna was the center of the British opium-growing industry in eastern India, but this included neighboring areas as well: Bengal, Bihar, Orissa and Benares. It is said that the best opium came from Bihar but Benares' output was highly regarded, too.[20]

Writing in 1858, a British opponent of the opium trade described how Bengal opium was produced. The fundamental principle of the British government's monopoly over opium production was that the Indian *ryot* (small tenant farmer) first had to get the government's permission to grow poppies: a heavy fine was imposed for any unlicensed cultivation. The *ryot* then received an advance from the Bengal authorities, which enabled him to plant poppies; in return he was obligated to sell the opium only to a government agency at a given price. He manured his land and planted white poppy seeds. When the poppies reached maturity, during the day he made incisions in the capsules of their heads with a three-pronged instrument shaped like a fork. At night a gummy substance oozed out of each incision; when morning came, men, women and children went back into the fields to scrape off and save this residue. The harvesting operation was repeated for three or four weeks, until the poppy could no longer produce opium.

This gummy residue was sometimes mixed with linseed oil to prevent evaporation and could be patted into flat cakes about three to four inches in diameter and then dried in the shade. The farmer sold these cakes to a local Indian dealer, who drained away the linseed oil and formed the cakes into balls. Each ball was wrapped in poppy leaves, 40 balls were put into a chest and every chest was sent to Calcutta to be auctioned off under the auspices of the British government.

The process of producing Malwa opium in the native states of central and western India was simpler because there was less direct involvement by the British. An Indian merchant would decide how many chests he wanted to send to Bombay. He then bought that number of chests from the local *ryots* and had them delivered to a government weighing station, where he paid an exportation tax on them. This tax was set high enough to cover the government's collection costs and to yield a profit as well, which went into the British treasury. After it had reached Bombay the opium was transshipped to China.[21]

THE ECONOMIC IMPORTANCE OF INDIAN OPIUM

Opium production in India itself grew very slowly until the drug became such a popular vice in China. In 1729, when the first Imperial antiopium edict was issued, as few as 200 chests of Indian opium were being sent to Macao each year; 40 years later this figure had risen to only 1,000 chests.[22] The explosive growth of the trade — that is, the large-scale production of opium in India and its well-organized delivery to ports in China — began early in the nineteenth century.[23] By the 1820s Indian opium had become an important source of income for British India and for Britain itself. In 1828 the income from opium sales paid for the entire annual British investment in the tea trade; opium was also indirectly responsible for about 10 percent of the British revenues coming in from the duty on tea.[24]

Between 1868 and 1878 the average price of a chest of opium sold at government auction at Calcutta was Rs (rupees) 1,400, but each chest cost only Rs 400 to produce. The resulting profit of Rs 1,000 per chest yielded a net revenue for the British of about £4,000,000 per year from Bengal alone, where 560,000 acres had been planted for opium.[25] A parliamentary report on India for 1871–1872 must have included the income from Malwa opium, too, because it put net revenue much higher — at an annual stream of wealth of £7,675,213.[26]

The State of Affairs in China

TRADITIONAL USE OF OPIUM

It is not true, as was sometimes asserted by the pro-opium lobby in the nineteenth century, that the Chinese had always smoked opium: historically speaking, this habit was in fact a late development. The Arabs probably first introduced opium into China around the middle of the fourth century, but the earliest reference to it in Chinese writings came in the first half of the eighth century, when a Chinese poet mentioned that poppies were growing in west China. Toward the end of the tenth century, the drug was being used for medicinal purposes.[27] In 973 it was listed in the official pharmacopoeia known as the "Herbalist's Treasury," with the advice that "Its seeds have healing power ... [people] may be benefited by mixing these seeds with bamboo juice boiled into gruel, and taking the mixture."

In the twelfth century the opium capsule itself (rather than just the seeds) was being used to make impure opium. The medical writer Lin Hung directed that the entire poppy head should be crushed, the juice filtered, boiled and then steamed; the gummy residue could then be "made into cakes shaped like a fish" and dried. By this time Chinese doctors were well aware that opium acted quickly but was also dangerous. "Great care must be taken in using it," wrote the physician Chu Chen-heng in the fourteenth century, "because it kills like a knife." It is only in the middle of the fourteenth century that we find the first mention of pure opium in China, made not by crushing the whole capsule but by carefully scoring it and then dehydrating the juice that flowed out.

Smoking Opium

The precise steps in the remarkable transition from the occasional use of opium taken orally for medicinal purposes to the widespread smoking of the drug purely for its narcotic effects are still unclear. The best guess is that the use of tobacco, which had been introduced by the Spanish into the Philippines, gradually spread west to the China coast, probably to Amoy, where opium was sometimes mixed with it. The Dutch may also have brought to China (from Java) the idea of fortifying tobacco with opium to produce a mixture known as *madak*. Another account, however, points to the island of Formosa (Taiwan), where opium was being smoked as early as 1620. Chinese soldiers were sent there in 1721 to suppress a local rebellion and may have brought the habit back with them when they returned to the mainland.

Opium smoking was initially confined mainly to Formosa and to the coastal province of Fukien [Fujian], since the Chinese government apparently had these regions in mind when it issued its first antiopium decree in 1729. This declared that dealers would be punished by having to wear a heavy wooden collar (known as the *cangue*) and would then be banished. Anyone found running an opium den would be sentenced to death by strangulation; growing or smoking opium would be punished by 100 lashes. There was an immediate protest from one opium seller, however, who claimed that he was only selling the drug for medicinal purposes. His claim was recognized as valid and the edict was never enforced.

The smoking of opium does not seem to have become a national problem until the early 1800s. Opium was not widely grown in China itself until after the first Opium War (1839–1842). After the war, however, the profits from growing it were so great and the Chinese government's authority was so limited that the poppy was widely planted in China itself.[28] Indeed, by 1858 a staff surgeon of the British Army could report that due to the West's "breaking down all local and Imperial opposition in China to the entry of opium," the cultivation of opium in China had grown with such rapidity that it was then equal to nearly one-third of the opium imports coming in from India.[29]

Once the semiprocessed Indian opium had been landed in China, it had to be refined for smoking. The thick juice taken from the interior of a ball of opium was slowly boiled with water in copper pans for three to five hours over a low fire and stirred frequently until it became stiff and thick. It was then pressed into thin sheets and dried. In addition, water in which raw opium had been steeped could also be boiled and stirred from four to seven hours until it, too, had thickened. The dross (unburned residues) from smokers' pipes was sometimes added during these processes. The net result: three pounds of raw opium yielded about two pounds of smokable opium.

To get the effects of the drug, the smoker reclined on a couch and, scooping up a tiny amount of opium with a long needle or a wire, heated it in the flame of a lamp to ready it for the pipe. A British writer in 1842 reported that an old, best-quality opium pipe had a cane stem, black from long use, 17 inches long and one inch in diameter. The mouthpiece was made of buffalo horn, and the opposite end of the stem was encased in copper inlaid with silver. The bowl itself, shaped like a flattened turnip, was formed of fine clay and was handsomely carved. It was nearly three inches in diameter and was located about three-quarters of the way down the pipestem.

This bowl had a small incision about the size of a pinhead on its upper side. The smoker himself, or a servant if he could afford one, held the hot ball of opium close to the incision on the bowl (or, in a different and less elegant kind of pipe, put the ball into a small metal bowl and then held the bowl over the flame of a lamp), inhaled deeply and held his breath. What he took into his lungs was not smoke itself as from a cigarette but a potent water vapor that contained the soluble alkaloids of opium in a volatile form. Two or three long pulls at the pipe were all most smokers needed to get the full effects of the drug, but hardened addicts had to have more.[30]

THE CIVIL SERVICE EXAMINATION SYSTEM

To understand why the opium trade flourished as it did and why the Chinese government was unable to stop it, we must look at conditions in China during the first half of the nineteenth century. The military and naval weaknesses of the Ch'ing [Qing] dynasty at that time will be discussed in the chapters on the Opium Wars. There is a more fundamental question at stake here: was there an underlying reason why China was so unable to resist the inroads of the West?

There is no easy answer to this question, and it would be simplistic to put all the blame for China's weaknesses on any one feature of traditional Chinese life. What is certain, however, is that most Chinese officials, from the emperor on down, failed to understand that the Western challenge was qualitatively different from anything China had ever experienced before and that their country was in danger of losing its independence and being partitioned into different "spheres of influence" (semicolonies) by the stronger states of the West.

These officials remained locked into a worldview in which China was the center of the universe and was surrounded only by barbarians. The Chinese routinely referred to Westerners by an unflattering term, *fan kwae*, which meant "foreign devils," "outlandish demons" or "barbarian wanderers."[31] Chinese traditionalists believed that the Altar of Heaven in Peking [Beijing] was the most sacred place in the empire; the center of the altar itself was regarded as the very center of the universe.[32] As late as 1850 the maps of the world used in Chinese schools continued to show the United States, Africa and the European countries simply as insignificant islands dotted around the vast mass of the Middle Kingdom (China itself).[33]

The mandarins who ran China on a day-to-day basis also believed that the emperor was the Son of Heaven and that he ruled not by force of arms or by the will of the people but by a cosmic concurrence known as the Mandate of Heaven. These officials were convinced that China's greatness flowed from its mastery of the principles of a harmonious social order, as studied and administered by learned sages and a benevolent emperor. Their failure to understand the nature of the threat posed by the West may well have been the result of China's rigid *examination system*, which offered almost the only gateway into the prestigious, lucrative world of the civil service.[34]

Confucius

The examination system itself and the nearly unshakable conservatism of the Chinese officials it produced was rooted in the teachings of a wandering teacher. This man, known to the West as Confucius [Kong Fuzi, 551–479 B.C.], systematized and passed on a body of philosophic ideas already current in his own time. Because the Chinese lived in small, crowded villages where the individualism so valued by Western culture would have caused endless friction, Confucius taught that the ideal human society should be based on harmony, which he believed could be achieved only by following certain carefully prescribed rites and rules of behavior.

According to Confucius, human society should operate, like the cosmic order, on the hierarchical and patriarchal premise that *no two people are equal*. This concept, based in practice on age and gender differences, meant that a son had to obey his father; a wife had to obey her husband; a younger brother had to obey an older brother; and, by extension, a younger friend had to obey an older friend. A common citizen had to obey a government official. A government official had to obey the emperor. The emperor had to obey "Heaven," i.e., the will of the cosmic order itself.[35]

When a disciple asked Confucius what was the first thing he would do if he ruled a state, Confucius replied, "Let the ruler be ruler, the minister minister, the father father, and the son son." This doctrine, known as "the rectification of names," meant that every name (e.g., ruler, minister, etc.) had certain behavioral implications that constituted the essence of that calling. According to Confucius, the reality should agree with this essence. In other words, if a ruler wanted to be truly a ruler and not a ruler in name only, he had to practice what we might call "rulerhood" and what the Chinese called "the way of the ruler."[36] Similarly, a true son had to follow the dictates of "sonhood," that is, by practicing filial piety (reverence toward one's parents).

Filial piety was a cardinal step in the attainment of the greatest virtue, known as *jen* (compassion or "human-heartedness"), which was supposed to be the goal of all well-educated men.[37] In the *Analects* Confucius urged his followers to attain *jen* by "conquering yourself and returning to ritual." Although he also urged them to be free from "opinionatedness, dogmatism, obstinacy and egoism," these were the very qualities that the civil service examination system tended to encourage.

The Examinations Themselves

The beginnings of the examination system were modest enough. By about 100 B.C. a rudimentary method to recruit competent officials had been established in China. Over the years this process became more and more complex, but it transmitted Chinese cultural values so successfully that it endured for virtually 2,000 years until finally being abolished in 1904. Let us see what the examinations involved.

Traditional Chinese society was divided into four classes. In descending order of importance these were government officials, farmers, artisans and merchants.[38] Only the first two of these, however, were considered fully respectable. The others—the artisans and merchants, as well as the "lowly people" and slaves—formed the bottom layers of the social pyramid. In theory the examinations were open to any man from a respectable class but in practice, given the long years of study needed to prepare for them, only the sons of government officials, of scholars or of prosperous farmers had much chance of passing. However, a bright boy from a modest background could also succeed, provided that a rich relative or his village or temple would support him financially so he could study full-time.[39]

Confucianism permeated the examination system. When a boy was only three years old he was taught how to draw 25 simple characters.[40] He could not read them then and would not actually begin his formal education until the age of eight or nine, but these beginner's characters contained an exhortation that he would understand sooner or later:

> Let us present our work to father.
> Confucius himself
> taught three thousand.
> Seventy were capable gentlemen.
> You, young scholars,
> eight or nine!
> Work well to attain virtue,
> and you will understand propriety.
> [that is, you will learn Confucian
> manners and patterns of thought].

The examination system reached its most complex and in terms of China's real needs its most irrelevant form during the years of the last dynasty, the Qing (1644–1912) — that is, just before and during the Western impact. By the time a promising boy had completed his education at age 15, he would have mastered archaic and difficult works: the *Analects* (of Confucius), the writings of Mencius, the *Book of Changes*, the *Book of Documents*, the *Book of Poetry*, the *Book of Rites* (which included the *Great Learning* and the *Doctrine of the Mean*) and the *Tso Chuan*. Taken as a whole, Chinese literature (ancient and modern together) is said to use about 50,000 characters; Chinese newspapers today can draw on a stock of roughly 6,000 simplified characters, but only about 600 of them are commonly used. By the time he was ready to take the preliminary examinations, a young scholar of the nineteenth century had learned up to 8,000 classical characters. He had also read long commentaries on the classics, had studied other historical and literary works and had practiced writing poems and essays along traditional lines.

Having mastered all this learning, an aspiring candidate for official office then faced a long series of difficult examinations, beginning at the district and prefecture level and culminating, for a chosen few, at the emperor's palace in Peking. Because a large number of candidates were usually competing for a small number of jobs, the competition was intense. The mandarins who graded the examination papers had come up through the system themselves and were not interested in reading original or creative responses to traditional questions: they only wanted to make sure the examination process was free from any irregularities or errors that could be blamed on them.[41]

For their part, the anxious and exhausted candidates, locked into an examination hall and each confined to a tiny cubicle, knew they could answer the questions by using only certain highly stylized formats and traditional responses. They knew they would be failed if they gave anything but the most time-tested answers. The examinations could be taken more than once, but if a candidate failed to pass them after repeated tries, he could find himself in a difficult situation — too refined, too weak and ultimately too old for physical labor but not qualified for a white-collar job as a government official.

Educated nineteenth-century Westerners, who were the product of a much more liberal academic tradition, considered the examinations to be stultifying. During the Qing dynasty, for example, candidates had to write an "eight-legged" essay (i.e., an essay divided into eight parts) based on short quotations from the Confucian classics. In 1838 the eminent phonetician Li Ruzhen, who had himself managed to pass only the low-level prefectural level examination, satirized the whole process in a novel, *Flowers in the Mirror*.

One of Li Ruzhen's mythical students is at first intimidated by the scholarly mien of the tutor of a fictional academy but soon realizes that this is all a farce. For example, when formally "broaching the theme" of an essay (that is, writing a brief introduction to it), the students are permitted to paraphrase the theme, rather than presenting it with any creativity. Li Ruzhen uses as a satiric example the theme "Having heard a beast cry, he cannot bear to eat it." The students successfully "broach" this simply by repeating the text with a few tiny changes: "A man who has heard a beast cry cannot bear to eat it."[42]

Another requirement was that candidates had to write out from memory and without making a single mistake the text of one of the 16 articles of an Imperial Rescript on Education issued by a Qing emperor who reigned from 1723–1736. Here is an earlier and shorter version of such an article:

> Do your duty to your parents.
> Honor your elders.
> Be at peace with your neighbors.
> Instruct sons and grandsons.
> Be content in your occupation.
> Do not commit offenses.

One error in writing any character of an imperial article would fail a candidate, no matter how good the rest of his examination paper was. Another requirement was that he had to avoid using not only the characters used to write the name of the current emperor but also those used to write the names of any of the preceding emperors of the same dynasty. By the time they had reached this advanced stage in the examination process, however, the candidates had such well-honed memories that they could think of other characters, identical in pronunciation, which could be substituted for those in the imperial names.

On the final examinations, in which the emperor was supposed to (but rarely did) grade the papers, the candidates had to end their answers, which had to be at least 1,000 characters in length, with a pro forma statement addressed to the emperor himself. This statement reflected the hierarchical society in which they were to play leading roles as senior officials: "I, Your humble servant, a superficial scholar newly advanced, not realizing where I was, have ventured to state my own views and am so ashamed of offending the Majesty of the Emperor that I do not know where to hide. I respectfully submit my answer."

The candidates who managed to pass the examinations were awarded various degrees, usually that of *chin-shih* ("presented scholar"), which was the equivalent today of a doctoral degree in a difficult subject, obtained with the highest marks from an excellent university. The *chin-shih* degree opened up to them the best jobs in traditional China — the prestigious, secure and profitable careers of the scholar-officials. What the examination system failed to give them, however, were the very qualities they would need to cope with the West — namely, originality, creativity and flexibility.

Commissioner Lin, whose seizure of foreign opium in 1839 precipitated China's first, disastrous conflict with Britain, was himself the son of a scholar and had earned such high marks in all his examinations that a brilliant career was already being forecast for him while he was still a young man.[43] A British observer who saw Lin at work said that he had keen dark eyes and that "his countenance indicated a mind habituated to care and thoughtfulness."[44]

The examination system assured that, as one of Commissioner Lin's colleagues remarked during the course of the first Opium War, "Our military affairs are in the hands of civil officials, who are likely very admirable calligraphists but know nothing of war."[45] Later, in a memorial to Prince Kung, the emperor's younger brother, a Chinese reformer made the same point:

> Our officials are plunged into the elucidation of classical texts and the refinement of calligraphy, while our military men are the most part ignorant dullards. Our education seems quite divorced from utility. When we are at peace we despise foreign inventions as worthless, while if trouble comes our way we exclaim that it is impossible for us to learn how to employ such mysterious contrivances.[46]

A Western solution would have been either to change the examination system to make it more relevant or to jettison it entirely. Chinese conservatives, however, feared that making any changes in the way officials were recruited would threaten their own status, which was based on their mastery of the classics. They were also afraid that radical reforms would invalidate Confucianism itself and undermine the legitimacy of the dynasty. Thus the examination system was not altered in any major way during the last years of the Qing dynasty and, as a result, China remained unable to defend itself militarily. Perhaps Lord Elgin, the British commander during the second Opium War, was not overstating the case when he wrote that because the Chinese did not know how to aim their firearms and had no training in tactics or discipline, "twenty-four determined men, [armed only] with revolvers and a sufficient number of cartridges, might walk through China from one end to the other."[47]

Chinese Dislike of Westerners

The shortcomings of the examination system were probably enough to ensure that China would not be able to defend itself against the West. If the mandarins themselves had felt any curiosity about the foreigners or had been interested in getting to know them on a personal basis, it is conceivable they might have learned something important — about the West's formidable military power, its social discipline and its economic resources. The problem was, however, that many Chinese officials genuinely disliked Westerners.

Ever since the first European vessel (a Portuguese ship) anchored off Canton in 1513, the potential for cultural clashes was evident. Diplomatic relations did not begin auspiciously: in 1517 the Portuguese ambassador and his assistants were imprisoned and left to die. Despite this setback, the Portuguese were followed by the Dutch and then by the English. In 1637 the English merchant-adventurer Captain Weddell, having been refused a landing at Macao by the Portuguese, bombarded the Chinese forts guarding Canton, even though England and China were not at war. In 1741 Commander George Anson, RN, moored his ship near Canton after a storm, believing the Chinese would treat him kindly. Instead, he met with endless bureaucratic delays and was charged outrageous prices for shoddy goods.[48]

To keep the foreigners at arm's length but still be able to do business with them, the Chinese government formed in 1720 a guild of roughly 10 well-established merchants, known individually as the Hong [hang] and collectively as the Cohong [gonghang], who were the only Chinese officially allowed to have any direct contact with foreign traders. Highly respected businessmen, the Cohong merchants played a key role as middlemen, shielding foreign traders both against the bankruptcies of Chinese firms and the whims of the Imperial government.

Although they could earn high profits by selling Chinese products (chiefly tea and silk) to the East India Company or to private Western traders, the Cohong was also responsible for collecting the government's customs duties from the foreigners and for paying some of the foreigners' mandatory fees to Chinese authorities. Their role as middlemen meant they could be "squeezed" (forced to contribute money) by the government and by foreign traders alike. Significantly, as early as 1754 the Hong merchants were also ordered to stand surety for the good behavior of the often-unruly foreign crews.

Given the background of refined Chinese scholar-officials, the opium trade made cultural clashes inevitable. Even English-language publications in China complained about the "licentiousness of the crews of the Opium vessels at Whampoa" and commented editorially that "everyone must know what sort of a community is likely to be formed by a body of seafaring men pursuing an illegal trade at the mouth of their own guns."[49] In the eyes of the mandarins, the crews of the opium clippers were ignorant, drunk, smelly, arrogant, aggressive, stubborn, greedy, sex-starved, ugly and hairy. (Because Western men had considerably more facial and body hair than Chinese men, the Chinese called them "the hairy ones." Chinese converts to Christianity were derided as "the secondary hairy ones.")[50]

The scholar-officials also deplored the comparative equality of Western men and women; thought Western clothes were outlandish and so tight-fitting that Western soldiers could never move freely enough in them to fight effectively once ashore; and thought that eating so much beef and heavy greasy dishes was a disgusting habit. They were also convinced that the foreigners needed to drink tea and eat rhubarb in order to survive.[51] They had little respect for the officers of the opium ships, who were seen as poorly educated and totally lacking the "human" (that is, Confucian) qualities common to all civilized men. Without these qualities — namely, flexibility, modesty, kindness, respect for others and knowing one's place in the cosmic scheme of things — harmonious business relationships between Westerners and Chinese were, from the Chinese point of view, difficult at best.[52]

Westerners were therefore dismissed simply as "foreign devils" — as unlettered barbarians who had little to teach the Chinese, except perhaps for a bit of technology (ship building, cannon casting, etc.). Instead, the mandarins felt that it was the responsibility of the barbarians to cast aside their brutish habits while in the Middle Kingdom and to learn from their Chinese superiors. This feeling of Chinese cultural superiority was so strong that it never, ever died. For 20 years after the treaties ending the two Opium Wars, the senior British representative in China was still referred to officially as the "English barbarian chieftain."[53]

Expansion of the Opium Trade in China

This assumption of cultural superiority seriously hindered the Chinese government in its efforts to stop the opium trade. Imperial edicts were issued and reissued frequently, but none of these proclamations had any lasting effect because they were not enforced: the trade was so lucrative that, as we have seen, almost all the Chinese officials along the eastern coast were involved in it. When Governor-General Yuan felt obliged in 1821 to crack down on the trade in Canton, this only forced the foreign opium merchants and their Chinese allies to shift their operations to the nearby island of Lintin, which lay outside the Governor-General's jurisdiction.

The expansion of opium trade had grave repercussions within China itself. In a briefing report of 1832, a British Select Committee advised a British admiral that

> Although the Trade in Opium is declared by Chinese laws to be altogether illegal, yet numerous officers of Government receive stipulated bribes for their connivance, and the very vessels appointed to counteract this commerce are frequently those by whose instrumentality it was carried on. Official reports are made twice in the course of every month to the Governor of Canton of the number of Foreign ships engaged in the Trade at Lintin, and at nearly simultaneous periods public assertions are made by the commanders of the Chinese war vessels that they have swept the seas of them. We need scarcely add that the [opium] ships remain undisturbed at their anchorage.[54]

By 1844, the effects of opium trade were even more evident. As a contemporary British observer remarked in that year,

> The enormous profits derived from the clandestine sale of opium induced many of the Chinese to embark on it as a speculation, who neither used it themselves, nor were habituated to any other commercial traffic. Official men both smoked and sold it;

hundreds of people gained a livelihood by the manufacture or sale of opium-pipes, and other apparatus connected with its use; and even the armed soldier often carried an opium-pipe in his girdle [belt], with the same unconcern as he did the fan-case which is very commonly part of his costume.[55]

The trade corrupted officials as well. As mentioned earlier, the governor-general of Canton used his own boat to bring opium ashore. John Francis Davis, the British governor of Hong Kong, was right in complaining in 1844 that "It is the universal corruption of the government officers of Canton, in the article of opium, that makes it so difficult to stop the rest of the contraband trade near that port."[56]

The Extent of Addiction in China

Although it is evident that corruption was widespread, it is more difficult to answer a related question: how many opium smokers were there in China in the nineteenth century? Estimates varied widely. An officer of the East India Company who served in China between 1831 and 1837 said, "From the personal experience I have had in both countries [England and China], I have no hesitation in expressing a decided opinion, that the injury to health and morals inflicted by the use of gin in England surpasses those [caused by] opium in China."[57] An American opium trader who spent his whole working life in China had even stronger views:

> The costliness of the prepared drug was such as to render a dilution of it (to bring it within the means of the masses) utterly harmless ... smoking was a habit, as the use of wine with us, in moderation. As compared with the use of spirituous liquors in the United States and in England, and the evil consequences of it, that of opium was infinitesimal. This is my personal experience during a residence at Canton, Macao, and Hong Kong of forty years.[58]

Other equally well-informed observers, however, pointed out that although only a small fraction (probably not more than 1 percent) of China's population smoked opium, there were about 400 million people in China at the time. Thus an upper estimate of the addict population was 4 million people, many of them in responsible positions. A Chinese memorial to the emperor in 1836 stated, "The great majority of those who at present smoke opium are the relatives and dependents of the officers of Government, whose example has extended to the mercantile classes, and has gradually contaminated the inferior officers, the military, and the scholars. Those who do not smoke are the common people of the villages and hamlets."[59]

In 1854 a British medical missionary estimated there were about 3 million smokers in China; in 1871 an official British report on East India Finance put the number at 3 to 4 million.[60] The distribution of smokers was uneven, being relatively high in the big cities along the coast and low to nonexistent in the hinterland, which made up most of China. In Shanghai itself, 55 percent of the men reportedly smoked opium, but this fell to 15 percent in the more rural province of Shantung and to 0 percent in many villages in the interior.[61] The practice continued to spread, however, to the extent that by the end of the 1930s as many as 40 million people (10 percent of China's population) were thought to be opium addicts.[62]

Notes

1. Owen, *British Opium Policy*, pp. 115–117.
2. Report by George Rorie, Foochow, 15 December 1863. Jardine Matheson archives, A8/92.
3. After Booth, *Opium*, p. 4
4. Cheong, *Mandarins*, p. 87.
5. Turner, *Kwang Tung*, p. 47.
6. De Quincey, *Confessions*, pp. 180–182.
7. Booth, *Opium*, pp. 88–90.
8. *Encyclopedia Britannica*, vol. 17, p. 537.
9. Cited by J. F Davis, *The Chinese*, p. 204.
10. Turner, *Kwang Tung*, p. 47.
11. Anderson, Cruise, p. 45.
12. Anderson, *Cruise*, p. 129.
13. Hehir, *Opium*, pp. 25–27; Owen, *British Opium Policy*, pp. 2–6.
14. Winius and Vink, *VOC*, p. 70.
15. Jeffereys, *British Army*, p. 7.
16. The establishment of the British East India Company was followed by the formation of similar companies: a Dutch trading company in 1602, a Danish company in 1611 and a Swedish company in 1612. The Dutch were selling opium in Indonesia soon after the founding of their own East India Company. See Van Ours, *Price Elasticity*, pp. 262–262.
17. F. S. Turner, *British Opium Policy*, p. 57.
18. Cited in the East India Company's *Collections*.
19. Cited in the East India Company's *Collections*.

20. Owen, *British Opium Policy*, p. 9.
21. Aberigh-Mackay, *Chiefs*, pp. lii–liv.
22. Owen, *British Opium Policy*, p. 52.
23. See also Wakeman, "Canton Trade," pp. 171–178, and Hobsbawm, *Age of Capital*.
24. Keay, *Honorable Company*, pp. 454–455.
25. Edwards, *Triple Curse*, p. 3; Owen, *British Opium Policy*, pp. 47–48; and Aberigh-Mackay, *Chiefs*, pp. lii–liv.
26. Cited in *Friend*, p. 41.
27. For a discussion of traditional opium use in China, see Morse, *Relations*, p. 170 ff.
28. Owen, *British Opium Policy*, pp. 10–17; and Morse, *Trade*, pp. 324–328.
29. Jeffereys, *British Army*, p. 6.
30. After Bingham, *Narrative*, pp. 127–128; and Fairbank, *Trade and Diplomacy*, p. 65.
31. H. W. C. (Hunter, William C.), *Fan Kwae*, p. 65. Westerners were also called *i* (pronounced "eye"), which meant "barbarian." A barbarian was defined as a man who could not read Chinese and did not understand the writings of Confucius. When the British objected to the use of *i*, the Chinese substituted less pejorative terms e.g., "western ocean men," "far-traveled strangers" or "men from afar." See Williams, *History of China*, p. 109.
32. Morrison, *Old Peking*, p. 58.
33. Dr. Charles Taylor, *Five Years in China*, pp. 212–213, cited by Hibbert, *Dragon*, p. 368.
34. If a man did not take the examinations or if he failed them repeatedly, this ended his hopes of an official career. But there was one exception — a "special entry" procedure for men who were known to have outstanding abilities in one way or another. If such a person came to the attention of the emperor or of a senior official, he could be directly appointed to a post. In this way the famous poet Li Po (701–762), who never took the examinations, was given a prestigious position at the Imperial Hanlin literary academy. See Cooper, *Li Po*, p. 39.
35. Eberhard, *History of China*, pp. 35–40.
36. Fung, *Chinese Philosophy*, pp. 41–42.
37. In the *Analects*, Confucius also taught a "golden rule"—"do not do unto others what you would not want others to do unto you"— but this was a less important precept for him than filial piety itself.
38. The low status accorded to merchants by traditional Chinese society contributed to the mandarins' dislike of Western opium merchants.
39. After Eberhard, *History of China*, pp. 76–77. The importance of academic pursuits was noted by Marco Polo, who reported in his *Travels* that the Chinese "surpass other nations in the excellence of their manners and their knowledge of many subjects, since they devote much time to their study, and to the acquisition of knowledge."
40. This citation and other details about the examination system are taken from Miyazaki, *China's Examination Hell*, p. 14 ff. Another useful source is Shen Fu, who failed the examinations himself and had to take a job as the legal

secretary to a magistrate. In his *Six Records of a Floating Life*, written in 1809, he gives (on p. 65) an insight into how deeply the examination system permeated Chinese life:

> With nothing to do in the long summer [c. 1792], we held examination parties.... We would draw lots, and the winner would become the examination master, sitting apart and being in charge of the proceedings ... [another guest] would be the official recorder, and also sat separately. Everyone else became an examination candidate, and drew a sheet of paper from the recorder, all properly stamped with a seal. The examination master would announce two lines of poetry, one of five characters and one of seven characters, and the candidates would then have the time it took for a stick of incense to burn in which to write lines rhyming with them.... When they had finished their couplets they put them into a box.... To prevent favoritism, when everyone had handed in his paper the recorder opened the box and copied the papers into a book [so that the writing of the candidates could not be recognized] which he then gave to the examination master ... the writer of the couplet selected as the best ... became the next examination master.

41. Another famous Chinese poet, Tu Fu (712–770), failed the examinations. He had been experimenting with new prose styles and had developed a unique but very difficult style which 53was judged unsuitable for bureaucratic use. See Cooper, *Li Po,* p. 39.
42. Li Ruzhen, *Flowers,* p. 262.
43. Hibbert, *Dragon,* pp. 112–113.
44. *Crisis,* p. 97.
45. Cited by Hibbert, *Dragon,* p. 144.
46. Cited by Hibbert, *Dragon,* p. 310.
47. Cited by Hibbert, *Dragon,* p. 234.
48. Anson was so incensed by this high-handed treatment that he published an account that was translated into several languages and that led to a groundswell of anti-Chinese feeling in the West.
49. Cited by Downs, *Golden Ghetto,* p. 333.
50. The reference to "hairy ones" is from Franke, *Chinese Revolution,* p. 53.
51. In an 1839 edict to Westerners in Canton, Commissioner Lin warned them: "Let our ports once be closed against you, and for what profits can your several nations any longer look? Yet more, — our tea and our rhubarb, — seeing that, should you foreigners be deprived of them, you therein lose the means of preserving your life — are without stint granted for exportation year by year beyond the seas. Favors have never been greater." Cited in *Crisis,* p. 3.
52. Ch'en, *China and the West,* p. 267; and Danton, *Culture Contacts,* pp. 4–7. The Chinese were also appalled that the foreigners paid no attention to *feng-shui* [fengshui], an ancient Chinese belief that means "wind-water" and that

can be defined as the subtle influence of the landscape, for good or ill, on buildings and people.

An English missionary reported that after the first Opium War, when Westerners demanded a foreign concession in Canton (that is, a place for them to live), the Chinese were amazed that they chose the island of Sha-meen. This was originally only a mud flat in the Canton river "in the very worst position Feng-shui knows of," wrote the missionary. Because of the concession's inauspicious location, the Chinese were not surprised when the Canton trade began to slacken; when every house built on Sha-meen was overrun with white ants, which defied all attempts to eradicate them; and when the English consul himself, although a special residence had been built for him in Sha-meen, decided instead to live two miles away — under the protecting shadow of a pagoda (a Chinese temple). See Eitel, *Feng-Shui*, p. 67.

53. H. W. C. *Fan Kwae*, pp. 63–65; and Fairbank, *Trade and Diplomacy*, p. 9.
54. Cited by Morse, *Chronicles*, vol. 4, p. 277.
55. Bernard, *Nemesis*, p. 184.
56. Davis, *The Chinese*, vol. III, p. 202.
57. Lindsay, *Is the War*, p. 29.
58. H. W. C. *Fan Kwae*, p. 80.
59. Cited by F. S. Turner, *British Opium Policy*, p. 253.
60. F. S. Turner, *British Opium Policy*, p. 253.
61. F. S. Turner, *British Opium Policy*, p. 253.
62. Booth, *Opium*, p. 168.

3

The Rise of the Great Trading Houses

Private companies played a pivotal role in the India-China opium trade. After the emperor's edict of 1729, the East India Company decided not to jeopardize its lucrative role in the tea trade by continuing to carry opium to China. Thus, with two exceptions discussed later on, opium was no longer carried in the Honorable Company's own ships, even as officers' personal cargo. Instead, private "country" traders (often Parsees or Scots) based in India or Western firms based in China itself bought the drug at government auctions in Calcutta and arranged for its onward shipment to China.[1]

The India-China opium trade could not have grown to its full dimensions without the managerial, financial and shipping skills provided by these trading houses. Their directors and ships' officers had to be expert judges of the economic and logistic factors involved in getting Indian opium quickly, safely and at a good profit into the hands of Chinese smokers. In return for being able to juggle these variables successfully, they were paid well and lived well.

The Major British Firm: Jardine, Matheson and Co.

Jardine, Matheson and Co. was the biggest, richest and best-known merchant house. At times an enormously profitable company, it was founded in China in 1832 and is still in business today, although it has not dealt in opium since the early 1870s.[2] Well into the twentieth century it was deeply involved in Chinese tea, coastal shipping, docks, railroads, mines and cotton mills. Now registered in Bermuda as Jardine Matheson Holdings, Ltd., the firm is a multinational enterprise consisting of eight core companies that are headquartered in Hong Kong and offer financial services, supermarkets, consumer marketing, engineering and construction, luxury automobiles (Mercedes-Benz), property and hotels. Jardine Matheson has commercial operations in more than 30 countries, but 75 percent of its earnings still come from Hong Kong and mainland China. It employs, directly or indirectly, about 200,000 people, and it may be the biggest foreign contractor working in China today. Jardine Matheson's net profits vary considerably from one year to another, but in the 1990s they seem to have averaged between U.S. $300–400 million annually.[3]

Dr. William Jardine (1784–1843) left Scotland in 1802 as surgeon's mate in the East Indiaman *Brunswick*. When his ship was captured by the French off Ceylon, he became a prisoner of war until he was exchanged (freed) in South Africa. During these adventures he met a young Parsee merchant, Jamsetjee Jejeebhoy, who became a lifelong friend and business associate.[4] After leaving the East India Company's service, Jardine went into the China trade on his own as a free merchant, working as an agent for firms in India. Between 1819 and 1823 he was loosely associated in business with T. Weeding, London, and Framjee Cowasjee, Bombay, but remained a free agent and in this capacity began to handle opium for Charles Magniac and Co. of Canton. He joined Magniac and Co. in 1825, and after James Matheson came aboard, this firm was renamed Jardine, Matheson and Company in 1832.

Jardine himself was a hard man, known locally (though not to his face) as "Iron-headed Old Rat"—referring to an incident at the Petition Gate in Canton when he was clubbed hard on the head from behind but did not so much as even turn around.[5] He had a lighter side, too. An American who had lived in China for 40 years remembered that at a dinner given for Jardine before his final departure for London in January 1839, there being no women present, "Then was seen what had never been seen at Canton before, Mr. Jardine himself and Mr. Wetmore attempting a Waltz."[6]

There was, however, little frivolity in this man's life, and he remained a hardheaded businessmen. In 1840 he defended his role as one

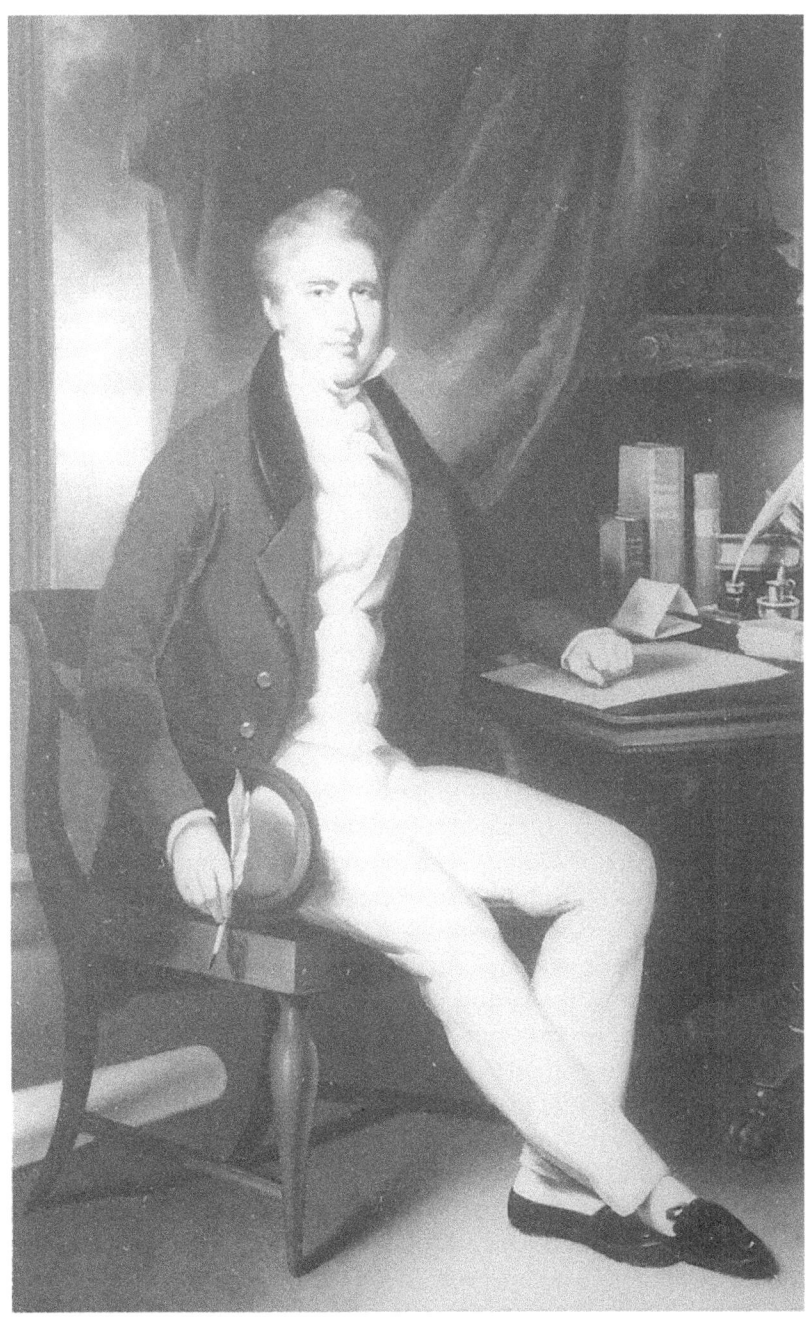

William Jardine (private collection)

of the world's leading opium merchants (at that time he had at least 12 ships in the trade) by citing the repeated conclusion of both Houses of Parliament, with — as he said, "all the bench of bishops at their back" — that it was financially inexpedient to abolish this controversial trade.[7] In any case, despite his critics Jardine clearly thought himself in the right and once urged a friend in Essex to invest in opium because it was "the safest and most gentlemanlike speculation I am aware of."[8] Jardine made a vast fortune in the China trade and retired to Britain to enjoy it and to serve as a member of Parliament from 1841 to 1842.

James Matheson (1796–1878), also a Scotsman, was educated at the University of Edinburgh and joined his uncle's business house, Mackintosh and Company, at Calcutta in 1815. By 1820 he was serving as the Danish consul at Canton and trading with Manila and Singapore. By his own account he was (in 1823) the first trader to run the great risk of selling opium along the Fukien coast north of the Canton estuary without any prearrangement with Chinese authorities there. In 1825 he joined Magniac and Co. and later became co-owner of the new firm of Jardine Matheson.

His first two coastal cargoes alone brought in a total of $212,000, and by 1838 his partner William Jardine could write from Canton to Captain John Rees of the bark *Austin*: "We are sadly at a loss for clippers just now, the demand for them, to deliver among the islands [off the central coast of China], being so great."[9] When Jardine retired in 1839 and went back home to enjoy his fortune, Matheson ran the company until he too retired to Britain with his own fortune and was a member of Parliament there from 1843 to 1862. His nephew, Alexander Matheson, took over the firm in China.

The company's operations in the Far East in the nineteenth century are documented in the Jardine Matheson archives, which total about 650 linear feet of material and include account books, ledgers, bills of lading, insurance certificates, miscellaneous reports and approximately 175,000 letters. All these may be consulted by researchers after they have obtained permission from Matheson and Co. in London (Jardine Matheson's London agents) and from the Cambridge University Library. These remarkable documents, often written in an elegant copperplate hand, reflect the daily buying, selling, accounting and shipping transactions that were the heart and soul of the opium trade. The Private Letter Books of William Jardine are especially valuable as a primary source because they contain copies of the many letters he sent from China to business associates in India and in the United Kingdom. The Jardine Matheson archives are, in short, a unique resource because they shed an intimate light on the daily operations of foreign merchants in China and reveal some of the inner workings of the opium trade.[10]

Other Trading Houses, British and American

After Jardine, Matheson and Co., the second most important British firm was Dent and Co., but it did not last long, going bankrupt during a banking collapse in 1865.[11]

American firms, for their part, played an active role in most aspects of the China trade. The *China Pilot* reported that of the 306 vessels that arrived at Canton in 1844, 57 were American.[12] By 1845 at least 46 American vessels were regularly engaged in the trade, usually carrying American exports to China and cargoes of tea back to New York.[13] American merchants, however, faced the same basic problem as their British cousins: the Chinese considered themselves entirely self-sufficient and had little interest in foreign products. The Americans had to find something to sell, however, to generate funds to buy the Chinese products, mainly tea and silk, that were in great demand in the United States.

Among the few American commodities that China would buy were blocks of ice from Boston's lakes, ginseng (an aromatic root) from New England, sea otter pelts and furs from the northwest coast (the coastline from northern California to Alaska), and sandalwood from the Sandwich (now the Hawaiian) and other Pacific islands. American silver dollars were always in demand. The Chinese market for most of these products soon became saturated and, looking around for a product that they could transport and sell easily at a good profit, some American traders turned

James Matheson (private collection)

to opium. The United States had previously financed its tea and silk imports from China both by its traditional exports to China and by the hard currency it earned by selling cotton to Britain. Now it was opium, paid for in silver by the Chinese, that helped to balance international trade.[14]

Because the British dominated much of the trade with India (the East India Company's monopoly on trade with India was not abolished until 1814 and with China until 1834), American merchants had to locate another source of opium. This they found in Turkey. The first captain to bring opium directly from Smyrna, Turkey, to China was Christopher L. Gantt, who carried a small amount of opium — "46 chests and 53 boxes" — to Canton in 1805 in the Baltimore brig *Entan*.[15] Although American traders subsequently acted as consignment agents in Canton for the "country" ships that carried Bengal and Malwa opium from India, they lagged far behind the British in their overall involvement in the opium trade. This can be seen from several overlapping estimates:

- Between 1818 and 1833 a total of 594 American ships brought $4,925,977 worth of opium into China. During the same period, however, 904 British ships brought in opium worth $104,302,948 (i.e., more than 20 times as much).[16]
- In the 28 years between 1806 and 1834 the Americans carried to China a declared total of 8,901 chests of opium; the real total must have been much higher, but it still constituted only a modest level of trade.[17]
- Americans are thought to have sold to the Chinese $133,000 worth of opium in 1824 and $275,921 worth in 1836, but this was insignificant compared to the $7.5 million and $9 million Americans spent in these years, respectively, for Chinese products, mainly tea.[18]
- Of the roughly 100 sailing vessels that were running opium into China on a regular basis, only 17 or 18 were American built. In chronological order, some of these were:[19]

Vessel	Built at	Year built
Dhaulle (pilot boat schooner)	Baltimore	1825
Ann McKim (clipper)	Baltimore	1832
Eagle (clipper-brig)	New York	1835
Anglona (pilot boat schooner)	New York	1841

Ariel (topsail schooner)	Medford	1841
Mazeppa (schooner)	Boston	1841
Zephyr (pilot boat schooner)	Boston	1842
Antelope (clipper-brig)	Boston	c. 1843
Minna (schooner)	Portsmouth	1851
Brenda (schooner)	Portsmouth	1852

Individual Americans did make some money in opium. (One of them was Warren Delano II, the grandfather of President Franklin Delano Roosevelt. Delano became the head of Russell and Co. in 1840). But, on balance, this trade was not of enormous importance to the United States economy as a whole and did not by itself produce any great American fortunes. The best guess is that at their high point the Americans had only about 10 percent of the Chinese market for opium.[20] By 1880 at the latest, American participation in the China opium trade (and in other freight carrying along the China coast) was over.[21]

Russell and Co.

The biggest American firm was Russell and Co., founded by Samuel Russell in 1818. He and Philip Ammidon ran the firm until 1830, when William H. Low and Augustine Heard became partners, too, and young John Forbes joined the staff.[22] Russell and Co. was chiefly an agency house; that is, it ran ships to and from India carrying cargoes belonging to others, not to the firm itself. It did not trade on its own account, although members of the firm could buy and sell opium on their personal accounts. By 1841, however, Russell and Co. may have changed its way of doing business, if only temporarily, and reportedly sent a cargo of tea to Mexico in a ship of its own.[23]

The agency trade itself proved to be exceptionally profitable: Russell and Co. earned more than $1,000,000 between 1834–1839 alone and ran at least four ships on the China coast and three others between India and China, all under the American flag.[24] One of the best American opium captains, Robert Bennet Forbes, was the head of this firm from

Howqua, the most famous Chinese merchant of the opium trade (private collection)

1839 to 1840. It soon became the biggest opium trader after Jardine Matheson and Dent, in part because two of Russell and Co.'s best clients were the well-known British bank of Baring Bros. and the Chinese Cohong merchant known to Westerners as Howqua or Houqua (Wu Bingjian).

Howqua was the leading Chinese opium dealer until 1821, when he apparently stopped investing in the drug, probably because the Chinese government had halted the trade at Canton and he did not want to risk offending the governor-general. He was so cautious in all his dealings with Chinese officials and foreign traders alike that he became known as the "Timid Old Lady." When Howqua and other senior Cohong merchants were squeezed by the local mandarin to contribute $200,000, Howqua himself was prepared to pay $50– $60,000 immediately and to go as high as $100,000 if necessary. When a $6 million ransom had to be paid to prevent a British attack on Canton, $2 million were squeezed from the Cohong merchants; Howqua himself paid $820,000.[25] He estimated his own fortune in 1834 at $26 million.[26] Howqua was very popular with American opium captains, probably because he was so honest and seemed to like them. He was the only Cohong merchant to have a clipper ship named after him. This was Russell and Co.'s 142-foot-long *Houqua*, built by Brown and Bell in New York at a cost of $36,000. The New York *Herald* was quite taken by this vessel, reporting that

> We never saw a vessel so perfect in all her parts as this new celestial packet [that is, a ship destined for the China trade]. She is about 600 tons in size [another account puts her at 450 tons]— as sharp as a cutter — as symmetrical as a yacht — as rakish in her rig as a pirate — as neat in her deck and cabin arrangements as a lady's boudoir. Her figure head is a bust of Houqua and her bows are as sharp as a pair of Chinese shoes.[27]

Captain Robert Bennet Forbes described Howqua himself in these glowing terms: "He had a most comprehensive mind, and united the qualities of an enterprising merchant and a sagacious politician. He was always a warm friend to the Americans, and through them was supposed to have carried on a considerable trade, on his own account, both to Europe and the United States."[28]

Historians of the opium trade are also indebted to Russell and Co. because one of its employees — William C. Hunter, who joined the firm in 1829 and became a partner in 1837 — has left us some of the most accurate and most readable accounts of how the trade was carried on.[29]

Scholars are also indebted to the American firm of Augustine Heard and Co., founded in 1840, which acted as opium and tea agents for Jardine Matheson and traded by using the clipper *Frolic* and other ships. The papers of this firm are now held by the Baker Library at Harvard University's Graduate School of Business Administration and constitute Harvard's biggest collection of business papers for any nineteenth-century firm.[30]

The Parsees

British and American companies were certainly not the only ones in the opium business: Indian (usually Parsee) firms were deeply involved in it, too, and by the time of the first Opium War in 1839, much of the trade was in Parsee hands. Colossal profits were made.[31] These merchants, who were often related to one another, generally exported Malwa opium from the west coast of India through the British port of Bombay or the Portuguese port of Daman, depending on which one offered the lowest rates, but they sent cargoes out of Calcutta as well.

The Parsee family of Pestonjee Bomanjee Wadia, for example, had been connected for centuries with western Indian shipping and had four vessels of its own in the opium trade.[32] Other well-known Parsee traders included Rustomjee Cowasjee Banajee, whose firm during 1812–1852 is said to have had 39 ships in the "country" and opium trades, as well as others along the China coast.[33] Jardine Matheson's big receiving ship moored in Hong Kong bore a Parsee name: *Comanjee Hormusjee*. One famous opium clipper, *Cowasjee Family*, was built in Calcutta in 1836 and became the favorite ship of the Parsee merchant Dadabhoy Rustomjee, probably because although it was nearly sunk in a clash with 15 Chinese war junks, it managed to escape. After its career in the opium trade the ship was sold to the Sultan of Muscat, who converted it into a man-of-war and renamed it *Prince of Wales*.

The Sassoons

The Sephardic Jewish Sassoon family originally came from Persia but settled in Bombay, where eight of its sons were eventually involved in the opium trade. The first member of the family to arrive in Canton was Elias, David Sassoon's second son, who went into business there in 1844. In the 1840s David Sassoon and Sons was still a small firm when compared with Jardine Matheson, which for several decades was the largest importer of opium into China. In the 1870s the Sassoons managed to corner the opium market in India — to such an extent that Jardine Matheson found it uneconomical to compete and decided to withdraw from the trade entirely.[34]

Juggling Economic and Logistic Variables

Jardine and Matheson themselves made great fortunes out of the opium trade, and many other traders did well enough to retire early and live comfortably. This was a speculative and risky business, however, and the price of opium fluctuated, like that of any other commodity, in response to market conditions. According to a contemporary source, the average price of a chest of opium in Canton was $1,325 in 1821; $723 in 1825; $587 in 1830; and $648 in 1832.[35] Some firms, especially the smaller ones, lost money in bad years. In the more frequent good years, however, they could expect to recoup their losses quickly enough because gross profits ran as high as $1,000 per chest.[36] Dealers who were willing to take risks and who had the foresight to buy opium immediately after Commissioner Lin's seizure of British opium in 1839, when the price temporarily fell to $150–$200 a chest, made what one commentator called "enormous fortunes" as soon as the price soared to $800–$1,000 per chest.[37]

Seen in overview, the opium trade was part of a triangular trade between India, China and Britain. It worked as follows[38]: First, Indian products — chiefly opium produced under the auspices of the East India Company but some cotton as well — were exported to China, where payment for the opium was made in silver. Payment itself was virtually risk free for the foreign trader because he was always paid in full and in cash before he handed over the drug. George Davis, the captain of the American opium brig *Eagle*, remembered how "The Chinese opium smugglers, when they required a supply of opium would run up alongside [a receiving ship], and, putting a bag of Spanish pillar dollars in one scale, it would be balanced by opium in the other, the price being weight for weight, and when they had obtained as much as they required would be off to dispose of their cargo [ashore]."[39]

Goods from China — notably tea but also some silk, sycee silver and financial instruments known as bills of exchange — were exported to England from Canton and other coastal ports of China.[40]

Proceeds from the sale of these products in England were used to pay for the Indian opium and the Chinese products, especially tea. These proceeds were also used to buy manufactured British goods, which were exported to India. British merchants dreamed of the day, which never arrived, when they would be able to sell large amounts of their manufactured goods in China itself. In the meantime, they were prepared to use opium to gain entry to this market. Thus in 1835 a former officer of the East India Company offered some advice to aspiring entrepreneurs: "The readiest and most effective method for introducing British manufacturers into China, through ports other than that of Canton, that is, by a contraband trade, must be by providing every ship fitted for that particular object, with a certain portion of opium as part of its cargo."[41]

In its day-to-day workings, the India-China trade could be quite complex. For example, one of the British presidencies (administrative units) in India could advance rupees to agency houses (the British trading firms controlling the "country" trade), which would use the rupees to buy Indian opium or Indian cotton. These goods would be sold in Canton for Spanish silver dollars. The dollars would be deposited in the East India Company's treasury in Canton, minus the "country" traders' profits. Alternatively, the East India Company's office in Canton could also accept specie from a "country" trader in exchange for bills of exchange on London or Bengal.

Yet another approach was to transfer credit "in treasury." This meant that if the Honorable Company owed an advance to a given Cohong merchant, he could use the advance to buy opium or cotton from a "country" trader. The merchant would then transfer his company debt to the trader, who in turn would remit it to London by a bill of exchange drawn on the company's court of directors.

Silver could be shipped from port to port, and this was often done. Sailing before the mast in 1834 as a common seaman, George Davis served in the American ship *Niantic* when it carried 150,000 Spanish pillar dollars from New York to Canton. Later, as *Eagle*'s captain, he loaded "an immense amount of treasure" in sycee silver and silver dollars at Shanghai and brought this booty safely to Hong Kong, where it was put aboard a British man-of-war bound for England.[42] To reduce the high costs involved in transporting and storing such a valuable cargo, Canton merchants and other traders often relied on bills of exchange, which could easily be cashed in London or in India. Before the first Opium War, many foreign merchants in China simply turned their silver over to the East India Company in return for these bills; the Company then used the silver to buy tea and silk.

So much money was to be made in the opium trade that many people tried to cash in on it. A certain Chinese inhabitant of Macao, for example, used to earn his living as a go-between. On the one hand, he accepted bribes from the Portuguese for allowing their opium shipments to enter Macao; on the other, he passed these payments on, minus his own commission, to the Chinese officials charged with suppressing the opium trade. In 1821, however, he became greedy and hired some local thugs to beat up one of his rivals. The Chinese authorities arrested him for this breach of the peace. What began as a minor incident soon escalated to the point where the local governor himself felt forced to intervene. Fearing that his own lucrative position would be in jeopardy if he did nothing to stop the illegal trade being carried on so blatantly in his jurisdiction, he ordered that Canton, Whampoa and Macao be closed to the opium trade.[43]

Although this was seen as a drastic step, it did not have much effect. The closure merely forced the ever-resourceful traders to shift their operations to the "outer seas," that is, to the waters beyond official Chinese jurisdiction. This they did by stationing receiving ships for the opium at the island of Lintin, about 40 miles from Canton, during the winter months and moving them during the southwest monsoon to the more secure Cumsingmoon or Hong Kong anchorages. A contemporary observer reported that

> Lintin is merely a roadstead, where the ships anchor, and are protected by the peak of Lintin from the violence of the northeast monsoon. Where there is an approach of threatening weather, or any great repairs are required, they go over to the opposite shore, and enter the haven of Cum-sing-moon.... You are very much surprised, however, at first, upon asking where such a vessel is, to be told that "she is in the moon," which is the abbreviation generally adopted by natives and foreigners.[44]

Although Lintin and the other anchorages were within or just at the entrance to the Canton estuary, they were conveniently treated by Chinese and foreigners alike as lying entirely within the "outer seas" and therefore not subject to Chinese control. In these congenial new settings the opium trade began to flourish. It was easier and much less risky to transship opium there; moreover, the prohibition of the drug now made it an even more desirable commodity for consumers in the Canton area and along the coast. Thus it was that after a slow start in the eighteenth century, the opium trade quickly picked up speed in the nineteenth century and reached its zenith in the 1870s. A temporary dip in the number of chests imported is evident when Whampoa was closed in 1821, but from then on the trade grew by leaps and bounds, although for many reasons other than the simple closure of the port itself:

Year	Estimated number of chests imported
1729	200
1767	1,000
1808–1820	an average of about 4,000–5,000
1821	3,137
1825	9,621
1826	12,000
1829	16,000
1830	18,760
1831	19,000
1832	23,670
1835	30,000
1848	40,000–45,000
1849	53,075
1855	78,354
1865	85,000
1870	88,683
1871	85,518
1872	93,364
1874	88,726
1885–1895	an average of about 82,000
1901–1905	an average of about 51,000
1908	61,900
1909	56,800
1910	51,700
1917	0[45]

Life in China for foreign opium merchants could be pleasant indeed, even though before the Opium Wars they could live only in Canton and reside there only in a carefully circumscribed area known as the

"Thirteen Factories." American opium trader William C. Hunter remembered that although stay-at-home Americans and British might have imagined that life in Canton was restricted, dangerous and uncertain, the reality was really quite different. The Chinese government's bark was much worse than its bite. Hunter tells us that foreign traders were

> threatened and re-threatened with the "direst penalties" if we continued to sell *foreign mud* to the people, whereby they were ruined in health and plunged into inanition, while the precious metals [sycee silver and silver dollars] oozed out of the country. Truly, "forbearance could no longer be exercised"; and we continued to sell the drug as usual. Our receiving ships at Lintin were no longer to loiter at that anchorage, but "forthwith come into port or return to their respective countries." The heart of the ruler of all within the *Four Seas* [the emperor] was full of compassion. "Yet now, no more delay could be granted, and cruisers would be sent to open fire on them with irresistible broadsides"; and in spite of these terrors the ships never budged.... And so, in numerous other ways, everything worked smoothly and harmoniously by acting in direct opposition to what we were ordered to do. We pursued the evil tenor of our ways with supreme indifference, took care of our business, pulled [rowed] boats, walked, dined well, and so the years rolled by as happily as possible.[46]

Notes

1. Parsees were the descendants of the Persian Zoroastrians who came to India in the seventh and eighth centuries to escape Muslim persecution.
2. The genealogy of Jardine, Matheson and Co.—e.g., its descent from Cox and Reid, founded in 1782—is sketched out by Greenberg, *British Trade*, p. 223.
3. Calculated from Jardine Matheson's *Group Profile, 1997 Annual Report* and *1997 Annual Results Presentation*.
4. Keswick, *Thistle*, p. 14.
5. Keswick, *Thistle*, p. 13.
6. Hunter, *Bits of Old China*, p. 269.
7. Greenberg, *British Trade*, p. 104.
8. William Jardine's Private Letter Book, 3 April 1830, cited by Greenberg, *British Trade*, p. 105.
9. Fairbank, *Trade and Diplomacy*, p. 66; and a 2 January 1838 letter from Jardine to Rees in William Jardine Private Letter Book. Jardine Matheson archives.
10. Greenberg, *British Trade*, pp. xi–xii.

11. Keswick, *Thistle*, p. 70.
12. *China Pilot*, p. 59.
13. Cutler, *Greyhounds*, p. 115.
14. See Layton, *Frolic*, p. 92.
15. Stelle, *Americans*, p. 15.
16. Morse, *Relations*, pp. 89–90.
17. After Morse, *Relations*, p. 170 ff.
18. Fairbank, *Trade and Diplomacy*, p. 22.
19. After Chapelle, *Baltimore Clipper*, p. 146, and *Search for Speed*, p. 317; also Davis, *Recollections*, p. 241.
20. Fairbank, *Trade and Diplomacy*, pp. 3, 4–5, 22. Most American traders stayed in Canton only long enough to acquire a "competency" (that is, one *lakh*, or $100,000). After returning to the United States, some of them invested their opium earnings in American railroads, textiles, etc., and parleyed these investments into substantial fortunes. (Private communication of 25 May 1998 from Dr. Jacques M. Downs.)
21. Stelle, *Americans*, p. 138.
22. For the history of Russell and Co. from 1823–1844, see H. W. C. (Hunter, William C.), *Fan-Kwae*, pp. 156–157; and Downs, *Golden Ghetto*, pp. 162–189.
23. For the source of this report, see Downs, *Golden Ghetto*, p. 182.
24. Russell and Co.'s earnings are computed from data in Downs, *Golden Ghetto*, p. 177.
25. Mackenzie, *Narrative*, p. 133.
26. H. W. C. *Fan-Kwae*, pp. 37, 48.
27. Cited by Cutler, *Greyhounds*, p. 111.
28. Forbes, *Remarks*, p. 14.
29. See H. W. C. *Fan Kwae*, and Hunter, *Bits of Old China*.
30. Layton, *Frolic*, pp. 18–21.
31. Coates, *Trade*, p. 52.
32. One of these vessels was the archaic *Pestonjee Bomanjee*, said to have been more that 100 years old. Found abandoned in the Red Sea in about 1850, its pointed prow, low waist, narrow poop, tapering yards and lateen-rigged gaff sails reflected a bygone age of shipbuilding. The ship continued to trade in the Indian Ocean until it was finally lost in a typhoon off Madras, India, in about 1879. See Lubbock, *Opium Clippers*, pp. 14–16.
33. Coates, *Trade*, p. 58.
34. Jackson, *Sassoons*.
35. Davis, *The Chinese*, p. 204.
36. Greenberg, *British Trade*, p. 185.
37. Bingham, *Narrative*, p. 160.
38. Useful sources on the triangular trade are Jardine Matheson, *Jardine Matheson*, p. 23; MacGregor, *Tea Clippers*, p. 9; Layton, *Frolic*, p. 92; and "Canton Trade and the Opium War," p. 168.
39. George Davis, *Recollections*, pp. 244–245. A pillar dollar was a Spanish coin bearing an image of the Pillars of Hercules. These were the two

promontories on either side of the eastern end of the Strait of Gibraltar: the Rock of Gibraltar in Europe and Jebel Musa in Africa. Davis neglected to mention that the Chinese opium smugglers would often pay *cumsha* to the captain of the receiving ship.

40. A bill of exchange is a written order from the writer (the "drawer") to the person to whom it is addressed (the "drawee"), authorizing him to pay a certain sum on a given date, either to the drawer or to a third person named in the bill (the "payee"). A bill of exchange was usually given for value received (e.g., for silver), and this was often stated on the bill itself. Bills of exchange were easier and safer to handle than cash, and they also paid interest.

41. Thompson, *Considerations*, pp. 132–133.

42. George Davis, *Recollections*, pp. 172, 246.

43. See *Notices*, pp. 65–70; and Williams, *Middle Kingdom*, vol. 2.

44. Downing, *Fan-Qui*, pp. 50–51.

45. All these figures are estimates and do not necessarily include the opium that was smuggled into China. My sources for them were Milburn, *Oriental Commerce*, pp. 294–295; J. F. Davis, *The Chinese*, vol. 3, p. 204; Morse, *Relations*, vol. 2, p. 556; *Friend*, p. 358; the International Opium Commission's *Report*, vol. 2, p. 178; Cheong, *Mandarins*, p. 21; Morse, *Trade*, p. 327; Beeching, *Opium Wars*, p. 11; Hobsbawm, *Revolution*; an "Opium in China" chronology in a 1978 study by the U.S. Department of Health, Education and Welfare entitled *Perspectives on the History of Psychoactive Substance Use* (Research Issues 24); and Owen, *British Opium Policy*, p. 286 ff.

46. Hunter, *Bits of Old China*, pp. 1–3.

4

Ships of the Opium Trade

The officers and men who carried opium from India to China or up the China coast were superb seamen and gunners who were ready to face death-or-glory adventures in return for high profits. Their gunnery and organizational skills made them superior to any defensive force the Chinese could muster. Over the years many different kinds of vessels were used in the opium trade. They included sturdy "country" craft, ornate East Indiamen, fast opium clippers, permanently moored receiving ships, rakish coasters and the multioared "centipedes" manned by Chinese smugglers. Faced with such a heavily-armed armada, it is not surprising that the cumbersome, ineffective war junks of the Chinese government rarely ventured far from their safe anchorages.

The "Country" Ships and East Indiamen

The British East India Company was trading directly with China as early as 1637. Opium was not officially listed in these early cargoes, but it was carried privately by employees of the company for their own profit and was carried by private passengers as well. As has been mentioned, the Chinese government issued in 1729 the first of a long series of edicts to curtail opium consumption. The Honourable Company decided not to risk compromising its profitable monopoly on tea and other Chinese exports by continuing to import opium, which had now become contraband. Thus in 1733 the company directed that — even though "it having been the usual thing heretofore for shipps [sic] bound from Fort St. George [on the Coromandel coast of India] to carry ophium [sic] with them for sale in China"[1] — henceforth its own ships, such as *Windlesham* and *Compton*, were forbidden to do so. Thereafter the company itself refused to carry opium, except on two ill-starred occasions.

The first was in 1781, when the armored sloop *Betsy* was engaged to carry Indian opium to the Malay Peninsula but was seized there by a French privateer. The second was in 1782, when *Nonsuch* carried 601 chests of Patna opium to China but had to sell it there at a loss because the market was depressed. With these two exceptions, the company otherwise washed its hands of the seaborne portion of the opium trade and left it entirely in the hands of the private entrepreneurs of the "country" trade.

The origins of this trade are obscure, but the term itself dates from the end of the seventeenth century. It refers in part to the trade carried out by vessels owned by British subjects (often Scots or Parsees) living in India. The captains of East Indiamen sometimes bought the ships they sailed and then used them to trade on their own account. The earliest record of English merchants in the "country" trade importing opium from Calcutta to Canton dates from 1773, though by then their trade as a whole was well established, and they had been involved in it for many years. Many of John Company's ships were sold in the Far East, usually to Parsee merchants. The Parsees were astute traders and liked to name their ships after members of their extended family. Thus we find in contemporary records frequent references to "country" ships with such sonorous names as *Jamsetjee Jejeebhoy, Rustomjee Cowasjee, Pestonjee Bomanjee, Cowasjee Family* and *Framjee Cowasjee*.

"Country" vessels were considered the finest fleet of merchantmen in the world in their time. The captain of a tea clipper reported that "country" ships "were kept in beautiful order, more like a man-of-war than a merchantman; the decks holystoned white; copper sheathing polished and oiled; yards all a-taught [tight]-o; and the furled sails rolled up in snow-white covers."[2] They were slow, heavy, broad-beamed ships with apple-cheeked bows and golden sails of Bombay canvas, built of tough, long-lasting, rot-free Malabar teak in the shipyards of Bombay and Calcutta. Below the waterline their hulls were protected from marine growths and wood-eating teredo worms by a thick mixture of fish oil and lime or by copper or "yellow metal" sheathing. Trading on their own

4. Ships of the Opium Trade

"Country" ship *Jamsetjee Jejeebhoy* (private collection)

account, they generally remained in Far Eastern waters, bringing Indian opium and cotton to China, as well as rice, pepper and tin from the Strait of Malacca. Sometimes they carried commercial dispatches and tea back to London. William C. Hunter, the American merchant who worked in China from 1825 to 1844, remembered them with affection in his *The 'Fan Kwae' at Canton*. (The Chinese called all foreigners *foreign devils* but distinguished between them easily enough. The English were the "Red-haired devils" and the Americans were the "Flowery-flag devils"—a reference to the stars and stripes of the American flag.) Here is Hunter's firsthand account:

> The local name for their business was the "Country Trade," the ships were "Country Ships," and the masters of them "Country Captains." Some of my readers may recall a dish which was often placed before us, when dining on board these vessels at Whampoa, viz. "Country Captain." [See Appendix I for a modern recipe for this excellent dish]. The ships were "Country" built as well, and of teak; they were not fast sailors, but comfortable and substantial. They made one voyage annually, rolling up the China Sea before the south-west monsoon and rolling down again with the north-east. Some of them, as the "Sulimany," the "Fort William," the "Futty Salaam," were not far from their eightieth birthday.... These formidable vessels were not of the modern clipper model, but broad-backed, with swelling sides and full bows. On board everything was neat, everything indicated system, discipline, and force [pp. 33–34].

Some of the East Indiamen that had been built in England were also used in the "country" trade. In 1793 the Company's monopoly on commerce with China and India had been partially ended. Trade with India was thereafter open to private individuals — provided, however, that they used the Company's ships and worked under its supervision. Private traders had to sail under a license issued by the company and were subject to the authority of its supercargoes (employees responsible for selling a ship's cargo in port and for keeping the accounts) once they reached Canton. In 1814 the company's Indian monopoly was abolished altogether, but the one in trade to China continued until 1834.

The Honourable Company's ships looked to some observers like a cross between a medieval castle and a floating warehouse. They had a top speed of only six knots (vs. 14 knots for a crack opium clipper) and were frequently bought by their captains or by Parsee merchants in India for use in private trade. In 1836 a British surgeon reported,

> The splendid Indiamen engaged in this service are an honour to the nation which sends them forth, and plainly point out the importance of the trade. They range from 600 to 1400 tons burden, and are fitted up in the best style for comfort and security. The inhabitants of these wooden castles consist of a captain, three or four mates, a surgeon, and from forty to eighty seamen, including petty officers. A few cannon are generally kept mounted, and small arms are in constant readiness. In the larger vessels, the uniform and etiquette of the Company's service are still kept up.[3]

Not much information on the early "country" ships has survived, but we know more about the East Indiamen. The most prestigious merchant ships of their day, they were big, heavy, slow, wellarmed (as many as 40 guns were mounted on the middle deck) and carried crews of up to 130 men. The passenger list included company employees who slept in their own spacious cabins and who dined with the captain, whereas less-favored travelers had to make do with makeshift cabins in the middle deck. The sailors themselves slept in hammocks mounted near the guns.

Today, visitors to the Netherlands National Maritime Museum in Amsterdam can go aboard the East Indiaman *Amsterdam*, a replica of the Dutch East India Company ship by the same name, which was built in Holland in 1749. She and her sister ships carried pepper and other products of the tropics, gold and silver in coins and ingots, Dutch textiles,

4. Ships of the Opium Trade

Dutch East Indiaman Amsterdam (photograph by the author)

French and German wines, and commodities for the Dutch East India Company in Asia — clothing, writing materials, bricks and tools. *Amsterdam* is 157 feet long, has a beam of 38 feet, a mainmast 183 feet high, a richly ornamented stern and is armed with 42 cannons.

One of the best examples of a British East Indiaman was the 1,330-ton ship *Thames*. Owned by Henry Blansard, a private trader who leased the ship to the East India Company for six voyages, this vessel was said to be one of the biggest and finest of her class, a claim confirmed by a contemporary illustration now in the British Library in London. She was launched at Blackwall on the River Thames in 1819. By that time so many ships had already been built in England that there was an acute shortage of compass timber — the naturally curved, immensely strong pieces of wood cut from a tree at the point where a major branch joins the trunk or where the trunk itself forks. To shore up her wooden walls, *Thames*'s builders were among the first to use iron knees (right-angled pieces of iron connecting the beams of a vessel to her timbers), iron breast hooks (these reinforced the ship's stem) and iron pillars (vertical supports for the deck beams and the deck itself).

The log of *Thames*'s maiden voyage has survived and can be consulted at the National Maritime Museum in Greenwich, United Kingdom. Although some of the entries are impossible to read now — all are written in the elegant copperplate handwriting of the nineteenth century, and many have faded over the years — it is clear that *Thames* sailed from England on 28 December 1819 and arrived at Bombay in early May 1820. The ship then headed for China, first touching at Penang, Malacca and Singapore to take aboard a load of pepper. It finally reached Whampoa on 20 August 1820.

Firm discipline must be maintained on all ships. *Thames* had not been in Whampoa for more than two days when a seaman named John Jones had to be "confined in irons [have his legs shackled to iron bars] for getting drunk when on duty in the gig [a light, narrow ship's boat] and endangering the safety of the boat, and the lives of those in her." The next month another seaman, Charles Rocks, stole pepper from his ship's hold and was caught red-handed trying to sell it over the side to a Chinese boatman. Thrown in irons for nine days, Rocks was no sooner released than he was back in irons again, this time for being insolent and threatening a midshipman.

With discipline reestablished, *Thames* loaded chests of tea at Whampoa, picked up passengers at Macao and on 22 November 1820 got underway for home. The log ends with its safe arrival in England on 9 April 1821. Records of later voyages appear to have been lost. What is known is that after *Thames*'s sixth trip on the company's behalf in 1832, Blansard sold her to Joseph Somes, a former company employee who was setting up under his own name one of the biggest British shipping firms of the early and middle nineteenth century. Somes then used *Thames* and other former company ships to trade extensively in the Far East.

The Opium Clippers

It was soon recognized that the big East Indiamen were not ideal for the India-China trade. An officer of the East India Company recommended that "smaller vessels, drawing much less water than the larger ones ... are much better suited for navigating the China seas, and the several passages leading to those seas ... particularly when the navigation occurs in those months which are considered more or less out of season."[4]

Gradually, beginning in the 1820s a new type of ship appeared in Far East waters and freed the opium trade from the tyranny of the monsoons. This was the early clipper, which can be defined as any fine-lined craft that was faster than the average vessel of her time. A clipper-built ship was sharp, rakish, sat low in the water and had forward-raking bows and masts raking aft. Most of the opium clippers were relatively small brigs and schooners rather than full-rigged ships with square sails on their three masts. Unlike the heavy-bowed "country" ships and East Indiamen, a clipper could beat to windward against prevailing winds of monsoon force. This enabled traders to send up to three cargoes of opium to China each year, rather than just one.

When the East India Company's monopoly of the China trade came to an end in 1834, speculators and seamen of every description flocked to get into the opium business. Businessmen had to have fast ships to stay in the game and, equally important, they had to be able to read the market well. Laying down the keel of a brig that was to become Jardine Matheson and Co.'s first coaster — the ill-fated 77-foot, 161-ton *Fairy*, built at Liverpool in 1833 and whose captain and officers were murdered at sea three years later — James Matheson was quick to see this:

> Our idea [in building a new opium clipper] is that the opium trade ... is [now] likely to be so much run upon by speculators of every description for the mere sake of remittance without a view to profit that it can hardly be worth our while pursuing on the old plan unless by operating on a large scale, and on the secure footing of always being beforehand with one's neighbors in point of intelligence [up-to-the minute commercial information].[5]

Matheson was certainly right: if competition had been fierce before, it now became cutthroat. In the wake of the first Opium War, a British observer could report in 1849 that

> The consumption of opium is rapidly increasing in China, and consequently the trade increases in proportion: there are six or seven fast-sailing clippers, constantly employed in carrying the trade from India to China; and, in addition to them, there are between twenty and thirty others engaged in the coast trade, that is in selling the contraband cargoes along the whole coast of China. But we must not forget the large receiving ships which are anchored off the various ports, and one at Hong Kong of seven hundred tons, and under the supervision of the British authorities; altogether, it is calculated, that between forty and fifty "clippers," or vessels of all sizes, all well armed, and manned, [are] employed in this hateful trade."[6]

The clippers themselves were fabulous ships. Richard Henry Dana, an American who spent two years before the mast in 1834–1836 in the California hide-and-tallow trade, first in the little brig *Pilgrim* and then in the ship *Alert*, at one point watched the long, sharp, 300-ton brig *Ayacucho*, built in Ecuador but at that time owned by a Scottish captain, get underway at Santa Barbara, California. This clipper had traded among South America, the Hawaiian Islands, California and Canton and was considered one of the fastest merchantmen in the Pacific.

When a storm came up suddenly at Santa Barbara and the ships moored there had to make sail at once and leave the anchorage before their anchors began to drag, Dana and his fellow seamen could see the *Ayacucho* "standing athwart our bows, sharp upon the wind, cutting through the head sea like a knife, with her raking masts and sharp bows running up like the head of a greyhound. It was a beautiful sight. She was like a bird which had been frightened and had spread her wings in flight."[7] Later, perched high above the water while working in the yards of *Alert*, Dana was well-placed to admire *Ayacucho* once again: "the Ayacucho had spread her wings, and, with yards braced sharp up, was standing athwart our hawse [crossing in front of *Alert*]. There is no prettier sight in the world," he recalled, "than a full-rigged, clipper-built brig, sailing sharp on the wind."[8]

Other experts, too, were unanimous in praising these fast ships. In 1840 a British resident in China who was a strong critic of the opium trade explained to Lord Palmerston, the foreign secretary, one of the reasons for the opium merchants' success: "Their fast sailing and weatherly vessels, effecting their passage from India at all seasons against high winds and head seas, with a celerity that was formerly thought impossible, have made many voyages along the coast of China, that no other class of ship, not excepting men-of-war, could have undertaken."[9]

The Aberdeen clipper *Torrington* was Alexander Hall and Sons' first opium clipper, and in about 1848 it became the talk of merchants and shipowners in Canton and Hong Kong because of its extraordinary passages.[10] A contemporary correspondent wrote that "The Torrington is still in all her glory — beating every ship on the [China] coast."[11] Hall also built other fine ships for the opium trade, for example the 264-ton schooner *Vindex* (1855) and the 109-foot *Salamander*, initially constructed in 1856 as a yacht for the Earl of Selkirk but used as an opium clipper on the China coast after 1859. Nathan Allen, an American with personal knowledge of the opium trade, agreed in 1853 that the clippers were among the best vessels found anywhere in the world. Toogood Downing, a British surgeon who lived in China in the 1830s, reported that the clippers averaged about 300 tons burden, were bark-rigged, fitted up in the first style and were "perfect models of naval architecture."[12]

Because of the great value of their cargoes, which included not only opium but also silver or gold specie, their officers were well paid. Downing explains how they earned their keep:

> Having all their cargo on board, they make the best of their way [from India] to China, often unmindful of the time of year, or the state of the weather. Obliged to "crack on," as it is called, or to bear a great press of canvas, they are in continual danger of losing their masts, or running, during the night, upon some of the reefs [in the Strait of Malacca] which so often stretch out from the land [pp. 52–53].

In *Two Years Before the Mast*, Dana has left us such a good account of what it means to "crack on" that it is worth citing here:

> Clouds look black and wild; wind rising, and ship [the brig *Pilgrim*] working hard against a heavy head sea, which breaks over the forecastle, and washes aft through the scuppers. Still, no more sail is taken in, for the captain is a driver, and, like all drivers, very partial to his top-gallant sails.... The second mate holds on to the main top-gallant sail until a heavy sea is shipped, and washes over the forecastle as though the whole ocean had come aboard.... By-and-by, — bang, bang, bang, on the scuttle — "all ha-a-ands, a ho-oy!" — We spring out of our berths, clap on a monkey-jacket and south-wester, and tumble up the ladder. — Mate up before us, and on the forecastle, singing out like a roaring bull; the captain singing out on the quarter-deck, and the second mate yelling, like a hyena, in the waist. The ship is lying over half upon her beam-ends; lee scuppers under water,

and forecastle all in a smother of foam.— Rigging all let go, and washing about decks; top-sail yards down upon the caps, and sails flapping and beating against the masts ... toward daybreak it moderates considerably ... and when the watch comes up ... [we] get the watch-tackle upon the top-gallant sheets and halyards, set the flying jib, and crack on to her again.[13]

In 1845 Montgomery Martin, the British colonial treasurer in Hong Kong, made a voyage "in the teeth of the monsoon," as he put it, down the China Sea to Java aboard the Jardine Matheson brig *Lanrick*. He reported,

> The vessels conveying the drug from India to China are probably the finest boats in the world. The Lanrick, of 283 tons register, built at Liverpool, cost £13,000 [and] is superior in sailing on a wind to any man-of war. Frequently we were running eight or nine knots close hauled, and carrying royals, when a frigate would have reefed her topsails and courses. In one of her voyages the Lanrick carried 1,250 chests of Bengal opium, valued at £200,000 sterling.[14]

Martin was so impressed by *Lanrick*'s master, Captain T. B. White, that he described him as "one of the most skilful and daring seamen who ever sailed." Captain White was cast from the same mould as most clipper captains, who according to Martin were educated men "of gentlemanly manners, very hospitable, of generous dispositions, well-skilled in seamanship, and of course of a courage and boldness unsurpassed."[15]

As mentioned earlier, the first ship to bring Turkish opium direct from Smyrna to China was American — the Baltimore brig *Entan*, in 1805.[16] It was followed in 1811 by another American brig, *Sylph* (not to be confused with the later Parsee clipper by the same name), which also carried opium from Turkey. Not long thereafter, fast American ships, usually pilot boat schooners, were being designed for the opium trade. One of these was the Baltimore schooner *Dhaulle*, which was described as "the most lovely vessel I ever saw" by a British naval officer who watched the ship abuilding, and which in 1825 was the first ship to beat to windward from the Strait of Malacca to China against the northeast monsoon. The 493-ton *Ann McKim*, built in 1832 by Isaac McKim of Baltimore and known as "the first real clipper," was another fine vessel.[17]

These pilot boat schooners usually ranged in length from about 54 feet to 114 feet; the 85-foot British-built opium schooner *Time*, launched in 1832, was a representative size.[18] A similar vessel, the 92-ton flush-decked fore-and-aft schooner *Anglona,* built by Brown and Bell in New York, was sent out to China for Russell and Co. in 1841. Another schooner, the 90- or 100-ton *Ariel,* was built in Medford, Massachusetts, that same year by Sprague and James. Captain Robert Bennet Forbes, who introduced pilot boats into the opium trade, described *Ariel* as a long, low topsail schooner with long hard pine masts and with the foremast stepped far forward. The hold was so shallow, he said, that a man could stand upright in it and still see the deck. After an inauspicious start (it capsized off Boston on its first trial and sank in seven fathoms of water), the ship was soon refloated, its sail area was reduced by cutting eight feet off the masts and it was sent out to China. There, in a 40-mile race around the island of Lintin, it beat *Anglona* and won a purse of $1,000.[19] While in the opium trade and when fully manned, *Ariel* carried 12 officers and a crew of about 42 men.[20]

SOME FAMOUS CLIPPERS

The opium clippers were the racehorses of their era. Let us look at seven of them, representing some of the major opium trading firms:

Ship	*Firm*	*Nationality*
Red Rover	Jardine Matheson	British
Falcon	Jardine Matheson	British
Sylph	Cowasjee	Parsee
Antelope	Russell	American
Frolic	Heard	American
Eamont	Dent	British
Wild Dayrell	Dent	British

FIRST OF THE BRITISH OPIUM CLIPPERS—RED ROVER

"The voyages of this vessel," enthused a correspondent of the *Bengal Courier* in 1831, "are quite astonishing and unparalleled, and until now considered perfectly incompatible from repeated failures of the finest men-of-war to make passage up the China sea against the monsoon." Built in Calcutta in 1829 in response to the Americans' success with *Dhaulle, Red Rover* was a rakish bark of 254 tons, 97 feet long, 24 feet wide. Its design was said to have been inspired by the long, low, narrow American schooner and privateer, *Prince de Neufchâtel. Red Rover* was skippered by Captain William Clifton, a pioneer of the British

Bark *Red Rover* in a storm (private collection)

opium traders. In 1833 Jardine Matheson bought a 50 percent share in her and later became her full owner.

Red Rover was flush-decked with minimum sheer and a sharply cutaway stem and stern and was judged "perfect in every respect" at her launching.[21] This clipper also proved to be fast, making a noteworthy passage from China to Bengal in 1834 in only 23 days, 19 hours, and another voyage from Calcutta to Lintin in 18 days. Before being lost at sea, she was a good moneymaker, possibly because Clifton himself had a nice personal touch. In 1834, for example, he wrote to a fellow captain:

> I beg to acknowledge the receipt of yours enclosing the Bill of Exchange for 40,000 Ds [dollars] drawn by Jo.s Goddard Esq. upon Messrs Hamilton and Co. which shall be invested with my opium free of all charges of commission and have no fear that your friends will do well with it, at least I am sure you will know it shall not be wanting for my best exertions that they will not, but I must mark it WC/RR [William Clifton/aboard the opium clipper *Red Rover*]. My own will be marked WC.[22]

Clifton was a tough man. On the eve of his own retirement in 1836, he urged Captain Wright, who was taking over command of *Red Rover*: "Do not forget my last words of advice, neither look to the right or left, but strait [sic] to the object of your voyage, and care for none or their wishes until your object fulfilled."[23] Captain Wright must have taken this exhortation to heart, for the next year William Jardine wrote to him: "We received with much satisfaction this morning the announcement of your arrival [at Canton], after so rapid a passage, and congratulate you most cordially on the occasion."[24]

Jardine Matheson's Flagship — Falcon. The first *Falcon* was an 84-foot bark or brig (accounts differ) of about 175 tons built at Cowes, England, in 1815 and owned by Lord Yarborough, then commodore of the Royal Yacht Squadron. Sold in 1824, it came out to Calcutta as an auxiliary steamer but had its engines and boiler removed there (the day of the steamer had not yet come) and was pressed into service in 1830 to become what local observers said was one of the "prettiest and fastest opium clippers out of the port of Calcutta."[25]

In the meantime, Lord Yarborough had commissioned a second bigger and better-known *Falcon*, which was to become the only full-rigged ship — i.e., a vessel with three or more masts, all of them square-rigged — in the opium trade. About 113 feet long and 27 feet wide, this 351-ton craft was built at the Isle of Wight in 1824 at a cost of £18,000 and was an impressive, well-armed ship with 22 small guns and a complement of 70 men. It was present at the Battle of Navarino, which was fought in 1827 by an Egyptian and Turkish fleet on one side and a combined British, French and Russian fleet on the other.

A British bank, Baring Brothers, bought *Falcon* in 1836 and later offered it for sale to Russell and Co. in Hong Kong, stating, "The ship seems admirably calculated for an opium ship between your port and Bombay or Calcutta. We believe she will sail faster than any other ship in that trade."[26] Jardine Matheson apparently chartered her around this time, too: early in 1837 William Jardine was urging Captain Reid of the bark *Austin* to make even greater efforts with his own ship because "The *Falcon* has been condemned in consequence of a severe gale off the Bashees [the Batan Islands in the Luzon Strait], so that we are one short of craft."[27]

Repaired after that gale, *Falcon* became one of the first British tea clippers, carrying a cargo of tea to London in 1837–38. Refitted at Liverpool in 1839, it returned to China in 1840, where Jardine Matheson made it the flagship of its rapidly expanding opium fleet. One can see why the ship was so fast: a fully rigged model, now in the Science Museum in London, shows that it had steep deadrise, sharp tapering ends and fine convex waterlines.[28] These characteristics made it a speedy ship and a good example of an early fine-lined clipper. *Falcon* remained in the opium trade until disappearing from shipping records in the mid-1850s. A vivid firsthand account of *Falcon* and its crew has survived and is reproduced in Appendix II.

The Indian Bark *Sylph*. Designed by Sir Robert Seppings, the surveyor of the Royal Navy, *Sylph* was built at Calcutta in 1831 for the Parsee merchant Rustomjee Cowasjee, who wanted a monsoon-conquering ship like *Red Rover*. Two contemporary paintings of *Sylph* show it to have been a heavily rigged ship with trysails on each mast and a tall high-peaked spanker. In one illustration, its topsails and topgallants are drying with the yards lowered and the sails "hauled a-bowline" (i.e., spread across the stays and braces). It was a 304-ton, 100-foot long bark that carried a complement of 70 men and was one of the fastest early opium clippers. This was a virtue much appreciated by Jardine Matheson, which chartered or bought *Sylph* from Cowasjee. Writing from Canton in 1831 to Hugh Matheson, his nephew, in Calcutta, James Matheson said that "if the *Sylph* is one of those sailing [from India], I think she will bid fair to beat the rest."[29]

This vessel carried opium to London in 1832 and made a fast passage in 1833 from Calcutta to Macao in only 17 days, 17 hours. That same year it also ran from Calcutta to Singapore in 9 days, 20 hours — a record held for some years. While sailing from Calcutta to China in 1835 with a full cargo of opium (995 chests), *Sylph* stranded on a shoal in the Malay Peninsula. The hull was damaged and the opium was soaked, but the ship and all but two of the chests were saved by the lucky appearance of the East India Company's sloop *Clive*. Refloated and later rebuilt at Singapore, *Sylph* was chased by Chinese junks in 1841 and came close to being captured. During the first Opium War, the Royal Navy offered a high price for this fast clipper, which would have made an excellent man-of-war, but its owners refused, preferring to keep the ship in the opium trade because each voyage meant such a huge profit.

After its masts had to be cut away during a typhoon that nearly overwhelmed the ship at the Cumsingmoon anchorage in 1848, *Sylph* was re-rigged at Hong Kong at great expense, the bill for repairs coming to 11,166.22 Mexican dollars — about half the cost of a new ship of the same size. As it turned out, this work was all for naught because the next year *Sylph* sailed from Hong Kong bound for Singapore and vanished without a trace. The best guess is that she was captured and burned by the pirates who frequented the island of Hainan.

Built in Boston — *Antelope*. This clipper was built in 1843 for

Captain Robert Bennet Forbes, who was a ship's captain by the age of 20 and a ship owner himself by the age of 28. *Antelope* was employed by Russell and Co. This 370-ton vessel began as a brig. Under the command of Philip Dumaresq, whom Robert Bennet Forbes believed one of the finest captains of his time, it was one of the few ships of the time that could beat against the northeast monsoon.

Under the command of Captain Watkins, it repelled an attack by Chinese war junks among the Ladrone Islands near Canton. In this incident, seeing that *Antelope* was becalmed, 20 to 30 Chinese sailors leaped onto the ship's low bowsprit and rushed aft at the boarding netting to cut an entrance through it with their knives. *Antelope*'s crew cocked their pistols, took deliberate aim and fired, driving about a dozen Chinese back to their boats. The crew then used pikes and boiling water to clear away the remaining boarders.

Captain Watkins was attacked again by war junks on his next trip but refused to heave to, that is, come to a stop. It is said that this time he ran down two war junks, whose crews drowned, and that he sailed into Macao Roads with a dead Chinese sailor hanging from each of *Antelope*'s yardarms. An excellent description of *Antelope* and its crew, written by a seaman who served aboard the ship, is given in Appendix III. Dismasted and nearly sunk by a typhoon in 1849, it was refitted as a bark at Hong Kong but was finally wrecked off the coast of China in 1852.

Frolic — Wrecked on the Coast of California. *Frolic* was a 99-foot long, 210-ton brig built in Baltimore in 1844. It usually carried Malwa opium from Bombay to the Canton area, returning to India laden with silver specie. With its sharp bows, tall raked masts and extreme deadrise, this ship was very fast, running between Hong Kong and Bombay in 35 days in 1845, the quickest passage of any vessel that year. What is most remarkable about *Frolic*, however, is that although its career was very short (only six years from launching to wreck), it is fully documented.[30]

The career of its captain, Edward Horatio Faucon, is also well known. This fine officer was a friend of Richard Henry Dana, who knew him in the California hide-and-tallow trade and who tells us in *Two Years before the Mast* that "Captain Faucon was a sailor, every inch of him; he knew what a ship was, and was as much at home in one, as a cobbler in his stall" (p. 256). *Frolic* itself had a varied career. In 1846 it carried over 10 tons of silver bullion, valued at $350,000, to India — almost all of it the proceeds from Augustine Heard and Co.'s opium sales along the

China coast. In 1849 it was dismasted, together with *Antelope*, in a great typhoon off Hong Kong; Captain Faucon had to cut away the masts to prevent the ship's being driven ashore. It was repaired but was later driven out of the opium trade altogether by the newly introduced steamers.

By then the California gold rush was in full swing, however, and San Francisco merchants would pay high prices for scarce luxury goods from China: shawls bought in southern China for $50 could be sold in San Francisco for as much as $180. Captain Faucon therefore loaded a cargo in China for the gold rush trade and set sail for California, carrying silks, cloth, a prefabricated house, paintings, lacquered ware, scales and weights, Chinaware (heavy duty stoneware bowls and saucers for the ham-handed gold miners), silverware, camphor trunks, candies and beer.

He reached the coast of northern California without incident, but his chart contained errors of up to 35 miles. Because of these errors and strong currents and a low-lying haze, on the night of 25 July 1850, Captain Faucon found himself too close to the coast and on the verge of running onto rocks. He tried desperately to head *Frolic* back to the open sea, but a strong swell picked up the ship and drove it stern-first into a rock. The impact broke the rudder and cracked the hull. The ship began to fill with water and soon had to be abandoned. Captain Faucon and his crew managed to survive. He made his way to San Francisco 10 days later, but by then the waves had carried *Frolic* off the rock and onto the beach, where it was plundered by the local Indians. Soon, knocked to pieces by the heavy surf, it disappeared forever.

A Topsail Schooner — *Eamont*. As mentioned earlier, in 1859 Lindsay Anderson, an ambitious young seaman looking for a job at Shanghai, a busy port where many foreign merchantmen called, signed on as third mate of *Eamont*. This was a trim, yacht-like 87-foot topsail schooner of about 120 tons. Built mainly of mahogany, *Eamont* had been launched at Cowes in 1852 and had a top speed of 14 knots.

Anderson found the ship "a perfect beauty as she lay there, with her boarding netting triced up all round her, and her guns run out and shining in the rays of the sun, so highly were they polished." He was pleased with the armament — four 18-pounders on a side, a long 18-pounder pivot gun in the forecastle and a 68-pounder pivot gun amidships.[31] Frequent gun practice — that is, firing at floating barrels or other targets in the sea — kept the crew ready for any emergency. *Eamont*'s sail plan was less to Anderson's liking, for as he reported with considerable understatement, "the main boom was one hundred and ten feet long, so that her mainsail was a swinger, and needed some handling."[32]

Anderson and his colleagues must have handled *Eamont* well enough because it had a varied career. Not only did the ship run opium, but it also fought off pirates, ferried negotiators between Shanghai and Nagasaki when Japan was being opened up to foreign trade, righted itself after being knocked on its beam ends by a typhoon and later ground its way over a coral reef en route to a remote Taiwanese port. Despite all these achievements, *Eamont* was eventually lost off the east coast of Japan, probably in a typhoon.

Wild Dayrell— One of the Last Opium Clippers. When Dent and Co.'s rakish 158-ton, 103-foot topsail schooner *Wild Dayrell* was launched at Cowes in 1855, a London newspaper singled it out for special mention and carried a flattering illustration. The yacht-like appearance of this vessel showed that it was in every respect worthy of the high reputation of its builders, John and Robert White. The newspaper reported,

> Her form for beauty, speed and seagoing qualities is most admirable; and she is so constructed, with extra fastenings and scantling where necessary, as to give her the greatest possible strength, to contend with the tempestuous weather of the China Seas, without detracting from her sailing qualities by overloading her with material. She has a heavy and most complete armament for protection against the swarms of pirates that now infest the Coast of China, and, in the event of coming athwart hawse of those junks, her "Long Tom amidships" will, no doubt, tell a tale. She is commanded by Captain Walter Macfarlane, a gentleman conversant with the coast, and who expects his *Wild Dayrell* to prove herself the fastest model afloat, and the forerunner of a fleet of similarly armed craft for that peculiar trade.[33]

The Receiving Ships

British surgeon Toogood Downing explained what happened to their cargoes of opium once the clippers reached southern China:

> Constantly moored in the roadstead, are armed vessels, which were formerly employed [to run opium], but which are now

kept as receiving-ships for the others. The opium is transshipped from the clippers into the *Jane*, the *Agnes*, or the *Bombay*, according to the house to which it is consigned, and is then sent up the country, in the night-time, by native boats, called, from the number of their oars, *centipedes*.[34]

Any former East Indiaman or broken-down "country" craft past its prime might well end its days as a floating warehouse somewhere along the China coast, fitted out with extra-heavy anchors, chain cables and hawsers to keep its place during the typhoons. To deter pirates and government war junks, these receiving ships bristled with weapons — everything from pikes and pistols to highly polished broadside guns. After the closure of Whampoa and Macao in 1821, a growing number of receiving ships owned by British, American and Parsee merchant houses soon dotted the "outer seas" close to Lintin. Additional receiving ships were moored at other locations as well. The opium trade became so profitable after the end of the first Opium War in 1842 that Jardine Matheson alone had eight receiving ships at various Chinese ports, as well as a cavernous depot ship (the 866-ton *Comanjee Hormusjee*) permanently anchored at Hong Kong. As the trade flourished, at least 20 receiving ships were eventually moored along the China coast.

The Coasters

The splendid sales made by the receiving ships at Lintin encouraged more adventurous merchants to ship the drug to the little ports north of Canton. Thus by the 1830s many small, fast, shallow draft brigs and schooners — known collectively as coasters — were carrying opium up to the island of Namoa and north along the Fukien coast. The first opium ship to be stationed north of the Canton area (in 1831) was Jardine Matheson's *Colonel Young*, for which *Fairy* served as a tender and ran between *Colonel Young* and Lintin. The opium stored in *Colonel Young*, as replenished by *Fairy*, was sold that same year for a third of a million dollars.[35] The Prussian missionary mentioned earlier, the Reverend Gützlaff, was such a good linguist that the Chinese declared him to be "a son of Han" (that is, Chinese himself). He sailed aboard *Colonel Young*, acting as an interpreter for opium sales in return for the opportunity to distribute Christian tracts along the coast.[36]

A good example of the coasting trade can be seen in the adventures of the Boston schooner *Rose*, owned by Russell and Co. A remarkable firsthand account of one of *Rose*'s voyages to Namoa has survived. The author was William C. Hunter, who spoke Cantonese fluently (like Gützlaff, he had studied Chinese in Malacca because the Chinese would not permit foreigners to learn it in China) and was himself a highly skilled sailor. Hunter decided in 1837 "to get a practical experience of the coasting trade, which was carried on with all the secrecy possible by the few who engaged in it." To this end he arranged a passage in *Rose*, a fast topsail schooner of about 150 tons that was carrying to Namoa nearly 300 chests of opium worth about $300,000.[37]

The outbound trip went very well. During a pleasant three-day voyage to Namoa, the sea was steady and the wind smooth, which was fortunate because *Rose* had so little freeboard that her scuppers were within two feet of the water. Because this was the typhoon season, Captain Forster and the ship's officers kept a sharp eye on the barometer. They were also wary of the fleets of fishing junks, "the crews of which," as Hunter explains, "were peaceable fishermen or cut-throat pirates according to circumstances."

Rose finally reached Namoa and anchored close to two English brigs—Dent and Co.'s *Omega* and Jardine Matheson's *Governor Findlay*—and awaited the expected arrival of a high-ranking mandarin. This official, the "Commodore" of a nearby war junk, was soon rowed over to the schooner, attended by servants who held a large embroidered silk umbrella over his head while others with fans kept the flies and mosquitoes away. Captain Forster received him graciously, offering wine and cigars, and on being asked why he had anchored at Namoa, claimed through an interpreter that it was only contrary winds and currents that had forced him to seek shelter at Namoa so that he replenish *Rose*'s supplies of wood and water.

This pro forma explanation was immediately accepted, and the mandarin played his own role with equal care, pulling from his boot a long red scroll containing the following Imperial edict:

> As the port of Canton is the only one at which outside barbarians are allowed to trade, on no account can they be permitted to wander about to other places in the "Middle Kingdom." The "Son of Heaven" [the emperor], however, whose compassion is as boundless as the ocean, cannot deny to those who are in distress from want of food, through adverse seas and currents, the necessary means of continuing their voyage. When supplied they

must no longer loiter, but depart at once. Respect this.
[signed] Taou-Kwang [the emperor's reign-title], 17th year, 6th moon, 4th sun [day]

The mandarin and his secretary then went down to the captain's cabin for refreshments, after which the mandarin asked Captain Forster, "How many chests have you on board? Are they all for Namoa? Do you go further up the coast?" After being satisfied on all these points, he then raised the key question of *cumsha* and was given to understand it would be the customary amount. Satisfied with this answer, too, the official then formally announced that he was about to depart. With his secretary he left *Rose* and was rowed back to his war junk.

Chinese merchants came aboard *Rose* as soon as the official visit had been completed, and their own trading junks appeared a day or two after they had taken delivery of the opium. It took much longer than expected for *Rose* to sell all her cargo, and after waiting for two weeks, Hunter finally decided he had to get back to Cumsingmoon and arranged a passage in Jardine Matheson's schooner *Harriet*. This was a small fore-and-aft vessel of about 100 tons, built in Macao by an American ship carpenter. It was making its way south along the coast after selling its opium at northern ports. For safety's sake, the proceeds of all the opium sold at Namoa up to that point by the three opium clippers were loaded aboard *Harriet* and sent down to the south. This proved to be a considerable treasure — gold bars and heavy mounds of silver worth a total of $430,000.

In 1841, laden with specie worth $180,000, *Rose* went down in a typhoon. Only one of her crew survived — a Portuguese helmsman who floated in the sea for three days on a plank until by an extraordinary stroke of good luck the Indian "country" ship *Good Success* picked him up.

Chinese Ships: "Centipedes" and Government War Junks

The Chinese ships directly or indirectly involved in the opium trade were of two general types.

The first were the smugglers' "centipedes," also known as "fast crabs," "scrambling dragons" or "smug boats." These fast craft carried opium from receiving ships to small harbors along the eastern coast of China. They were powered by oars and were manned by 20 to 70 or more Chinese boatmen, described by British observers as excellent sailors and "desperadoes of the worst and lowest class." John Morrison, who was employed by British merchants in Canton as their Chinese translator in the 1830s, explained how they took delivery of the opium:

> The Chinese smuggling boats are fine vessels; they are well manned and armed, and carry a great number of oars.... When the smugglers come alongside [a receiving ship], the orders [for opium] which they bring are immediately attended to; the opium is taken out of the chests in which it is packed; and after examination is removed by the boatmen in matted parcels, of a size that they can easily carry off, if in danger of being pursued. The fee on opium, of one dollar per chest, paid for the connivance of the officers of the imperial preventive squadron, is left by the smugglers in charge of the commanding officer of [the receiving ship], on whom the imperial officers call for what is due to them.[38]

Local Chinese officials lived in terror of these ruthless smugglers and reported to the emperor in 1836 that they "ply their oars as swiftly as though they were wings" and had "all the overbearing assumption and audacity of pirates." Their armament might include a sizable cannon at the bow of the boat, small swivel guns, flintlock muskets, spears, shields, knives and "plenty of round stones, wherewith to repel the curiosity of any Government war-boat, which might be inclined to approach closer than the smugglers liked." If cornered, the smugglers would never surrender. As the captain of the American opium clipper-brig *Eagle* remarked, if a government junk actually managed to close with the smugglers' boat, "a bloody and determined resistance was inevitable, for, if captured, the smugglers were certain of death by strangulation, or being pressed to death between two planks or bamboos, and of course they preferred death in fight. Thus, figuratively speaking, 'fighting with a halter around their necks.'"[39]

The second type of Chinese vessel was the government war junks. These were usually bigger versions of the smuggling boats but not so ably manned. On rare occasions they made token efforts to suppress the opium trade. It is worth quoting Downing again for his on-the-spot description:

> By the time the opium season is over, there is generally collected together at Lintin a little fleet of clippers. Having discharged their cargo, they wait until they are all ready, and then start

> homewards in a body, with the north-east monsoon in their favor. The chief mandarins, who well know the time at which they usually depart, take advantage of it to impress the minds of the natives with a high sense of their power and authority over every other nation on the face of the globe. For this purpose, an order comes down at the time from Pekin [sic], for the Admiral of his Celestial Majesty's fleet to put to sea, and drive these troublesome Fan-quis [sic] from the coast.
>
> As soon as the clippers have got underway [to return to India with the northeast monsoon], twenty or thirty Chinese men-of-war junks are seen creeping slowly out from Chuen-[p]ee and other places inshore, and making towards them.... The lumbering junks, some of them more than 600 tons burden, follow them as far as the Ladrones [two small islands near the mouth of the Canton estuary], but never close enough to be within reach of a cannon-ball.... After they have seen [the clippers] fairly away, and almost out of sight, they then begin their warlike maneuvers, and keep up their cannonade until the report of their guns can no longer be heard.[40]

The caution of the mandarins who commanded these war junks is understandable: they were trying to save face and not get themselves killed. Western captains were much better trained and more disciplined than their Chinese counterparts and had faster ships. The war junks were also lightly armed. The few cannons they carried were poorly made, loaded with weak gunpowder of Chinese manufacture and of relatively small bore, firing only 12-pound balls. These guns were mounted on rigid wooden carriages without quoins, the wedge-shaped blocks of wood needed to raise or lower cannon barrels. This meant that at long range the Chinese guns would shoot too low and at short range too high. As a result their broadsides were usually ineffective. In a 7 January 1841 clash at Chuenpi [also spelled Chuenpee in Wade/Giles and Chuanbi in Hanyu pinyin] during the Opium War, for example, most of the junks' shots flew high, slicing through the sails and rigging of the Royal Navy's ships *Hyacinth* and *Volage* but never hitting their hulls.

Notes

1. Owen, *British Opium Policy*, pp. 52–53.
2. Cited by Lubbock, *Opium Clippers*, pp. 14–16.
3. Downing, *Fan-Qui*, pp. 3–4.
4. Thompson, *Considerations*, pp. 80–81.

5. Letter of 10 March 1831, James Matheson's Private Letter Book. Jardine Matheson archives.
6. Sirr, *China*, vol. 1, p. 266.
7. Dana, *Two Years*, p. 109.
8. Dana, *Two Years*, p. 285.
9. *Rupture*, p. 36.
10. Hall is known for introducing the famous "Aberdeen Bow." In technical terms, this design had two characteristics: the rabbet followed the curve of the stem rather than curving upward, and the hull had hollow waterlines. In simpler terms, an Aberdeen Bow was graceful, long and narrow. The first vessel with this feature was the clipper-schooner *Scottish Maid*, built in 1839. See Chapelle, *History of American Sailing Ships*, p. 248.
11. Cited by MacGregor, *Fast Sailing Ships*, pp. 114–115.
12. Downing, *Fan-Qui*, pp. 52–53.
13. Dana, *Two Years*, p. 440 ff.
14. Martin, *Opium in China*, p. 87.
15. Martin, *Opium in China*, p. 87.
16. The American trade in Turkish opium was conducted only on a small scale. Fragmentary statistics suggest that it peaked in 1830–1831, when 1428 chests valued at $806,827 were imported, and came to an end about 1838. See Downs, *Golden Ghetto*, p. 355.
17. Bowen, *America Sails*, pp. 313–314.
18. Chapelle, *Baltimore Clipper*; and Gardiner, *Sail's*, p. 51.
19. Lubbock, *China Clippers*, p. 151.
20. Lubbock, *Opium Clippers*, p. 19.
21. In nautical jargon, sheer is the difference between the design trim freeboard at any point and that of the midships section. The sheer line is the line of intersection of the main or weather deck with the side of the ship. More simply, sheer is the fore-and-aft upward curve of the hull of a vessel. An East Indiaman or a junk had a great deal of sheer and was therefore slow but dry; an opium clipper with very little sheer was fast but wet. See Gillmer and Johnson, *Naval Architecture*, p. 41.
22. From a 2 November 1834 letter from Captain William Clifton, aboard *Red Rover* at Lintin, to Captain Cheverley. Jardine Matheson archives.
23. From a 27 January 1834 letter from Captain William Clifton, aboard *Red Rover* at Canton, to Captain Wright. Jardine Matheson archives.
24. From a 13 October 1837 letter from William Jardine at Canton to Captain Wright aboard *Red Rover*. Jardine Matheson archives.
25. Coates, *Good Old Days*, p. 37
26. Cited by MacGregor, *Tea Clippers*, p. 36.
27. 17 January 1837 letter from William Jardine at Canton to Captain Austin. William Jardine Private Letter Book, p. 164. Jardine Matheson archives.
28. Deadrise, also known as the rise of floor, is technically the athwartship rise of the bottom from the keel to the bilge. A vessel with steep deadrise of 25 to 29 degrees had a hull that was more V-shaped than U-shaped. This gave it more speed but less cargo-carrying capacity: pilot boat schooners were good

examples. American ships often had steeper deadrise than their British counterparts. The reason was that American ships were not expected to take the ground (that is, rest on the mud of a harbor at low tide) and therefore did not need to have flat bottoms. The tidal range in Boston, New York and Baltimore is much less than that of London and other British ports, where British ships routinely had to take the ground. See Gillmer and Johnson, *Naval Architecture*, p. 41; and MacGregor, *Fast Sailing Ships*, p. 44.

29. 4 November 1831 letter from James Matheson to Hugh Matheson in Calcutta, James Matheson Private Letter Book. Jardine Matheson archives.

30. *Frolic*'s career is documented in the Heard collection at the Baker Library of Harvard University's Graduate School of Business Education. See Layton, *Frolic*, p. 18 ff, the source for my discussion of this ship.

31. A cannon was described not by how much it weighed but by the weight of the shot it fired. Thus an 18-pounder usually fired a solid 18-pound cast-iron ball.

32. Anderson, *Cruise*, pp. 34–35.
33. *Illustrated London News*, 10 November 1855.
34. Downing, *Fan-Qui*, p. 53.
35. Beeching, *Chinese Opium Wars*, p. 68.
36. H. W. C., *Fan Kwae*, pp. 70–71.
37. For details of this trip, see H. W. C., *Fan Kwae*, pp. 66–72.
38. Morrison, *Commercial Guide*, p. 29.
39. George Davis, *Recollections*, pp. 244–245.
40. Downing, *Fan-Qui*, pp. 54–55.

5

The Opium Wars

In April 1838 Captain Charles Elliot, RN, the British superintendent of trade in Canton, reported to Lord Palmerston, the British foreign secretary, "In the course of the last two months the number of English boats employed in the illicit traffic has vastly increased, and the deliveries of opium have frequently been accompanied by a conflict of fire-arms between those vessels and the government preventive craft."[1] The rapid expansion of the opium trade was clearly putting Britain and China on a collision course.

Matters came to a head almost one year later. In March 1839 a newly appointed imperial commissioner, Lin Tse-hsü, demanded that all the opium illegally brought into Canton by foreign traders be turned over to him for destruction. The traders grudgingly complied and in May 1839 surrendered more than 20,000 chests of opium — the exact number was either 20,291 chests or 20,283, depending on which contemporary source is consulted. The opium in these chests, which was later officially valued by Lord Palmerston at 6,189,616 Spanish silver dollars, was publicly destroyed near Canton.[2] A British naval officer who arrived in China shortly thereafter reported,

> On the lst of June [1839], the high commissioner [Lin], the governor [of Canton], and all the officers, civil and military, of the black-haired race of Han [the Chinese], proceeded to Chunhow, near the Bocca Tigris [literally, the mouth of the tiger, named after Tiger Island near the narrowest part of the Canton estuary];

and on the 4th, commenced operations for the *forcibly-seized* British property; large trenches, lined with stone, were dug, the opium being decomposed in them by the use of quicklime, rock salt, and water, when the mixture was allowed to run into the sea.³

By this drastic measure Commissioner Lin hoped to end the pernicious opium trade once and for all. He had been sent to Canton because after long debates in Peking, the emperor had finally sided with the mandarins, who wanted to stamp out the opium trade entirely rather than legalize it in hopes of getting some control over it and at the same time increasing the government's customs revenues. The antiopium lobby carried the day, arguing that addiction was already spreading rapidly and would continue to expand unless the trade was stopped. In addition, they pointed out, there were already too many foreign merchants and ships along the south China coast and that more would surely be coming if the trade was allowed to continue.

Despite his intelligence, his energy and his good intentions, Commissioner Lin miscalculated badly. The destruction of their valuable property infuriated the British (7,000 chests were in the name of Jardine Matheson alone⁴) and prompted calls at home for sending a "thoroughly coercive" military expedition to China to ensure "complete reparation for the past, as well as of improved arrangements for our commercial relations in the future."⁵

It precipitated China's first armed conflict with the West (from 1839 to 1842)—a clash that even the *Times* of London and British journalists were soon calling an "opium war"—and it was an important underlying factor in China's second war with the West, which followed not long thereafter (from 1856 to 1860). This latter conflict has many names. I will refer to it here as *the second Opium War,* but it can also be called, with equal justice, the *Arrow* war, the second China war, China's second antiforeign war or the lorcha war.

Commissioner Lin's seizure and destruction of the opium had consequences far beyond what he could have imagined at the time. In a letter of 14 June 1839 from Macao, an executive of one of the great trading houses (probably Jardine Matheson) reported that as a result of this seizure the opium trade had passed from the established houses in Canton "to a class of men prepared to carry on the traffic at all hazards, to overcome all obstacles that may oppose their purpose by the weapons of war, and who for this purpose, at this time, both here, [at] Manila, and at Singapore, are fitting out vessels in such a manner as will defy all the naval power of China."[6] Moreover, driving the opium trade out of Canton made every coastal port to north of that city a center for local drug sales. It also corrupted virtually all the local officials, who were only too happy, thanks to the bribes they received from opium captains and the fines they could levy on Chinese opium dealers, to turn a blind eye to the coasters moored so visibly in their jurisdictions.

In this chapter we will first look at the role opium itself played in the struggle between China and the West from 1839 to 1860. We can then focus on the respective weaknesses and strengths of the Chinese and the British forces. The next chapter will demonstrate the fatal consequences (for China) of these weaknesses and strengths in the heat of battle, during nine engagements in the Opium Wars. To recapture the death-or-glory flavor of these times, I will, as usual, let the participants speak for themselves rather than try to paraphrase their vivid firsthand accounts.

Did Opium Cause the Two Wars?

From the perspective of our own day, an evenhanded explanation of the causes of the Opium Wars might run along these lines:

- The increased Western presence and influence in southern China, which was almost entirely due to the opium trade, had a corrosive impact on the Confucian patterns of thought and the traditional way of life on which Chinese society was based. Few of the mandarins had ever been outside China itself; virtually none of them had ever been to the West. Culture-bound, self-righteous and stubborn, they were convinced that China was the most civilized country on earth. The opium trade aggravated their already strong xenophobia to the point that they were willing to fight rather than give in to the barbarians and allow this illegal trade to continue and to expand.

- Western opium traders, for their part, were also culture bound, xenophobic, self-righteous and stubborn. They firmly believed their own societies were the best on earth and that they had an inalienable right to trade with any country in the world, including China. If this alleged right was denied them, they felt entitled to use force to uphold it.

- If there was to be any balance of trade between China and the West, however, British and American merchants had to offer for sale in China something the Chinese themselves wanted to buy. Opium was the one foreign commodity for which there was a potentially insatiable demand and which was easy to produce and, being so compact, was cheap to ship to China. Because the opium trade generated truly enormous profits, Westerners were ready to fight to preserve it.

Such an explanation, however, would have pleased none of the nineteenth-century protagonists. Passions at the time ran high. Chinese officials insisted that opium was the sole cause of the first war. They were steeped in a tradition that defined foreign trade as "barbarians bearing tribute to the Emperor." In 1793 Emperor Ch'ien Lung [Qianlong] had made this perfectly clear to Lord Macartney, a British emissary: "The Celestial Empire," the emperor announced, "possesses all things in prolific abundance and lacks in no product within its borders. There is therefore no need to import manufactures [sic] in exchange for our products."[7] Foreign trade was always seen as a privilege, not as a right or as a mutually profitable relationship between two sovereign and equal states.

The personal pride of Chinese scholar-officials was deeply involved in this process, too. In his picaresque account of the Opium Wars, a modern British novelist puts these fictional but entirely believable words into the mouth of his roguish hero, Colonel Harry Flashman:

> To their chagrin [the Chinese] discovered that their God-given superiority, their highly-refined taste in eggshell pottery, and their limitless lines of ancestors, availed nothing against any Dundee [Scottish] pirate with a pistol on his hip and a six-pounder [cannon] in his bows who was determined to run his opium in. Which made the Manchoo Mandarins wild with outraged pride, and more high-handed towards foreigners than ever.... You have to understand this Chinese pride — they truly believe that they have dominion over us, and that our rulers are mere slaves to their Emperor ... fiercer and stronger, perhaps, but infinitely lower in the scale of creation. That's how the Chinese think of us.[8]

Contemporary Western observers insisted that the real cause of the wars was not opium but the principle of free trade. Many of them sincerely believed this to be the case. At the end of the first Opium War a British military engineer in China was convinced that the opium question should be regarded merely as a spark blown into a mine [an encased explosive charge], which, during the past half century, the vindictiveness and insufferable arrogance of the Chinese government had been gradually charging [filling]; and it can no more be considered the primary cause of the war than the match, which ignites the train [of gunpowder], be styled the cause of the breach made by the explosion. That the quarrel was an unhappy one, and for many reasons to be deeply deplored, does not admit of a doubt, but that it was on our part just and unavoidable, and that the demands of our government were reasonable, and based on the principle of reciprocity in commercial discourse, all must allow, after a dispassionate consideration of all the circumstances.[9]

An English missionary to South China made the same point:

The circumstances which give rise to the war are a matter of eternal regret; but even those who most strongly deprecated the trade in opium, declare that the war was necessary on other grounds. The native authorities refused again and again to receive foreign visitors on terms of equality, in order to negotiate with them a satisfactory basis for trade, and nothing but force could bring them to listen to any proposals.[10]

Despite these protestations of innocence, however, at least four important commercial issues were at stake in the Opium Wars:

1. The stream of wealth generated by the opium trade was irresistibly attractive.
2. Britain wanted to help finance its empire in India and its tea trade with China by selling Indian opium to China.
3. The Chinese were worried not only about the corrosive effect of opium on their people but also about the adverse financial effects caused by the loss of customs revenue: duties could be imposed on other imports but not on opium itself because it was an illegal commodity (until 1858).
4. The Chinese government was also concerned that the flow of silver out of China — i.e., the proceeds from the sale of opium — would fuel inflation and further impoverish the country. This is in fact what happened.[11]

Opium was directly or indirectly involved in all these considerations. For this reason, referring to China's first two conflicts with the West as "the Opium Wars" is not only a convenient literary shorthand but also historically defensible.

Weaknesses and Strengths

The long, desultory and complicated saga of these wars has been chronicled so painstakingly by contemporary and modern writers alike that there is no need to replow the same ground here: the interested reader is invited to consult the bibliography.[12] For our purposes it is enough to understand only the broad outlines of these two conflicts.

The First Opium War (1839–1842)

After Commissioner Lin destroyed the opium in 1839, minor skirmishes began between the Chinese and the British.[13] In 1840 the British decided to send out an expedition to punish China. This expedition sailed from Hong Kong north along the coast trying to present officially to the Chinese government a letter from Lord Palmerston containing a formal demand for reparations. The letter was at last delivered to Kishen, the grand secretary to the emperor, but the emperor himself was angry with Commissioner Lin because the barbarians were by that time already at the Peiho [Hai] River, only 100 miles from the gates of Peking. Lin was dismissed in disgrace; Kishen took his place, with instructions to negotiate with and soothe the barbarians.

Despite repeated diplomatic efforts, no lasting settlement of the dispute could be reached.[14] The British laid siege to Canton in 1841, demanding and receiving from the Chinese a ransom of $6 million for sparing the city itself, but the Cantonese later counterattacked. The British then carried their military campaign northward, easily capturing some small Chinese cities along the coast (Amoy, Tinghai, Ningpo) and, after getting more reinforcements from India, compelled Wusung [Wusong], Shanghai, Chinkiang [Jinjiang] and Nanking [Nanjing] to surrender in 1842. The Treaty of Nanking (1842) ended this first war.

Quite remarkably, however, the Treaty of Nanking said nothing at all about opium itself. As a result, this illegal trade not only continued but actually flourished as new markets were opened up along the Chinese coast after the war. In 1844 alone, 306 foreign vessels arrived at Canton, of which 228 were British and 57 American; many of them were carrying opium.[15] Jardine Matheson was said to have had eight receiving ships stationed at coastal ports, one large receiving ship moored permanently in Hong Kong, four or five coasters, and five other ships bringing opium from India.[16] Dent and the other traders were adequately if less elaborately equipped. The net result of these collective endeavors was that the number of chests of opium smuggled into China reportedly rose from about 20,000 in 1839 to about 52,000 in 1850.[17] This increase called for more opium clippers, and between 1840 and 1845 at least 48 additional vessels entered the trade.[18]

The Treaty of Nanking had also failed to resolve the important question of whether Westerners (many of whom were associated with the opium trade) would be permitted to enter the walled city of Canton. Tensions grew as strong antiforeign feelings welled up among the Cantonese and among the Chinese gentry in the neighboring province of Kwangtung [Guangdong]. Governor-General Yeh Ming-ch'en encouraged the angry Cantonese to expel the uncultured barbarians, who in the eyes of Confucian traditionalists were little better than the Japanese pirates who had terrorized Chinese coastal cities in the fourteenth century.[19]

The Second Opium War (1856–1860)

These antiforeign sentiments finally came to the breaking point in October 1856, when the Canton police seized the lorcha *Arrow*—a British-registered but Chinese-owned ship flying the British flag—and accused its Chinese crew of being pirates and smugglers.[20] The crew was later freed at Britain's request, but the Chinese refused to apologize for seizing a British ship because they believed one member of the crew might have been a pirate. This incident was used by the British as a convenient excuse for war.

Both the British and French were resolved to open up China even further to Western trade and influence. The British therefore dispatched a fleet to fight its way up to Canton. Using as their own excuse the fact that a French missionary, Père Chapdelaine, had been executed by the Chinese, the French joined forces with the British, who were further strengthened by the arrival of a military expedition from England. Joint Anglo-French forces captured Canton in 1857 and the next year took the Taku [Dagu] forts and marched to Tientsin [Tiajin].

Four treaties to end the war were negotiated at Tientsin in 1858, but in 1859, as the British and French emissaries were sailing toward Peking to sign them, their ships were repulsed with heavy losses by cannon fire from the Taku forts. In retaliation, an allied force attacked Peking itself in 1860. The British — after discovering that three of their own soldiers, a British diplomat, a correspondent of the *Times* and eight Sikh (Indian) soldiers had all been captured and horribly tortured to death by the Chinese — burned to the ground the emperor's fabulous Summer Palace, located seven miles northwest of Peking. In October 1860 the Peking Convention, signed by Lord Elgin for the British side and by Prince Kung for the Chinese side, finally brought the second Opium War to a close.

Under the terms of the Peking Convention, the Chinese were forced to abide by the provisions of the four treaties they had agreed to earlier at Tientsin. Like the Treaty of Nanking, these agreements were also silent on the subject of opium. But in November 1858 and with the full consent of the Chinese negotiators, the opium trade was quietly legalized as opium was added to the list of dutiable imports.[21] Even after this legalization, however, so many thorny problems about opium still remained — such as taxation, smuggling and the special position of Hong Kong — that it took fully 20 years of continuous negotiation between the British and Chinese officials before they were finally resolved in 1887.[22]

Chinese Weaknesses

With this overview in mind, we shall see that the reasons why China could not stop the opium trade were also the reasons why it could not defend itself militarily against the West. Having been in power since 1616, the once-powerful Qing dynasty was by the time of the Opium Wars much enfeebled and suffering from terminal weaknesses. The first signs of the decay of this dynasty were popular uprisings in 1774–1775, stimulated by harsh demands from local officials and landlords and by the indolent life led by idle Manchus in the cities, who did no work but drew comfortable pensions from the government. New uprisings occurred frequently — in 1813, 1825 and 1845 — and culminated (during the years discussed in greatest detail in this book) in the convulsive Taiping Rebellion of 1850–1864, which will be outlined below.

There were other signs of dynastic decline as well: inept leadership at the top, a corrupt bureaucracy, a tripling of the population (resulting, ironically, from the earlier eighteenth century prosperity of the Qing), and perhaps most fatally, China's ancient ethnocentricity and xenophobia, which served as intellectual blinders to the dangers presented by the

West. Using a good analogy, the Communist theoretician Karl Marx once likened the Manchu empire to a mummy in a hermetically sealed coffin suddenly exposed to the open air: as soon as the Qing dynasty was exposed to Western influences, its decay was rapid and inevitable.[23]

During the Opium Wars, many Chinese officials were aware of the weaknesses of their country and advocated a strategy that can be summarized as "talk first; then if possible, delay." Whether in the hope that their bold words might take the place of military action or merely to save face, the Chinese were prone to issue verbal broadsides. In a long letter of 1839, for example, Commissioner Lin warned Queen Victoria that

> there is a tribe of depraved and barbarous people, who, having manufactured opium for smoking, bring it hither for sale, and seduce and lead astray the simple folk, to the destruction of their persons, and the draining of their resources.... When your majesty receives this document, let us have a speedy communication in reply, advertising us [sic] of the measures you adopt for the entire cutting off of the opium in every seaport. Do not, by any means, by false embellishments evade or procrastinate.[24]

In 1840 another letter from Lin to the Queen (or perhaps a different version of the one cited above) was printed and widely distributed in China, but the Queen herself apparently never read it. This letter gives a clear idea of how the Chinese government traditionally addressed other — i.e., tributary, vassal, barbarian — rulers:

> During successive months and years has been the wide increase of this poison [opium], and its stench and uncleanness have ascended upward until the wrath of heaven has been excited, and the gods themselves have become indignant!... Now, just reflect, that if you, barbarians, brought no opium here, then from whence could the flowery natives [the Chinese] traffic in it? and from whence procure it to smoke? It is evident that it is you, abandoned foreigners, who have really resolved in death the natives of this flowery land [China]!... *After you have received this document, do you immediately put an entire end to Opium and its causes, and forthwith proceed to send us a reply.* Do not be evasive or dilatory for this is a dispatch of the highest importance.[25]

When words failed the Chinese, delays often followed. As a British chief superintendent in China put it, rather than fight, the Chinese "were far more likely to follow their usual plan of gaining time, and attempting to disarm us by pretenses of negotiation."[26] This was certainly a wise strategy because as another on-the-spot Englishman observed: "The art of war in the Celestial Empire [China] is probably at as low an ebb as it can possibly be ... The military tactics seem to consist mainly of placing soldiers in curious positions, and at every evolution to make them 'pousse un grand cri' [give a great shout] to the sound of the tambour [drum]."[27] Other British observers came to the same conclusions. Two British officers explained why Commissioner Lin placed such great faith in the power of the 10,000 "double-sworded men" under his command:

> The double-sword is a weapon of a very remarkable and singular construction. The blades are carried in the same sheath, and necessarily the inner side of both is quite flat, while the opposite one is triangular ... clashing and beating [their twin swords] together and cutting the air in every direction, accompanying the action with abuse, noisy shouts, and hideous grimaces, these dread heroes advance, increasing their gesticulations and distortions of visage as they approach the enemy, when they *expect* the foe to become alarmed and flee from them.[28]

Chinese troops carried spears, bows and arrows and matchlocks (a primitive kind of muzzle-loading rifle fired by applying a glowing cord to the priming). A soldier armed with a matchlock carried around his waist a cotton or leather case containing 14–16 wooden tubes, each holding a loose charge of gunpowder. There was a great danger, however, that careless handling could cause the glowing cord to set fire to his cotton clothes or to the gunpowder and blow the man up. For this reason many soldiers preferred the bow to the matchlock.[29]

Chinese cannons were of enormous weight in proportion to their caliber. Some pieces of ordnance captured by the British weighed as much as seven tons but fired balls weighing only 42 pounds. Chinese gunpowder was similar in chemical composition to British powder and was almost as powerful, but it was coarse and badly made. For this reason or perhaps because the cannons themselves were overcharged, they frequently burst despite their enormous thickness of metal.[30]

An even more serious military failing, however, was that Chinese officers often ran away during a fight. The diary of a Chinese poet who lived outside the walls of Chinkiang contains this damning account:

> Today [21 July 1842] at the hour of the Snake [9:00 A.M.] the foreigners disembarked. The Assistant Commissioner Ch'i-shen

and the Commander-in-Chief Yun-hsiao hastily marshaled the troops whom they had secluded in a fold of the hills, and directed operations sitting in carrying-chairs. Our troops fired several rounds; but the foreigners continued to advance. The two generals left their chairs and fled on horseback; whereupon all their men broke into a general stampede up hill and down dale, in the direction of the Tan-yang high road, to the great amusement of the foreigners.[31]

Such dereliction of duty was frequent, and it continued throughout the course of the second Opium War. An 18-year-old British midshipman, however, took a more charitable view when he concluded, "Not but what the Chinaman is a brave man if properly led, which he never was, the mandarins having invariably a pressing engagement elsewhere when the fight was at its height; so the poor soldiers followed their example, and I believe that those of any other nation would do the same if their officers were the first to fly."[32]

If China's land forces were weak (an English missionary reported that "their enormous armies broke and ran before little bands of organized western troops"[33]), China's navy was in much worse shape because the Japanese pirates who raided China's coast in the fourteenth century had effectively prevented the development of a competent navy. The Chinese could do little more than make a symbolic, face-saving show of force. A British commentator thought that "the navy is even more contemptible than the army; the whole fleet of men-of-war having been known to fly before a single, unarmed, foreign merchantman. The arms are in addition badly made, the cannon formed of base metal and ill cast, and the gunpowder so weak that the cannonballs appear often to fall out of the mouth of the guns."[34]

Government war junks bristled with weapons, but these were more impressive in appearance than effective in reality. War junks could carry 14 or more small cannons of various calibers, mostly of Chinese make, as well as several large *gingals*. (The spelling of this word varies but the weapon itself was a heavy-duty matchlock which weighed about 12 lbs. It had a barrel seven feet long that could hold as many as 19 two-ounce balls and was fastened to crude mountings on the bulwarks of the junk.) Fishing nets were sometimes draped over the bulwarks of the junks in hope of entangling boarders, who could then be finished off with spears. As personal weapons the crews were armed with spears, swords and matchlocks. Even the most formidable war junk, however, could not possibly survive the crushing effect of the concentrated fire of British line-of-battle ships.[35]

Another Englishman reported,

> Their war-junks, or "soldier-ships," as they are called, are about two hundred tons burden, with two masts, and as many sails, which are hoisted and lowered in a series of tiers and folds. Their form is more compact than of the common junks, but still very awkward and unwieldy ... the guns are few in number, and inconsiderable in size — the largest not more than a twelve-pounder. They are mounted upon wooden carriages, and are incapable of elevation or depression.[36]

In view of these serious shortcomings, Commissioner Lin believed he could do little more than offer his captains "Seven General Rules for the Extermination of the Barbarian Forces":

1. Attack the prow and stern of barbarian ships, where they have the fewest guns.
2. Attack in two squadrons "in the form of the wings of a goose."
3. Hurl a great number of stink-pots [primitive but effective Molotov cocktails] from your mastheads down onto the decks of enemy ships.
4. After boarding their ships, decapitate the barbarians and cut the ships' lines and rigging to render them helpless.
5. Men must obey the orders of their commanding officer: "Decapitation is the penalty of disobedience."
6. Prepare fire-boats to be nailed to the sides of enemy ships.
7. "Valour and courage are the quantities most in esteem in defeat of the enemy.... Should any withdraw during the contest, their heads will be instantly taken off and suspended on poles as a warning to all!"[37]

Despite his brave exhortations, however, Commissioner Lin himself singularly failed to put adequate defenses in place around Canton. His successor reported to Peking that this key city was poorly defended. The forts protecting it were all located on small islands that could easily be blockaded by the British. Enemy ships could also approach Canton by other channels out of range of the forts. Many of the forts' guns were obsolete and out of commission; moreover, they covered only the frontal approaches to the forts, leaving the sides undefended. Chinese marines suffered badly from seasickness, and Chinese soldiers were of poor quality. Military discipline in battle had proved to be so tenuous that Admiral Kwan, a key naval commander during the first Opium War, had to pawn his own richly embroidered robes to give each soldier two foreign dollars so that he would not desert.[38]

Chinese Strengths

There is a positive side to the ledger as well. The Chinese could be clever and resourceful. When British troops captured the city of Amoy, the Chinese managed to save all the silver in their treasury by hiding it in hollowed-out logs, which coolies then carried to safety out through the city gates under the very noses of the barbarians.[39] A few Chinese small brass guns were strong, wellcast and smoothly bored. The mandarins also tried to have heavy cannons made and big vessels built along the lines of the British line-of-battle ships, but these projects were beyond their managerial and technical capabilities. They tried to compensate for their weaknesses by assembling fire rafts, loading two or three junks with combustible materials, chaining them together and setting them afire on an outgoing tide in hopes they would drift into British ships and burn them to the waterline. They even tried to copy their enemy's most advanced naval technology — the paddle wheel steamers such as *Nemesis*, discussed below — by building five "wheel-boats." Each was commanded by a high-ranking mandarin and was powered by four wooden paddle wheels turned by capstans worked by the sailors by hand. These could give the boat a top speed of 3.5 knots.[40]

The Chinese could also be brave. Their best fighters were the Tartar troops, officially termed the "tiger-hearted" soldiers by the Chinese.[41] To see what stern stuff they were made of, it is worth learning how they stood fast when the British attacked the Chapu [Zhapu] joss-house (i.e., a Chinese temple) near the Yangtze River on 18 May 1842 during the first Opium War. This firsthand account comes from a British military engineer [42]: "The Tartar soldiers silently awaited the attack of our detachment, and as soon as the leading files and officers had passed through the entrance [of the joss-house] ... they opened upon them a fire which sent a perfect shower of matchlock balls into their ranks, killing and wounding most of those who had passed the fatal barrier."

In this fight, the British were at first forced to retreat, but then they rallied and used a 50-pound bag of gunpowder to blow a hole in the wall for an assaulting party. Their second attack also failed because "the Tartars, cool and undismayed under all the horrors which had accumulated around them, received the storming party with so well-directed and heavy a fire from behind the trelliswork [that] the assailants were once more compelled to retreat with loss." The British soldiers did not give up easily. They shot down the Tartars who were trying to escape, blew another breach in the wall, set fire to the joss-house, stormed it with bayonets and finally carried the day. The Tartars' spirited defense, however, soon won the grudging admiration of the British, who respected these men who "though totally unaccustomed to and unpractised in modern warfare, and doubtless brought now for the first time under the fire of artillery and musketry, could yet maintain to the last such steady coolness and indomitable valour."

Other observers praised the Tartars, too. During the 7 January 1841 attack on the forts guarding Canton, a British naval officer reported,

> "The Hie-tie, or brigadier Chin Leenshing, fell at his post, being shot through the breast, when trying to rally his men.... Many of the mandarins sustained the character of brave men; and on the whole the Chinese troops stood better than they did on any subsequent occasion in this river; they were principally Tartars, and the *elite* of the troops."[43]

The chronicler of the steamer *Nemesis*'s operations during the first Opium War agreed:

> As far as personal bravery could aid them, [the Chinese soldiers] were by no means an enemy to be despised. The spear and bayonet frequently crossed each other ... and in not a few instances, the *long* spear was more than a match for the shorter bayonet. Hand-to-hand encounters with the Tartar troops were not uncommon towards the close of the war; and, indeed, many of our men learnt, to their cost, that they held the Chinese far too cheap. Instances occurred in which the powerful Tartar soldier rushed within the bayonet guard of his opponent, and grappled with him for life or death.[44]

And in one of the last engagements of the first Opium War, long after it was clear the Chinese had been defeated, the Tartars still proved themselves indomitable fighters, killing or wounding 168 British troops during the fall of Chinkiang on the Yangtze River upstream from Shanghai on 21 July 1842.[45]

British Weaknesses and Strengths

The only weaknesses the British displayed in this era seem to have been the products of an unshakable Victorian self-righteousness. These failings might be said to include overconfidence, intolerance and contempt for Chinese military forces — all of which contributed to the heavy losses the British suffered at the Taku forts in 1859.[46] This action, described in the next chapter, was the first and only significant defeat they encountered during the whole course of the two Opium Wars. For unlike the Chinese, the British had the advantages of a vastly superior technology, thanks to the Industrial Revolution, and of strict military discipline and personal accountability, thanks to the long and generally successful experience of the Royal Navy and the British Army in other parts of the world.

Their evident strengths encouraged the British to take a more forward-leaning (that is, more combat-ready) posture. If the Chinese strategy usually was "talk first; then if possible, delay," the British countered this with their own strategy of "talk first; then if necessary, fight." On 3 July 1840, during the early stages of the first Opium War, a British fleet under the command of Captain Charles Elliot attempted to deliver to the Chinese government the letter from Lord Palmerston, which demanded, among other things, that the Chinese pay in cash for the more than 20,000 chests of opium destroyed by Commissioner Lin. When the 42-gun British ship *Blonde* sent a British interpreter ashore in a small boat to deliver the letter, Chinese soldiers fired several shots at the boat. Seeing that the soldiers were about to follow this up with a full volley from their matchlocks, the British did not resort to soothing words. A British naval officer tells us how

> at the instant, two of the Blonde's thirty-two pound shot went bowling into the midst of these valiant fellows, and "Sauve qui peu[t]" [every man for himself] became the cry — the whole mass, officers, soldiers, and spectators flying for their lives, leaving five or six of their number dead upon the beach. The Blonde's guns were now turned on the forts [which were protecting the city of Ting-hai on Chusan (Zhoushan) Island, south of the estuary of the Yangtze River] and war-junks, in consequence of their having opened fire upon her, which she soon effectually and quickly silenced, riddling the former and sinking the latter.[47]

The British were willing to fight because they were confident that their ships and naval firepower were much better than those of the Chinese.

Although badly outnumbered on the ground (during a May 1841 attack on Canton, British land forces totaled about 2,753 men vs. about 49,000 Chinese troops),[48] the British dominated the seas and controlled access to all the Chinese coastal ports. Even if the Opium Wars were not big wars by Western standards, the British naval order of battle was still impressive. At the end of the first Opium War, the British squadron consisted, by one early count, of 32 ships, plus two survey vessels, nine wooden steamers and five iron steamers.[49] A later tally made by the governor of Hong Kong showed that when the Treaty of Nanking was signed in 1842 the British had 70 vessels and 12,000 fighting men in China.[50]

Given China's weaknesses, Britain's advanced technology was bound to prevail. This was never clearer than in the case of the iron steamers, such as *Nemesis*, especially when they were armed with the formidable Congreve rockets, named after the British officer who invented them in 1804. *Nemesis* was a sturdy flat-bottomed iron paddle wheel steamer of 700 tons' burden, 184 feet long, 29 feet wide and 11 feet deep. She had 120 horsepower steam engines, which consumed 11 tons of coal a day, carried a complement of 90 officers and men and drew only a little more than five feet of water. Her officers testified to the fact that in the fight at Anson's Bay near Canton on 7 January 1841,

> one of the most formidable engines of destruction, which any vessel, particularly a steamer, can make use of is the Congrove [sic] rocket ... especially when there are combustible materials to act upon. The very first rocket fired from the Nemesis was seen to enter the large junk against which it was directed, near that to the admiral, and almost the instant afterwards it blew up with a terrific explosion, launching into eternity every soul aboard, and pouring forth its blaze like a mighty rush of fire from a volcano.[51]

The shallow draft of *Nemesis* was also a great asset to the British and allowed the ship to thread its way up the winding channels of the Canton River. Handling a big ship in such a narrow inland waterway took steady nerves and seamanship of a high order. During the 26 February 1841 attack on Canton, "In many parts the river was so narrow that the steamer's bow had to be forced into one side of the river's bank to be enabled to clear the other, and in many places she had not an inch of water to spare."[52] Another British officer reported, "The astonishment of the Chinese who dwelt in the villages along ... the banks at the sight of a gigantic vessel moving, independent of wind and tide, close to the doors and windows of their dwellings may hence be conceived."[53]

Notes

1. Cited by Morse, *Relations*, p. 183.
2. It was almost impossible at the time, and is even more so today, to arrive at a fair estimate of the value of the opium that Commissioner Lin destroyed. Lord Palmerston's calculation of more than 6 million Spanish silver dollars was thought by some opium merchants to be much too high, but other estimates were high as well (e.g., $10–11 million, £2 million, etc.). Whatever the exact figure, it is clear that British and other foreign merchants did indeed sustain a heavy loss. See Owen, *British Opium Policy*, p. 185; Turner, *Kwang Tung*; and *Crisis*, p. 27.
3. Bingham, *Narrative*, p. 125. Emphasis in original.
4. Of these 7,000 chests (two-thirds of which contained Malwa opium and one-third Turkish opium), only 2,000 belonged to Jardine Matheson itself. The rest belonged to other trading houses and individuals, many of whom were Parsees. See Fay, *Opium War*, p. 157.
5. Graham, *The Right, Obligation, and Interest*, p. 24.
6. Cited by Alexander, *Rise and Progress*, p. 27.
7. Cited by Booth, *Opium*, p. 112.
8. Fraser, *Flashman*, pp. 16–17. The xenophobia and moral superiority felt by the Chinese toward Westerners sometimes had an ambivalent quality. In an Imperial edict of 5 June 1842, for example, the emperor admitted that the fighting abilities of his troops were not equal to "the barbarous dispositions of the rebellious barbarians." Cited by Murray, *Doings*, p. 234.
9. Ouchterlony, *The Chinese War*, pp. 36–37.
10. Turner, *Kwang Tung*, pp. 45–46, citing Williams, *Middle Kingdom*.
11. A contemporary British observer said that in 1838 the British bought about £3.1 million worth of goods from China (teas and silks) and sold about £5.6 million worth of goods to China (opium, metals and cotton). This left a balance of trade of about £2.5 million in favor of the British, which was paid for in sycee silver. "Thus we see," he wrote, "what was the chief and true reason for [the Chinese] attempting to stop the trade in opium, and accordingly the [emperor's] edicts previously or subsequently to this year, enlarged more on the abstraction of the sycee than on the morals of the people." See Bingham, *Narrative*, pp. 69–70.

Because large amounts of silver were exported from China to pay for the opium, the result was inflation. In 1852 a Chinese official reported to the emperor that "the price of silver is too high, and it is difficult to pay the taxes [which had to be paid in silver] ... Previously an ounce of silver was worth a thousand copper coins [agricultural products were sold for copper coins, not silver], so that for a picul [133 lbs.] one received three ounces of silver. Today an ounce of silver is worth two thousand copper coins, so that for a picul of rice one receives only one and a half ounces of silver." See Franke, *Chinese Revolution*, p. 22.

12. For contemporary accounts of the wars, see Bernard, *Nemesis*; Bingham, *Narrative*; Davis, *Sketches*; Kennedy, *Hurrah*; Ouchterlony, *Chinese War*;

Mackenzie, *Narrative;* and Murray, *Doings*. For modern accounts see Beeching, *China's Opium Wars;* Fay, *The Opium War;* Fraser, *Flashman and the Dragon;* Holt, *The Opium Wars;* Owen, *British Opium Policy;* and Waley, *The Opium War Through Chinese Eyes*.

13. The first of these skirmishes occurred on 4 September 1839 and was known, perhaps sarcastically, as the "Battle of Kowloon." Elliot lost his temper when the Chinese at a waterside village refused to sell supplies to his men. The American opium captain Robert Bennet Forbes happened to be on the scene. The next day, in a letter written to his wife (cited by Kerr in *Letters*, p. 167), he reported that the clash

> was an action between Capt. Elliots [sic] Cutter mounting four guns, the Brig Pearl with as many more, a boat well armed from the frigate, and four men of war junks each mounting guns ... Hearing the firing I took a small fast pulling [rowing] gig and went round a point of land with my long spy glass to see the fun, while many ships sent their armed boats, & the frigate got underway to protect them, it was quite a farce — I kept a mile off not intending to mix up in this quarrel — The Chinese fired bravely & it is reported today [5 September 1839] that several are killed & a Mandarin among them — Capt. Elliot had a small ball pass through his hat, & Capt. Douglas of the Cambridge one through his arm, one sailor shot through the jaw & one in the leg, all doing well today including the hat ... The junks retreated but fired bravely & what is wonderful they were left in quiet possession of the field at dusk.

14. In January 1841 a document known as the Convention of Chuenpi (or Chuenpee) was drawn up and signed by Elliot and Kishen, but this agreement was soon angrily repudiated by both China and England. Because the convention gave Hong Kong to the barbarians, the emperor decreed that Kishen be taken from Hong Kong in chains, condemned to death at a trial in Peking (this sentence was eventually commuted to exile in Tibet) and have all his property (valued at £10 million) confiscated to help pay for the war. On the British side, Lord Palmerston called Elliot "disloyal" and "neglectful"; Queen Victoria herself was furious with him. Elliot was replaced by Henry Pottinger and was exiled in disgrace to such obscure posts as the Republic of Texas, Bermuda, Trinidad and St. Helena. See Kerr, *Letters*, pp. 266–267.

15. *China Pilot*, p. 59.
16. Owen, *British Opium Policy*, p. 197.
17. Kerr, *Letters*, p. 114, citing Collis, *Foreign Mud*, pp. 246–54.
18. MacGregor, *Tea Clippers*, pp. 102–103.
19. Eberhard, *History of China*, p. 252.
20. After the Treaty of Nanking, to facilitate trade (including the smuggling of opium), the British allowed some Chinese junks to get a license in Hong Kong that would permit them to fly the British flag. Thanks to the British ships-of-

war stationed on the southeastern coast of China, this gave them protection from the pirates infesting the region and to some extent from Chinese government war junks as well. See Eberhard, *History of China*, pp. 299–300.

21. Morse, *International Relations*, p. 323 ff. Foreigners, however, were to sell the drug only in the treaty ports; the Chinese handled sales within China itself. See Johnson, *Far China Station*, p. 99.

22. Waung, *Controversy*, p. 1.

23. Marx is cited by Fraser in *Flashman*, p. 314, but no source for the quote is given.

24. *Crisis*, pp. 50 and 51.

25. Peggs, *A Voice*, pp. 31–35. Emphasis in original.

26. Davis, *Sketches*, vol. 2, pp. 270–271.

27. Downing, *Fan-Qui*, vol. 3, pp. 324–325.

28. Mackenzie, *Narrative*, p. 145. Bingham makes the same point in his *Narrative*, p. 131–132.

29. Mackenzie, *Narrative*, pp. 143–144.

30. Mackenzie, *Narrative*, pp. 149–150.

31. Waley, *Opium War*, p. 197.

32. Kennedy, *Hurrah*, p. 76.

33. Turner, *Kwang Tung*, pp. 45–46.

34. Downing, *Fan-Qui*, vol. 3, pp. 324–325.

35. Bernard, *Nemesis*, pp. 241, 278–279.

36. Lay, *The Chinese*, p. 97.

37. Taken from Kennedy, *Hurrah*, pp. 71–76.

38. After Waley, *Opium War*, pp. 134–135.

39. Ouchterlony, *Chinese War*, pp. 175–176.

40. Bernard, *Nemesis*, p. 354.

41. "Tartary" is the historical name of a vast but poorly defined region of Eastern Europe and Asia that was overrun by Tartars (members of various Mongolian or Turkish tribes) in the Middle Ages. In his *Travels*, Marco Polo says the Tartars "are stout fighters, excelling in courage and hardihood ... they are of all men in the world the best able to endure exertion and hardship and the least costly to maintain and therefore the best adapted for conquering territory and overthrowing kingdoms." They were such fierce fighters that even today the "Tartar" still implies a savage, intractable person. The reference to "tiger-hearted" Chinese troops is from Mackenzie, *Narrative*, p. 78.

42. Ouchterlony, *Chinese War*, pp. 277–281.

43. Bingham, *Narrative*, pp. 107–108.

44. Bernard, *Nemesis*, p. 236. Emphasis in original.

45. Bernard, *Nemesis*, p. 418.

46. One of the best examples of these Victorian attitudes was provided by Commander J. Elliot Bingham, RN, who in 1840 was the First Lieutenant on HMS *Modeste*. This is taken from his *Narrative*, pp. 1–2:

> Ho! for China, was the cheering sound heard on board the Cape Squadron, on the morning of April [date missing], 1840, when

we received the news that our worthy admiral (the Hon. G. Elliot, C.B.) was appointed commander-in-chief of the India station, and would take command of the expedition fitting out at Calcutta, which was destined to act against the Chinese; and happy fellows were they whose ships were selected to join that force — Melville 74 [number of guns] flag [flagship], Modest 18, Columbine 16....

47. Bingham, *Narrative*, pp. 202–203.
48. Bingham, *Narrative*, p. 167.
49. Bernard, *Nemesis*, pp. 551–552.
50. Davis, *China*, p. viii.
51. Bernard, *Nemesis*, p. 271.
52. Bingham, *Narrative*, p. 180.
53. Ouchterlony, *Chinese War*, pp. 124–125.

6

The Heat of Battle

The fatal combination of Chinese weaknesses and British strengths can be seen most clearly in the clashes, both afloat and ashore, between the two sides during the Opium Wars. *Battles* is probably too strong a word for most of these low-level military and naval engagements, which pale in comparison with the major campaigns of, say, the Crimean War of 1853–1856 or the American Civil War of 1860–1865. It is instructive, nevertheless, to look at contemporary accounts of some of these bloody fights.

Because the wars were so carefully documented by the British, there is no shortage of such accounts, but we can choose nine of them — five in the first Opium War and four in the second war — as typifying the rest.[1] These engagements were only isolated incidents in the nine-year-long course of the wars, but they will help us see later on how repeated Chinese humiliations during the Opium Wars caused many of China's later problems with the West. The best summary of these humiliations was provided by the British scholar Hosea Ballou Morse in 1910: "As a result [of the Opium Wars], the Chinese learned, and they accepted as their law, that, whereas formerly it was China which dictated the conditions under which international relations were to be maintained, now it was the Western nations which imposed their will on China."[2]

The First Opium War

War Junks and Fire Rafts Off Chuenpi (3 November 1839)

As it approaches Canton, the Canton River narrows about 45 miles from the sea to a constricted channel less than two miles wide. As has been mentioned, this area was known as the Bogue or the Bocca Tigris and was studded with small islands such as Chuenpi, North and South Wangtong, Boat Island, Taikoktow, Tiger Island and Anunghoi. On some of these islands the Chinese had built powerful forts to protect Canton. It was in the waters off their fort on Chuenpi that the first major engagement of the first Opium War occurred on 3 November 1839.

After a good deal of palaver and unsuccessful diplomatic maneuvering by both sides, the Chinese drew up at Chuenpi a fleet of 16 war junks and 13 fire rafts that the British believed had hostile intentions and therefore opened fire on. An officer of HMS *Volage* who took part in the fight describes it vividly:

> The first vessel to receive our fire was one of their fire-rafts; we threw a few shot [sic] upon her in passing, and in a few seconds observed her to settle in the water, and almost immediately go down. One of the war-junks was now on the beam of the Volage, and fired a couple of guns at her, which passed over. These were immediately returned, several of the shot telling on the junk; and almost instantly we heard an explosion, and looking round saw through the envelope of the smoke the fragments of the unfortunate junk floating as it were in the air. She had blown up ... the [18-gun ship HMS] Hyacinth came in astern of the Volage, passed her, and got among the denser part of the junks.... The firing was now indiscriminate upon any vessel where the guns would tell....
>
> [Chinese] guns and powder must have been good, from the distance they carried; but not being fitted for elevation or depression, all their shot were too high to have any effect, except on the spars and rigging. The Volage got some shot through her sails, and the Hyacinth was a good deal cut up in her rigging and spars; a 12-pound shot lodged in her mizen-mast, and one went through her main-yard, requiring it to be secured. Their wretched gunnery hurt no one. The firing commenced about twelve, and at one they were all sunk, dispersed, or flying.... The result of the whole was three junks sunk, one blown up, many deserted, and the rest flying.[3]

Chinese fire rafts were feared by Western merchant captains but actually did little damage. On Commissioner Lin's orders the Chinese tried three times to attack with fire rafts the fleet of foreign merchantmen off Canton. A British chief superintendent in China recounts that

> It so happened, that the last attack of fire-rafts occurred on the night of the 9th of June [1840], the very day on which [HMS] Alligator, being the first ship of the approaching expedition, arrived off Macao. That frigate was in fact guided to the anchorage at [Cumsingmoon] by the light of the burning rafts, and her boats were employed in towing them away from the fleet. The attack had been concerted with all imaginable secrecy, and scarcely had the signal of danger been made than the fire burst out from nearly twenty rafts, or rather boats, chained together two-and-two, so that they might swing athwart our ships with the tide, which, as well as the wind, was in their favour.... The confusion was considerable among the merchant shipping; most of them slipped their cables in the hurry to move out of danger.... No serious injury, however, was sustained.[4]

THE CAPTURE OF TING-HAI (5 JULY 1840)

The British military expedition later sailed north for eight days along the China coast to take possession of the Chusan [Zhoushan] group of islands near the Yangtze River. The Chinese defenses there were feeble at best — a few war junks had been stationed off Ting-hai, the capital city of the islands, and Chinese soldiers had been put to work building shoreside batteries protected by canvas bags filled with grain. The British demanded that Ting-hai surrender peacefully but by 5 July 1840,

> no overture for a peaceful occupation [of the city] having been received ... a shotted gun was fired from the [HMS 74-gun line-of-battle ship] Wellesley.... It was immediately returned by one from the junk of the Chinese admiral; and the fire shortly became general along their line of defence, and from their junks abreast of the town [Ting-hai]. The first broadside of the Wellesley almost annihilated the wretched craft opposed to her; and the [HMS 28-gun ship] Conway, directing her guns against some temporary works thrown up on the slope of a hill to the right of the town, speedily silenced their fire...When the smoke cleared away, the junks were seen dismasted, or driven on shore, and the soldiers on the wharves dispersed.... The [British] troops, the first division of whom had been put into their boats previous to the commencement of the action, were now directed to land....

There were the first European troops who had ever landed on the shores of China as conquering invaders.⁵

ATTACK ON THE BOGUE FORTS (7 JANUARY 1841)

Negotiations with the Chinese having again failed, the British decided to mount an attack on the Bogue forts near Canton. On 7 January 1841, more than 1400 troops were landed, initially without opposition, but then they came under heavy fire. The British soon outflanked the Chinese defenders, however, and the quick volleys fired by British marines and by Indian sepoys (that is, soldiers)

> told fatally amidst the densely-crowded Chinese, a number of whom fell. The rest rushed back into the fort for safety, shutting the gates, and locking themselves in. The gates, however, were quickly blown open by the muskets of their pursuers, who, as they entered, dealt death on every side. The blue jackets [British sailors] scaling and entering the fort at the opposite end, resistance became useless, and about one hundred [Chinese] asked for, and received, quarter. The remainder locked themselves into sheds and out-houses, seizing every opportunity of firing from them upon their victors when they thought they were not being perceived. This drew down on them indiscriminate slaughter. In many cases they betook themselves to the water, and attempted to fire at our men; failing in which they would ask for quarter, but in these cases rarely obtained it.⁶

While all this was going on, British ships were attacking the Bogue fort at Taikoktow:

> ...terrific were the effects of the concentrated broadsides of the [HMS 44-gun ship] Druid's long guns, whole masses of masonry falling before them. The buildings of the fort were soon in ruins, and its defenders were escaping by tens and dozens at a time through holes that our shot had made in the walls, the gates having been all securely locked, for the double purpose of keeping them in and us out.
>
> Perceiving that the fort was now nearly silenced, the boats of the [HMS 26-gun ship] Samarang and the [HMS 18-gun vessel] Modeste landed under the south end of the wall, when Mr. Lugard, mate of the former ship, and myself [the author of this account was the First Lieutenant on Modeste], scrambled through the breach in the wall ... then running along the platform, we drove about thirty Chinamen before us, so excessive was their

panic.... The Chinese lost about twenty killed, and, no doubt, many wounded, our loss being very inconsiderable.... The whole of the fighting did not continue more than an hour and a half.[7]

In this battle the steamer *Nemesis* had her first chance to prove how useful small shallow-draft iron vessels could be in coastal warfare:

> After disembarking the whole of the 37th regiment below Chuenpee, she ran alongside the [Taikoktow] fort, and threw shells into the upper fort ... taking advantage of her light draught, she ran up close to the sea battery, and poured through the embrasures destructive rounds of grape as she passed; then pushing on over the shallows into Anson's Bay, in the midst of the war junks lying at anchor, she threw three Congreve rockets with startling effect, the very first having set fire to the largest of them, which blew up, with all of her crew on board. Aided by a flotilla of boats from the squadron, she proceeded on her course across the bay, setting fire to junk after junk, until the whole fleet, eleven in number, was destroyed, except for two which remained unhurt, moored to the shore on the far side of the bay; but Captain Hall [*Nemesis*'s captain] went over, grappled them, towed them into deep water, and set fire to them, before the Chinese could sufficiently recover from their surprise and consternation, to offer any resistance to the bold maneuver.[8]

This demonstration of British power proved to the Chinese just how vulnerable Canton was, and it forced them to sit down and negotiate. Under the terms of the Convention of Chuenpi, signed by both sides on 20 January 1841, they agreed to pay the British a $6-million ransom to save Canton, to cede Hong Kong to them and to allow trade to resume. Yet by the middle of February 1841 the Canton trade had still not reopened, and the Chinese were observed to be making additional warlike preparations. These prompted the British to attack the remaining Bogue forts.

Another Attack on the Bogue Forts (26 February 1841)

In this 26 February 1841 action, *Wellesley*, *Druid* and *Modeste* shelled the battery on North Wangtong while *Calliope*, *Herald*, *Samarang* and *Alligator*, each with 26 guns, poured their starboard broadsides into the lower Wangtong battery as they passed by it. The line-of-battle ships *Blenheim* and *Melville* shelled the South Anunghoi fort. "The firing of these ships," reported a British officer, "was most splendid: nothing could withstand their deadly aim.... Truly it was an awful day for the black-haired race of Han [the Chinese]."⁹ Three hundred seamen and marines then landed and occupied the fort. British casualties were very few, but Chinese losses were estimated at 500 men. Poignantly, "there fell, on that day, one chief, near the gate of Anunghoy, bravely but vainly endeavoring, with a handful of men who still adhered to him, to resist the entry [of a British officer] and his seamen — this was the valiant old Admiral Kwan, whose body was found among the slain."¹⁰

Clash at the Chusan Islands (10 October 1841)

In the summer of 1841 the British sent an expedition north along the coast to recapture Tinghai and Chinhai in the Chusan Islands, which had been returned to Chinese control earlier that year. Lieutenant Alexander Murray of the 18th Royal Irish regiment was one of the many British officers and men who showed remarkable coolness under fire. On 1 October 1841, during an attack on Tinghai a Chinese soldier drew his sword and ran at Murray, who later wrote that "having no confidence in my regulation spit [sword], or perhaps in my own skill as a swordsman, I stuck my sword in the mud beside me, took steady aim with my pistol, and shot him."¹¹

On 10 October 1841 two advancing columns of British troops caught the Chinese forces in a pincer movement. A British officer tells us what happened next:

> A dreadful scene of slaughter was enacting on the right bank of the river, where the Chinese troops, retiring before the advance of the center column [of British troops] ... in hopes of retreating across the river ... came unexpectedly upon the head of the left column....
>
> It is not difficult to conceive the scene which ensued. Hemmed in on all sides, and crushed and overwhelmed by the fire of a complete semicircle of musketry, the hapless Chinese rushed by hundreds into the water; and while some attempted to escape the tempest of death which roared around them, by consigning themselves to the stream, and floating out beyond the range of fire, others appeared to drown themselves in despair.... The loss of the Chinese was immense in killed and wounded.... On the side of the British but few casualties occurred.¹²

The first Opium War ground on into 1842 as the British continued their advance toward Nanking, where a treaty ending the war was finally signed on 29 August 1842. The significance of this treaty and of the other treaties ending the second Opium War will be discussed in the concluding chapter. At this point it is important to remember that, after the first Opium War was over but during the course of the second war, there occurred in China what has been called "the worst civil war in history, and the second bloodiest of any kind, being exceeded only in casualties by the Second World War, with its estimated 80 million dead."[13] This was the great Taiping rebellion of 1850–1864, a convulsive upheaval that weakened the Qing dynasty even further. Indeed, the agriculture and industry of the lower provinces of the Yangtze River had still not recovered fully even 50 years later.

The Second Opium War

Militarily, the second Opium War was something of a replay, albeit on a bigger scale, of the first war. The basic equation remained unchanged: a weakened and corrupt Chinese dynasty was incapable of fending off the advanced technology and superior discipline of Western forces.

YET ANOTHER ATTACK ON THE BOGUE FORTS (12 NOVEMBER 1856)

William (later Admiral) Kennedy, then an 18-year-old midshipman in the 84-gun, teak, line-of-battle ship HMS *Calcutta*, the flagship of the commanding officer of the East Indies and China station, has left us a firsthand account of this assault on the Bogue forts. In addition to *Calcutta*, five other British ships — the frigate *Nankin* (50 guns), the corvette *Encounter* (14 guns), two sloops (*Hornet* with 17 guns and *Barracuda* with six guns) and the small paddle steamer *Coromandel*, which mounted four howitzers but was used as a tender — were all involved in this action:

> At daylight ... the ships cleared for action [i.e., cleared the decks], and took up their appointed station, the Calcutta having the post of honor, abreast of and within a few hundred yards of the South Wantung [fort], mounting 100 guns. Our position was so well chosen that only a few guns could bear upon the ship. The Chinamen, with incomprehensible stupidity or indifference, allowed the ships to take up their positions and

moor head to stern, right under their guns without firing a shot, nor was it till we had carefully laid our guns and delivered a concentrated broadside that they condescended to reply. The results of these tactics was that we had it all our own way.... After an hour-and-a-half's firing the batteries were silenced, having been crushed from the beginning by the terrible fire from the ships.[14]

Breaking the Boom on the Peiho River (20 May 1858)

During the first British attack on the Taku forts, located in northern China on the Peiho [Hai] River about 70 miles from Tientsin, this time William Kennedy was in charge of the left wing of the British forces storming the forts:

> The Chinamen had stretched a boom across the mouth of the river to keep hostile boats from entering. This boom was composed of spars, chains, and hawsers, and was sufficiently strong to keep out boats or junks, but not a steam vessel going at high speed. The [steamer] Cormorant ... led the way in gallant style, snapping the chains like thread. As each vessel passed the narrows where the boom had been she received a heavy fire [from the Taku forts], as the Chinese had concentrated their guns on that spot, and did not seem able to fire in any other direction.... The Chinamen stuck to their guns well, and returned the [British] fire with spirit, hulling each vessel repeatedly as she entered the river; but once inside, they turned their attention to the next.... [When British troops stormed ashore] the Chinese no sooner saw us coming than they bolted, the mandarins leading the way on horseback.[15]

Western Envoys Are Repulsed at Taku Forts (25 June 1859)

In June 1858 the British had captured the Taku forts but did not occupy them permanently. As a result, the Chinese took possession of them again and over the next year worked hard to make them more secure. The *Times* of London reported that "the number of booms had been increased, the forts rebuilt, enlarged and strengthened ... and the result is a powerful and almost impregnable fortress."[16] On 25 June 1859, a joint task force consisting of 16 British ships (a heavy man-of-war, two frigates and 13 gunboats) and two French ships (a frigate and a gunboat) were carrying British and French negotiators en route to Peking to sign the treaties negotiated at Tientsin. This fleet tried to force its way past the Taku forts but was repulsed with heavy losses.

Walter White, a British sailor assigned to HMS *Scout* on the China Station, was not present at this fight himself, but after listening to the yarns of many other bluejackets who were in it he got a clear picture of what happened there. His account tallies with official reports and shows us the Chinese defenses at their best.

White says that two of the British gunboats, *Plover* and *Opossum*, steamed at full speed at the strengthened boom but failed to snap it. This was the signal for the forts to open a heavy fire on the ships. Another gunboat, *Starling*, grounded on the muddy tidal flats opposite a fort that mounted 58 guns. These quickly sank a fourth gunboat, *Kestrel*, and put a round shot through *Starling*'s starboard bow that killed eight men who had been serving the pivot gun and wounded three others. The badly wounded British commander, Admiral Hope, was transferred from *Plover* (which was first disabled and then sunk by Chinese fire) to *Opossum*, but while he was on deck a cannon ball carried away the chain by which he had been supporting himself and he fell heavily, breaking his ribs and arms and bruising his side.

Despite these setbacks, British troops succeeded in landing in small boats under the guns of the forts and immediately found themselves bogged down in mud up their knees. Using "we" in a collective rather than a personal sense, White continues the story:

> We struggled on towards the batteries until we came to a broad deep ditch, with five or six feet of water. In we plunged, men falling at every step, still we pushed on until we came to another ditch filled with sharp pointed stakes. We could get no further and were all this time exposed to a cruel fire of gingal balls, bullets and even arrows.... Every now and again the Chinese threw out their fire balls which lighted up the place like a day for a few moments, and gave them the chance of firing on us.... Before morning the Chinese had burnt the Plover and taken all they could from the other gunboats. We lost in the ships 25 killed and wounded and in the attack on shore 64 were killed and 345 wounded in this desperate fight.[17]

The Fall of Peking and Burning of the Summer Palace (October 1860)

Realizing that unless Peking itself were captured the Chinese would have little incentive to negotiate a speedy end to the war, British and French forces pressed on toward the capital. An anonymous Chinese scholar, now known to us only as "a certain Doctor of Letters and member of the Hanlin Academy," kept a diary during these troubled days:

> Rumors began to circulate that the barbarians had already reached Taku.... During the next few days, people began to leave Peking, for the report was spread that our troops had been defeated at Taku, and that a Brigadier General was among those slain; the garrison had fled to Pei T'ang and the forts were in the hands of the barbarians ... our troops engaged the barbarians outside the Ch'i Hua gate, the van [the foremost division] was composed of untrained Mongol cavalry, who had never been in action. No sooner had the barbarians opened fire than they turned as one man, broke their ranks and stampeded upon the infantry in their rear. Many were trampled to death, and a general route followed, our men falling in every direction and the barbarians pressing on to the city walls.... Suddenly, a little after mid-day, the immense blaze was seen to the north-west, and speedily it was reported that the barbarians had seized Hai-tien and the Summer Palace. Our army was said to number half a million men, and yet it seems that not one of them dare oppose the barbarians' advance ... vast columns of smoke were rising to the north-west, and it was ascertained that the barbarians had entered the Summer Palace, and after plundering the three main halls, leaving them absolutely bare, they set fire to the buildings....[18]

During the siege of Peking, the Chinese had tortured to death some British and Indian prisoners. Lord Elgin, the British commander, decided that the emperor's Summer Palace (the Yuanming Yuan) near Peking should be destroyed in retaliation for these brutal and senseless acts. After being looted, the Summer Palace and the other adjoining royal palaces were therefore set on fire. These lovely buildings burned for two days, with clouds of smoke hanging over them like a pall and drifting into Peking itself. Lord Elgin justified his decision by stressing that

> it was the Emperor's favorite residence, and its destruction could not fail to be a blow to his pride as well as to his feelings.... The punishment was one which would fall, not on the people, who may be comparatively innocent, but exclusively on the Emperor, whose direct personal responsibility for the crime committed is established, not only by the treatment of the prisoners at Yuenming Yuen, but also by the edict in which he offered a pecuniary reward for the heads of foreigners.[19]

Notes

1. There appears to be only one readily accessible English translation of contemporary Chinese documents on the Opium Wars. This is Waley's *The Opium War Through Chinese Eyes*, which has been used here.
2. Morse, *Relations*, vol. 1, p. 617.
3. Bingham, *Narrative*, pp. 153–155.
4. Davis, *Sketches*, vol. 2, pp. 263–264.
5. Ouchterlony, *Chinese War*, pp. 44–45. A similar but less detailed account can also be found in Davis, *Sketches*, vol. 2, pp. 272–279.
6. Bingham, *Narrative*, pp. 103–107.
7. Bingham, *Narrative*, pp. 111–114.
8. Ouchterlony, *Chinese War*, pp. 98–99.
9. Bingham, *Narrative*, pp. 143–144.
10. Ouchterlony, *Chinese War*, pp. 114–118. A similar account of the fight, but not of Admiral Kwan's death, appears in Bingham, *Narrative*, pp. 143–148.
11. Murray, *Doings*, p. 33.
12. Ouchterlony, *Chinese War*, pp. 188–192.
13. Fraser, "The Taiping Rebellion" (Appendix I), in *Flashman*, pp. 293–296. Because of the importance of this rebellion in nineteenth-century China, a short description may be of interest.

In addition to strong anti-Western sentiments in Kwangtung province (south China), there were communal tensions, too. The local inhabitants (Taipings) were hostile to immigrants (Hakkas) who had settled among them. However, having lost prestige by its defeats in the first Opium War, the Chinese government was unable to keep the peace between these rival groups. Hong Xiuquan, a Cantonese clerk who had fallen into a religious trance after failing his civil service examinations, believed himself to be a son of God. He founded a mass movement known as the Heavenly Kingdom of Great Peace (Taiping Tianguo). Many of his followers were Hakkas, but his rebellion also attracted starving peasants, outlaws, members of secret societies and a handful of very able organizers and military leaders.

At first the Taipings were successful, capturing Nanking in 1853 and threatening Tientsin soon thereafter, but gradually they were suppressed by government troops who had been reinforced by Chinese mercenaries equipped with modern Western rifles. These mercenaries were led first by an American soldier of fortune, Frederick Townsend Ward, and then by a British officer, Charles George ("Chinese") Gordon. When the Taiping Rebellion was finally put down in 1864, whole provinces had been devastated, 600 towns had been laid waste, Hung had committed suicide by taking poison, all the other Taiping leaders had been killed in action or executed, and a minimum of 20 to 30 million people had been killed. See "The Taiping Rebellion" in the *Encyclopedia Britannica*'s article, *China*, vol. 16, p. 125–126.

14. Kennedy, *Hurrah*, pp. 50–51.
15. Kennedy, *Hurrah*, pp. 106–108.

16. Cited by Levenworth, *Arrow War*, p. 130.
17. White, *China Station*, pp. 40–41.
18. Bland and Backhouse, *Empress Dowager*, pp. 14–24.
19. Cited by Williams, *History*, p. 333.

7

Pirates of the South China Sea

In the early and mid-nineteenth century, the Sailing Directions for the Canton River (which was also known then as the Pearl River) began with a sober warning: "Ships approaching the Coast of China, particularly those of small size, ought always to have some guns ready, in order to repel any attacks that may be made by Ladrones [pirates], or other piratical boats, which are sometimes mistaken for fishing boats."[1]

Opium clippers and coasters ignored this advice at their peril. Pirates were truly an occupational hazard. Ships in this trade were considered extraordinarily rich prizes by the pirates because their cargo was invariably opium, specie or both. Even when these ships were well manned and well armed they could still fall prey to the swarms of pirates who infested the China coast. Great caution was needed because it was often impossible for opium clippers and other ships to know whether approaching junks were crewed by harmless fishermen or by cutthroat pirates. A British officer complained that

> The fishermen along the whole [southern] coast of China, as far as Canton, are rogues, pirates, smugglers — in short, ready to take advantage of any opportunity, honest or otherwise, of benefiting themselves. They will perhaps appear quite friendly at first; and, if they think a vessel is not prepared to resist, or if they think that they could overpower her, the chances are that

they would not hesitate to make the attempt, when least expected.... It is at night that the Chinese would be most likely to make the attempt, and for this reason the opium clippers are always well armed and manned.²

A Familiar Menace

Long before the opium trade began, pirates were a serious problem in Chinese waters. One of the greatest captains of Chinese pirate history was Ching-Chi-ling. Before his capture and execution in 1661, his fleet of 1,000 pirate junks was the best organized maritime force between the Yangtze and Canton and was far more potent than the lightly armed and undermanned Chinese navy. Upon Ching's death, his son Koxinga assumed command of the fleet and raided the coast so savagely that the population had to be evacuated as far as 12 miles inland. Koxinga's own descendants, however, were unable to hold the fleet together, and gradually it divided into small flotillas run by local warlords.

Toward the end of the eighteenth century, as European trade with China increased and more European ships began to ply Chinese waters, piracy became a growth industry. The first recorded pirate attack on an opium ship occurred in 1793. Thirteen years later, Alexander Dalrymple, who was for many years the hydrographer of the Royal Navy and the editor of the Canton Secret Consultations of the East India Company, could report that "from the earliest times of the European Navigation to Canton, it appears, from the name *Ladron*, i.e., *Thief*, given by the Portuguese, to the Southern Island, on the East Side of the Entrance to Canton River, that there were Freebooters infesting these Parts."³

Another important pirate lair was the island of Hainan, from where small fleets of their junks sailed northward each year with the summer monsoon to pillage the coast and attack shipping west of Taiwan and off the Luzon Strait. Dalrymple estimated in 1806 that there were as many as 600 to 700 pirate vessels, about 200 of which were based along the east coast of China, with the remainder in the waters near Hainan. He drew up a list of contemporary pirate attacks:

In 1795 the small vessel *Leebow*, en route from Manila to China, was overpowered among the coastal islands by a fleet of 26 pirate junks. Her captain, Robert Funter, was captured and tortured to death. One of *Leebow*'s crew escaped to tell how this unfortunate officer met his end.

Funter was "spread out at length, and bound naked, exposed to the Sun, in which state he was kept alive for some days, putting into his mouth occasionally a little water and some rice, with a Man with a Knife frequently threatening to cut his head off."[4]

The next year a small Portuguese vessel sailing from Cochin China (the southern tip of Vietnam) bound for Macao "was boarded by the Pirates; who, not content with plunder, murdered eight of the Crew." By 1802 pirates based near Macao were assaulting ships heading for Canton. A year later the American brig *Ohio* was attacked by four large junks, but the Americans gave them what was called a whiff of grape — that is, "two or three rounds [of grapeshot] being fired with considerable effect, which compelled the Boats to sheer off."[5]

In 1804 the Portuguese gunners manning the forts near Macao lived in fear that pirates would capture the city itself. This was a valid concern for two reasons: first, the Portuguese themselves were such poor shots that their cannon balls rarely fell within a quarter of a mile of any pirate junk, and, second, "the Mandarin Boats, stationed for the protection of the Rivers, fled on the appearance of the Pirates, and left the Passages, and unarmed Inhabitants, entirely at their Mercy." Thus it is not surprising that when 70 pirate boats appeared off Macao in 1805 and were taken under fire by a Portuguese ship, they were still able to capture and plunder a large merchant junk anchored within four miles of the city. At times the presence of so many pirates even brought the opium trade itself to a temporary standstill.

Pirate Junks

Pirate junks ranged in size from big three-masted vessels, 80 feet long and with a beam of 18 feet, to smaller two-masted boats about 40 feet long. The captain lived with his family in the poop, where for his own safety he also kept all the muskets and pistols. The crew and their families lived wherever they could in the hold or on the decks themselves. The ship's magazine, where gunpowder was stored, was in the hold. A primitive galley was located on the afterdeck.

When pirates captured a trading junk they could easily convert it to their own purposes simply by adding guns. The big junk of one pirate chief mounted as many as 38 guns — two long 24-pounders, eight or nine 18-pounders, and the rest 9- and 6- pounders. Gingals were used both on land and in small junks. They were effective against unarmed merchant junks at close range but were no match for the heavy cannons and well-drilled crews of Western ships, so pirates usually looked for crippled or weakly manned European ships to attack.

To compensate for their shortcomings in gunnery, the pirates tried to come alongside a prize and then bombard it with stink-pots. These were made of sealed earthen pots, half-filled with gunpowder sometimes moistened with high-proof Chinese gin, and topped by pieces of lighted charcoal. Thus prepared, stink-pots were slung in bags on the rigging of pirate junks, where they came readily to hand and could be tossed onto the deck of a ship under attack. When they landed, they shattered and burned fiercely. Even if the deck itself did not catch fire, the crew of the vessel under attack might well be choked or blinded by the acrid smoke, leaving them vulnerable to a pirate boarding party armed with swords, knives and spears.

Daily life aboard a pirate junk was far from pleasant. In 1809 Richard Glasspoole, who was then a lowly fourth mate on the East India Company's ship *Marquis of Ely* but later rose to the command of its ship *Buckinghamshire*, was captured by pirates off Macao. Glasspoole was held prisoner for 11 weeks until finally rescued by the company's cruiser *Antelope*. This is how he described pirate life:

> The Ladrones [pirates] have no settled residence on shore, but live constantly in their vessels. The after-part is appropriated to the Captain and his wives; he generally has five or six. With respect to conjugal rights they are religiously strict; no person is allowed to have a woman on board, unless married to her according to their laws. Every man is allowed a small berth, about four feet square, where he stows his wife and family. From the number of souls crowded into so small a space, it must naturally be supposed that they are horridly dirty, which is evidently the case, and their vessels swarm with all kinds of vermin. Rats in particular, which they encourage to breed, & eat them as great delicacies; in fact, there are very few creatures they will not eat. During our captivity we lived three weeks on caterpillars boiled with rice. They are much addicted to gambling, & spend all their leisure hours at cards and smoking opium.[6]

Ching Yih and His Successors

By the early nineteenth century the charismatic pirate leader Ching Yih had organized such a large fleet that it dominated the waters around

Canton and was stronger than the emperor's disorganized and feeble navy. As a contemporary Chinese scholar explained,

> There have been pirates from the oldest times in the eastern sea of Canton; they arose and disappeared alternately, but never were they so formidable as in the years of Kea-king [a prince who became emperor in 1796], at which time, being closely united together, it was indeed very difficult to destroy them.... The pirates divided themselves into different squadrons, which sailed under various colors. There existed six large squadrons, under different flags, the *red*, the *yellow*, the *green*, the *blue*, the *black*, and the *white*. These wasps of the ocean were called after their different commanders.[7]

In 1806 John Turner, chief mate of the British ship *Tay*, was captured by Ching Yih and held for ransom for five months. During his captivity, Turner learned that Ching Yih had between five and six hundred vessels in his fleet, some of which mounted 12 guns. These big junks also carried a number of small boats that, armed with swivel guns and carrying twenty men each, were used to board other ships or to attack villages along the coast.

The pirates beat Turner frequently and threatened to kill him. He was treated leniently, however, when compared with the fate reserved for captured officers of the Chinese navy. Turner's account of these atrocities is not for the squeamish: "I saw one man ... nailed to the deck through his feet with large nails, then beaten, with four rattans twisted together, till he vomited blood; and after remaining some time in this state, he was taken ashore and cut to pieces. [Another prisoner] was fixed upright, his bowels cut open and his heart taken out, which they afterwards soaked in spirits and ate ... The dead body I saw myself."[8]

After Ching Yih died in a typhoon in 1807, his widow — Ching Yih Saou, also known as Ching Shih — took his place as commander of the Red Squadron. Her lieutenant and lover was Chang Paou, who had been a favorite of her late husband. The pirates under their joint command were required to be on good behavior — at least with one another. Chang Paou laid down three rules:

1. If any man goes privately on shore, or what is called "transgressing the bars," he shall be taken in and his ears perforated in the presence of the whole fleet; repeating the same act, he shall suffer death.
2. Not the least thing shall be taken privately from the stolen and plundered

goods. All shall be registered, and the pirate receive for himself, out of ten parts, only two; eight parts belonging to the storehouse, called the general fund; taking any thing out of this general fund without permission, shall be death.
3. No person shall debauch at his pleasure captive women taken in the villages and open places, and brought on board the ship; he must first request the ship's purser for permission, and then go aside in the ship's hold. To use violence against any woman, or to wed her without permission, shall be punished by death.[9]

Richard Glasspoole estimated on his release that the pirate fleet of Chang Paou and Ching Shih consisted of 500 vessels of different sizes. He also saw how pirates recruited new crews. Landsmen who offered no resistance when captured could join the pirates simply by taking an oath, but those who refused to comply were treated cruelly: "Their hands were tied behind their backs, a rope from the mast-head rove through their arms, and hoisted three or four feet from the deck, and five or six men flogged them with rattans twisted together till they were apparently dead; then hoisted them up to the mast-head, then lowered them down again, 'till they died or complied with the oath."[10]

The pirates gave their enemies no quarter. Glasspoole relates how 300 pirates attacked several government war junks moored near Whampoa. The pirates all swam ashore, each man with a short sword securely lashed to his body under his left arm, and boarded the junks, killing many of the panic-stricken sailors. Like any good commander, Chang Paou always tried to spur his men on to greater efforts:

> The Ladrones were paid by their Chief ten dollars for every Chinaman's head they produced. One of my men turning the corner of a street, was met by a Ladrone running furiously after a Chinese; he had a drawn sword in his hand, and two Chinaman's heads which he had cut off, tied by their [pig]tails, and slung around his neck. I was witness myself to some of them producing five or six heads to obtain payment![11]

Because they were not armed, the men and women of coastal villages were easy prey. Few of them could fight back, although the "boxing master" (martial arts teacher) of one village managed to kill several pirates before he himself was cut down. Some women chose suicide rather than dishonor and tried to take their attackers with them:

> Mai ying, the wife of Ke choo yang, was very beautiful, and a pirate being about to seize her by the head, she abused him exceedingly. The pirate bound her to the yard-arm; but on abusing him yet more, the pirate dragged her down and broke two of her teeth, which filled her mouth and jaws with blood. The pirate sprang up again to bind her. Ying allowed him to approach, but as soon as he came near her, she laid hold of his garments with her bleeding mouth, and threw both him and herself into the river, where they were drowned.[12]

The pirates themselves were soon riven by internal jealousies. In 1809 the commander of the Black Squadron, Kwo Pow Tai, fell out with Chang Paou. Their respective fleets fought a short, bloody battle. Although Chang Paou was defeated, losing 16 junks and 300 men, Kwo Pow Tai feared that since Chang Paou had more pirates at his command, he would ultimately be the winner in the struggle for supremacy. So Kwo Pow Tai quickly made his peace with the local Chinese authorities and surrendered 8,000 men, 126 ships and 500 light cannon to the governor-general in Canton, who promptly pardoned him and made him a minor official.

With Kwo Pow Tai on his side, the governor-general declared that "with the pirates I will destroy the pirates." Ching Shih and Chang Paou both saw the writing on the wall, and in 1810 they too surrendered and were pardoned. The governor-general later sent Chang Paou against the remaining pirates, who were based near Hainan and along the coast of Vietnam. These were defeated and forced to surrender or had to retreat to the Philippines. The emperor rewarded the governor-general by making him a guardian of the prince, giving him a hereditary title and allowing him to wear gorgeous peacock feathers with two "eyes." Chang Paou himself was made a major. The Chinese chronicler of this affair was thus able to end his account on an upbeat note: "From that period till now ships pass and repass in tranquillity. All is quiet on the rivers, and people live in peace and plenty."[13] His optimism proved premature, however, for as the following accounts will show, piracy remained a serious threat to Western shipping along the China coast into the 1860s and even beyond.

In 1835 the English ship *Troughton* was dismasted in a gale 100 miles southwest of Macao and was forced to anchor off Hainan. The *Singapore Chronicle* reported that from 30 nearby junks, 300 fishermen/pirates swarmed aboard her, tied up the crew, plundered the ship — which was carrying specie worth $50,000 and merchandise worth an equal amount—and tried to burn her. When the news of this attack reached Macao, the Chinese government reacted with unusual speed and effectiveness. It recovered most of the goods and specie, even though the pirates had concealed it cleverly: about $4,000 were hidden underwater in a sack made fast to the anchor of a junk, several thousand dollars more were mixed in with the sand and gravel ballast of another boat, and other amounts were recovered from boxes buried 10 feet deep on the beach. Chinese authorities captured 40 to 50 of the pirates, brought them to Canton in chains and beheaded them there.[14]

The mysterious disappearance of the brig *Fairy*, which had been designed as a private courier vessel for Jardine Matheson but was in practice used as their first coaster, was initially thought to have been the work of pirates. In September 1836 William Jardine wrote to Captain J. Rees of the bark *Colonel Young*, "We are still in a state of extreme anxiety, respecting the *Fairy*, having had numerous reports of her having been attacked by Pirates, and the whole of the crew murdered."[15]

What had actually happened was that the six Manila seacunnies (that is, helmsmen) aboard *Fairy* had mutinied, killed Captain McKay and his officers, thrown their bodies overboard and forced the rest of the crew to take to the brig's longboat. The crewmen managed to reach the coast, but their boat capsized in the heavy surf, where several of them drowned. Fifteen, however, survived and were taken into custody by the local Chinese authorities.[16]

After news of *Fairy*'s fate reached Canton, Jardine wrote to his agent in Manila, John Shillaber, in January 1837, "I am glad you have discovered the murderers of poor McKay, and shall be anxious to hear the results of the investigations. The *Fairy* had a good many gold bars on board ... about two inches long, one broad and ½ to ¾ of an inch thick ... worth from $195 to $200 each."[17]

Ironically, it was this same gold, valued at about $70,000 and bearing Chinese *chops* (that is, stampings), that led to the seacunnies' undoing. As soon as the longboat carrying *Fairy*'s crew was out of sight, the mutineers made sail for the coast of Luzon. There they hid the treasure and scuttled the brig. Later, when they foolishly tried to sell in Manila what were unmistakably Chinese gold bars, they were arrested on suspicion of robbery, forced to confess their crimes, condemned and executed.

From Jardine Matheson's point of view, the *Fairy* incident, although tragic, ended as well as could be expected. In a letter to his London counterparts in 1838, James Matheson wrote that "the loss of our vessel the *Fairy*, which you allude to was a very sad event, but her cargo being insured we suffered but little in a pecuniary view — As if to afford another proof that Providence never permits such foul deeds to go unpunished, the mutineers and murderers have all been apprehended and executed at Manila."[18]

In 1839 HMS *Pylades* came on pirate junks at anchor and decided to attack them. Six officers and 41 British seamen piled into *Pylades's* small boats — the cutter, gig, pinnace and jolly-boat — and on reaching the junks were met with "a heavy but ill-directed fire from match-locks, ginjals, and guns." As British seamen tried to board the junks, they were knocked back into their boats with pikes and hooks, "numerous stink-pots being thrown in at the same moment, the sulfurous vapor of which rendered some of the men temporarily inefficient." The boats then dropped back well clear of *Pylades*, which from her big guns sent "some heavy and well-directed volleys" into the crowded junks. When *Pylades's* boats advanced a second time, "our brave tars [sailors] mounted the sides of the [nearest] junk, her crew flying before them, and jumping into the sea." The remaining junks fled. In this brief encounter two British seamen were killed and five wounded; their shipmates reported that "the carnage on board the junk had been tremendous."[19]

In 1840 James Matheson wrote to his colleagues about two pirate attacks. The first was on *Hellas*, which had joined the opium fleet in 1838, had a crew of 50 men and was heavily armed:

> [*Hellas*] was attacked near Chusan, a little East of Namoa, by Nine Junks having the appearance of Merchant Vessels & supposed to be Pirates, who severely wounded her Commander, Captain Jauncey, in the Chin, besides several of her crew. The Junks anchored near the *Hellas*, at night, and there being nothing to attract suspicion, no particular notice was taken of them until they unexpectedly commenced their attack in the morning, the *Hellas* was almost unmanageable, besides being entangled among fishing stakes.

The ship successfully beat off the attack, and Matheson added that

> it seems the Coast is swarming with Pirates, in consequence of which the merchant Junks are afraid to move about except in convoy, for mutual protection, and Captain Jauncey supposed his assailants to be a peaceable fleet of that description, till he was undeceived by their unexpected attack. It is a severe blow to the

Coast Operation, but we must persevere against every difficulty.[20]

Less than two months after this attack, Matheson complained that "the Mandarins & pirates are becoming alarmingly formidable. The *Black Joke* (a clipper of Messrs D & M Rustomjee & Co.) was attacked by 16 junks off Chinchew, which chased her ten miles off land, keeping up a sharp fire all the time. Their sails were a good deal cut, and one Lascar badly wounded."[21]

Painted sea-green so that she could not be easily seen at a distance, the Boston-built 90-ton pilot schooner *Gazelle* was actively involved in the opium trade. George Davis, an American sailor who served aboard this ship, remembers that she carried

> such a crowd of canvas that when under all sail, with a beam wind or close-hauled with stiff breeze, she would lay over, and the captain would carry sail until the water would almost reach the main coamings, and her long, tapering yellow pine masts would bend until they formed an angle of twenty degrees, especially when any suspicious piratical-looking junk or lorchas hove in sight.

A contemporary portrait, showing *Gazelle* under bare poles during a storm, suggests she had good sea-keeping qualities.[22] With a crew of 80 well-armed men, *Gazelle* also took aboard millions of dollars worth of sycee silver, picking up these ingots from receiving ships stationed off the coast and carrying them to Whampoa or Canton for onward shipment to England. George Davis left a good account of how *Gazelle* repelled a pirate attack in the 1840s:

> One night, on our second trip to Canton or Whampoa, loaded with treasure to the planksheer almost, and while riding at anchor in Cumsingmoon passage in a dead calm with a strong ebb against us, the *Gazelle* was attacked by a number of pirates, about one hundred and fifty of them having stealthily jumped overboard from junks anchored further up-stream, and, dividing into two lines so as to come alongside on both sides simultaneously, drifted silently down on us with the swiftly-running tide, seemingly as much at their ease in the water as on the land, and, heaving fire-balls and stink-pots on our decks attempted to board us.

But Davis and his crew were not caught napping: "We had our boarding netting triced up, but [the pirates] being bold, daring fellows, about fifty or more succeeded in getting a footing on our decks, only to be repelled after a desperate struggle. We drove them back into the water, that is, those who were not killed or so wounded that they were unable to escape." In this attack one of *Gazelle*'s crew was killed and many others were seriously wounded. Davis himself received flesh wounds "which, although not dangerous, were sufficiently severe to leave scars and marks which will last me as mementos of the fray as long as I live."[23]

The Last Great Pirate Fleets

The Chinese navy was so weak and ineffective that between 1834 and 1869 the only organized efforts to suppress piracy were made by the British. In 1849 an expedition led by Commander C. Dalrymple Hay, RN, was sent out to destroy the last great pirate fleets—those of Shap-'ng-tsai and of his lieutenant, Chiu Apoo—which were terrorizing the coast between Fukien and Hainan.[24]

Chiu Apoo was based at Bias Bay, 50 miles east of Hong Kong. In an attack that began on 28 September and ended on 1 October 1849, Hay, who was commanding the operation aboard the fastest ship in the Royal Navy, HM *Columbine*, an 18-gun brig, cornered him there and killed more than 400 pirates. In this operation Hay was ably assisted by two steam-powered vessels—the Peninsular and Oriental (P&O) Steam Navigation Co.'s *Canton* and HM gunboat *Fury*. Hay's men destroyed 23 pirate junks and set the pirates' shipyards and arsenal on fire. Chiu Apoo himself was wounded in the battle but managed to escape. Ultimately, he came to a bad end: two years later his followers betrayed him to the authorities, and he committed suicide in prison.

In early October 1849, Hay followed up this initial success. Accompanied by eight junks of the Chinese navy and by *Fury* and the East India Company's paddle steamer *Phlegethon*, Hay, still aboard *Columbine*, chased Shap-'ng-tsai's fleet of 64 junks for more than a thousand miles, finally driving it up into the Tonkin River. Moored half a mile upstream behind the river bar, the pirates must have thought themselves safe, but at high tide Hay's ships forced their way over the bar. The pirates opened fire with a 240-gun fusillade, but their junks had shifted with the tide and most of the shots were high or wide.

Some of the shots did go home—*Columbine* was hit by 39 round-shot and *Fury* by 41—but in reply Hay's flotilla sent broadside after broadside crashing into the pirate fleet. Shap-'ng-tsai's flagship met a spectacular end, blowing up and resembling a powerful explosion of fireworks. The final tally was 58 junks destroyed and as many as 1,700 pirates killed. Shap-'ng-tsai and 400 of his men got away in small boats and fled to a base on Hainan. There they continued pirate attacks at a low level until Shap-'ng-tsai was bought off by the Chinese government and rewarded with a job as a naval mandarin.

Piracy Continues

The days of the big pirate fleets may have been over, but small-scale fights still went on, sometimes at the rate of up to 14 a month, for many years. The records of many of these incidents have been lost, but the scope of the problem can easily be seen: the index to a contemporary periodical, *The Chinese Repository*, has 40 entries under "Piracy" for the years 1832–1851 alone. Here are some examples from other contemporary reports.

In 1853, Arthur Mellersh, RN, the commander of HM steam sloop *Rattler*, pursued and destroyed a force of pirate junks off the Fukien coast and was promoted to captain for this successful action.[25] In 1856 the *Sailing Directions for the Coast of China* still had to remind captains who were nearing Canton: "We now begin to perceive our proximity to the river of Canton; and are entering upon the extensive archipelago, which lying off the embouchures of this river, is frequently the resort of pirates, and for the most part inhabited by a class of people ready at any time to lay aside their peaceful occupations for the sake of plunder."[26]

As if to prove this point, that same year *Alligator* had to stand by helplessly (because she was becalmed) as not far from her a pirate lorcha brazenly opened fire on and hurled stink-pots onto a fishing junk, which soon burned to the water's edge. The crew of the fishing junk presumably perished. That same year HM steamer *Coromandel* struck a small blow against the pirates by sinking two of their junks in the archipelago off Canton.[27]

SEAMAN BROWN AND THE PIRATE CHING AH-'LING

In October 1857 a British sailor, Edward Brown, was hard up on the beach (ashore and unemployed) because of the outbreak of the second

Opium War. He first joined the Hong Kong police force but left after only three months, accepting instead — although his former boss, the superintendent of police, advised against it — the dangerous job of master of the British-registered lorcha *Shunloi*.

Before going to sea in February 1857, he bought half a chest of Benares opium for 210 dollars to trade along the coast of Vietnam for his own profit. Off Cape Verala — about midway between the present-day Qui Nhon and Nha Trang — Brown ran into seven large Canton-built pirate ships, which opened fire on his lorcha. A good man with a cannon, he managed single-handedly to damage two of the pirate junks, but the other five drew alongside the lorcha. Brown's crew was terrified and hid in the hold. He himself remained on deck, revolver in hand, "determined to take the life of the first man who should hold a boarding pike, or present a musket at me." The pirates boarded the lorcha and told Brown they would not harm him. The owner of the lorcha, however, did offer some resistance, and this infuriated the pirates. They slashed the owner with their knives and, to intimidate him further so he would confess where any valuable cargo was hidden, they drank some of his blood. The lorcha's cargo was of little value, however, so the pirates brought Brown and his men before their own chief, Ching Ah-'ling, in Verala Bay.

Brown described Ching as a handsome man, 35 to 40 years old, taller than most Chinese and who would have been physically very strong were it not for his excessive use of opium. Claiming he was not a pirate at all but a Taiping rebel, Ching asked Brown to teach pirate crews how to handle ships' guns so that the Taipings would be able to attack Canton itself. Brown tried his best to turn his pirates into well-disciplined gunners but found that when he took his pupils into action they "entirely forgot their stations, and paid no attention to my orders, but fought (if it could be called fighting) in the greatest disorder."[28] Soon Brown was manning the guns by himself; and during one hard-fought engagement, with three shots from a swivel gun he helped the pirates capture a large Fukien trading junk that was making a passage from Chin-chew, a Chinese port about 40 miles north of Amoy, to Vietnam.

During this attack, the pirates showered stink-pots on the junk, which set fire to her sails, and then "jumped on board, with their knives and spears; and with a frightful yell, commenced their work of butchery." When Brown himself boarded the junk — after first putting a quid of tobacco into his mouth to prevent nausea from the sights he suspected lay before him — he was utterly appalled: "Oh, what a slaughter-house! There were more than fifty bodies lying mangled on the deck, some without heads, some without arms or legs, others run through and weltering in their gore; in fact, the picture is too dreadful to describe. There had been no quarter given; young and old alike were slain; they had not left one alive."

Of Brown's own boat crew of 137 pirates, 10 were killed and 12 severely wounded; the pirate fleet as a whole lost more than 100 men killed or wounded. The prize was a rich one: the junk's cargo consisted of merchandise, opium, Chinese money, sycee silver ingots, gold bars and packages of gold leaf worth a total of about $50,000. Not long after this incident, Brown managed to escape from the pirates but in the process was severely wounded in the thigh by a musket ball. Aided by friendly Vietnamese villagers, he eventually made his way to the British brig *Punch* and in 1858 resumed his nautical career as a mate in the British bark *Kim-quan-seng*.

Lindsay Anderson and the Pirates

In about 1859, during the second Opium War the topsail opium schooner *Eamont* came under fire from a Chinese battery on a hill, which was protecting several pirate junks moored beneath it. *Eamont*'s captain immediately put his own ship on a course that would take him almost within pistol-shot of the junks. "Man your port broadside guns," he ordered the first mate, Mr. Jule; "withdraw your shot and load with grape, and pitch right into the junks when I call out 'fire' … pass the word along for [third mate Lindsay] Anderson to do the same."[29] Anderson tells us what happened next:

> Our captain, standing close to the man at the wheel, cons [steers] the *Eamont* till he brings us within two hundred yards, then I hear him calling out, "Ready there, all?"
>
> "Ready," each of us reply, as we keep our guns trained on the junks.
>
> "Fire!" and as the word leaves the captain's mouth, our guns belch forth their arguments, and we are greeted from the junks with yells and roars, accompanied by a futile discharge of their guns, that is a sufficient answer to us that our shot has landed in the right place.

Eamont then brought her starboard guns to bear on the junks and gave them another broadside of grape and canister shot. The pirates replied with a few ineffective shots and although still under fire from the shore battery, whose shot fell far short of the target because the Chinese gun carriages could not be elevated, *Eamont* made sail and was soon out of range.

AN ANONYMOUS OPIUM TRADER

In 1860 an Australian officer, who had formerly been the captain of the opium schooner *Eamont*, assumed command of the brig *Sin Tauka*, which had been chartered by Jardine Matheson as a receiving ship at the Taiwanese port of Takow. Writing under the pseudonym of "Sin Tauka," this anonymous trader has left such vivid accounts of fights with pirates that they are worth citing at some length.[30]

After Sin Tauka moored his receiving ship at Takow, the leading mandarin of the port asked for help in suppressing local pirates, who had captured several trading junks belonging to a nearby village. Sin Tauka quickly fitted out two cutters for this expedition. The first was the 35-ton *Pearl*, a fast sailor of great beam and shallow draft that had been built expressly for running opium. She was armed with one long 12-pounder swivel gun amidships and two brass cannonade 6-pounders on a raised quarter deck. The second boat was Sin Tauka's own cutter, powered by 12 oars and armed with a 6-pounder in the bow. Fourteen lascars (that is, East Indian sailors), six Manilamen, three European seamen and three officers made up the crews. For close-quarters combat they were armed with muzzle-loading and breech-loading rifles, revolvers and swords.

The pirates were based at a fortified town northwest of Takow. Hoping to negotiate with them, Sin Tauka took both cutters over the bar at the estuary leading to the town. Then he took his own cutter farther up the narrow serpentine channel but soon grounded in the shallows and was immediately set upon by the pirates:

> They rushed at us and endeavored to obtain our rifles and guns, at the same time discharging a gingal at us; one shot carried my cap away and two of our men were wounded. I ordered half our party to open fire, while the remainder backed stern out so as to give our six-pounder in the bows working power. The crowd on the beach was very dense and quite close to us. I gave the order "fire" and almost while I spoke a "bang and deafening yells" showed that our charge of grape had done its work; and sure enough it had cleared quite a lane through them; the rest ran for

the cover of the banks near the forts, and we assisted them in their flight with a dose of round shot.

Sin Tauka retreated downstream and returned to *Pearl*, which opened fire on the town itself. At low tide some of the pirates crept close to the cutters and shot at them with matchlocks and gingals, killing a lascar and wounding an interpreter. Other pirates fired from the banks, wounding Sin Tauka himself and killing a Manilaman, but were then beaten off: "We slewed round the swivel in double-quick time, and gave them a heavy dose of grape, which left the sand bank covered with dead and wounded; a second shot of grape completed the work we had commenced so well, and now the vagabonds ceased firing and made for the town."

The next day the pirates attacked just before dawn but were again repulsed. When the weather, which had been bad, deteriorated into a typhoon, Sin Tauka and his colleagues knew they had to escape. First, *Pearl* ran out a kedge (that is, they put a small anchor in place) to help her negotiate the bar. The pirates saw what she was doing and came on in full force: "Some swam to the kedge line to cut it, but rifles turned them over one after the other. One had succeeded in getting hold of the line, but was killed with a revolver bullet just in time to save the line.... We repulsed several determined attacks before 8 A.M., and must have killed an immense number as all our shots told well."

By 9:00 A.M., *Pearl* managed to warp up to the kedge (that is, the men hauled on the kedge line until the cutter was close to the bar). They then got Sin Tauka's cutter alongside, tripped the kedge (i.e., hoisted the anchor), ran up a close-reefed mainsail and stood straight for the bar. The pirates made a last-minute rush to stop the boats, but they were too late. The cutters cleared the bar with only a few feet to spare and made good their escape. Reflecting on this episode, Sin Tauka knew how close they had come to disaster:

> We had gone thither underrating the Chinese who fought well and stood any amount of killing; and, had we been half-an-hour later in getting away we should probably have been lost in the typhoon; besides which our ammunition was exhausted.... Pirates will always be found among these sand banks, and all vessels trading on this coast ought to be well manned and armed, and always ready for action.

Two years later, while carrying opium to Taiwan and oil cake and rice back to Amoy, Sin Tauka ran into a heavy fog and heard a heavy surf breaking dead ahead. He steered his ship clear of this reef but was immediately attacked by pirates who were sure he had struck the reef and was disabled:

> We were all at our quarters prepared for them, and directly the first junk showed through the fog we gave it to them from the forecastle swivel-gun which had been loaded with grape. The junk was sweeping across our bows, when the discharge demolished his quarter with a tremendous crash and put her crew into a great state of confusion. They fired their forward guns without aim, and then turned tail.

Not long after this incident, a pirate chieftain offered a reward for Sin Tauka's head, but this intrepid Australian sailed straight through a pirate fleet that was lying in wait for him, hoping that his ship would not be recognized. He had just cleared the last junk when the pirates realized who he was and opened fire. Their cannonballs holed his studding sails, shot away the starboard boom and hit the hull, scattering splinters in every direction. Sin Tauka held his course, however, did not return their fire and was soon out of range.

Sin Tauka also gives us an account of how another opium trader, McPhail, defended himself in 1863 while offshore in an open boat. When attacked by a pirate junk,

> McPhail laid down in the boat, and with a rifle, double-barrel gun [a shotgun], and a revolver, positively beat them off; in fact, he fired at them until he had killed them nearly all, the junk drifting ashore and becoming a prize to the fishermen. McPhail was a plucky little Scotchman, and a good friend, and was rewarded by the mandarin of Obay for having destroyed one of the most troublesome pirates on the coast.

The most active period of foreign efforts to suppress Chinese pirates was between 1832 and 1869. Thanks to the Royal Navy, by the end of this period the pirate threat in the South China Sea was much reduced. After 1869 the Navy's policy was to chase down pirates off the China coast only if they molested foreign shipping, leaving to local Chinese authorities the task of dealing with "the foam of the sea" (pirates) when Chinese vessels were attacked.

In later years there were other incidents involving Chinese pirates, some of whom were reportedly led by an American (Eli Biggs) or by an

Englishman (William Fenton). Piracy, however, has never died out in the South China Sea. In the late 1990s, for example, bands of robbers, based on Indonesian islands and equipped with fast boats and automatic weapons, clambered up the sides of lumbering tankers crewed by a handful of unarmed officers and men. The pirates forced the officers to open the ships' safes. They stole money from the crews and sometimes pushed them over the side. Occasionally they even hijacked a ship and sold its cargo at the nearest port. [31]

Notes

1. Horsburg, *India Directory*, p. 378.
2. Bernard, *Nemesis*, pp. 485–486.
3. Dalrymple, *Memoir*, p. 1.
4. Dalrymple, *Memoir*, p. 5.
5. A muzzle-loading nineteenth-century cannon normally fired one heavy cast-iron ball designed to punch a hole in a ship or a fort at long range. But this gun could also fire grapeshot — a cluster of small balls, used at close range as an antipersonnel weapon.
6. Glasspoole's account of the pirates is in Wilkinson, *Sketches*, pp. 192–221.
7. Yung Lun-Yen, *History*, pp. 1–5.
8. Cited by Cordingly, *Pirates*, p. 108.
9. Yung Lun-Yen, *History*, pp. 13–14.
10. From Glasspoole's account in Wilkinson, *Sketches*, p. 209.
11. From Glasspoole's account in Wilkinson, *Sketches*, pp. 213–214.
12. Yung Lun-Yen, *History*, p. 48.
13. Yung Lun-Yen, *History*, p.
14. Hunter, *Bits of Old China*, pp. 200–202.
15. From James Matheson's Private Letter Book, Jardine Matheson archives.
16. The loss of *Fairy* is described in Williamson, *Eastern Traders*, pp. 147–153.
17. From James Matheson's Private Letter Book. Jardine Matheson archives.
18. From a 30 April 1838 letter from William Jardine to Messrs. Magniac, Smith and Co., London; in James Matheson's Private Letter Book. Jardine Matheson archives.
19. *Pylades*'s attack on the pirate junks is described by Bingham, *Narrative*, pp. 202–204.
20. This and the preceding citation are from a letter of 29 May 1840 from James Matheson to his partner in Calcutta, Charles Lyall. James Matheson's Private Letter Book. Jardine Matheson archives.

21. This citation is from a letter of 10 July 1840 from James Matheson to Henderson, his agent in Macao. William Jardine's Private Letter Book. Jardine Matheson archives.

22. Davis, *Recollections*, p. 250.

23. Davis, *Recollections*, pp. 249–250.

24. Cordingly, *Pirates*, p. 112; and Beeching, *Chinese Opium Wars*, pp. 169–172.

25. Mellersh, correspondence.

26. Williams, *Commercial Guide*, p. 10.

27. The Hong Kong [sic] Shipping List of 4 August 1856 describes the *Alligator* and *Coromandel* incidents.

28. All the quotes involving Brown come from *Captivity*, p. 28 ff.

29. All quotes involving Anderson, come from *Among Typhoons*, pp. 31–32.

30. All quotes in this section are from "Sin Tauka," *Jottings*, pp. 1–24.

31. A BBC broadcast of 21 September 1998 reported that the oil tanker *Petro Ranger* had been hijacked by pirates in the South China Sea.

8

Typhoons, Monsoons and Hazards to Navigation

A typhoon was one of the most lethal dangers of the opium trade. However, another weather pattern of the tropics — the northeast and southwest monsoon — could speed a ship's passage if properly used. In addition to knowing as much as possible about the likely tracks of typhoons and the onset and duration of the monsoons, the master of an opium clipper had to be aware of all the hazards to navigation in the Indian Ocean and China Seas — the poorly charted islands, rocks, reefs, shoals, strong currents, eddies, tides, fog and the limits of nineteenth-century navigation itself. Coping with these dangers required experience, steady nerves, seamanship of a high order and a fair amount of luck if a ship was to survive. A mariner had to know the language of the sea. As Joseph Conrad said in *Typhoon*, "The China seas north and south are narrow seas. They are seas full of every-day eloquent facts, such as islands, sand-banks, reefs, swift and changeable currents — tangled facts that nevertheless speak to a seaman in clear and definite language."[1]

Typhoons

Drawing on his own experiences as an officer in the British ships *Vidar* and *Highland Forest*, Conrad never forgot the awesome power of a typhoon. It was, he remembered, "something formidable and swift, like the sudden smashing of a vial of wrath. It seemed to explode all round the ship with an overpowering concussion and with a rush of great waters, as if an immense dam had been blown up to windward."[2]

The word *typhoon* itself comes from the Chinese words *tai* (great) and *fong* or *hong* (wind).[3] These great winds are intense tropical revolving storms and have a variety of names: they are known in the western Pacific as typhoons, in the Indian Ocean as cyclones and in the eastern Pacific as hurricanes. Regardless of what name they are given locally, however, they are born six to eight nautical miles above the surface of warm seas. Heavy cumulonimbus clouds spread out at about 50,000 feet and gradually begin to rotate in the same direction as local winds closer to the surface. Both high- and low-level winds are soon turning together. Air is pulled down from the stratosphere into the calm, cloudless eye of the storm. Extremely strong winds rush in from the outskirts of the storm toward the eye but are deflected upward by the funnel-shaped cloud walls surrounding it. Typhoons play a noticeable role in redistributing the world's atmosphere because they move large quantities of warm, moist air from low to middle latitudes; indeed, it is estimated that as much as 3.5 trillion tons of air can be moved each hour.

Typhoons occur in the South China Sea on average about nine times a year from July through November, with July and September being the most hazardous months, and can severely damage coastal cities by their torrential rains, huge waves and high winds. Weak buildings can be flattened, roofs plucked off and trees snapped. These storms last from five to ten days and during this time they can travel thousands of miles. The Royal Observatory's track of Typhoon Elsie in 1975 showed that in six days this storm moved 2,000 miles. Born in the Pacific Ocean north of the Caroline Islands, it roared westward through the Bashi Channel between Taiwan and the Philippines, came ashore at Hong Kong and finally petered out north of Macao.[4]

Sailing ships are especially vulnerable to typhoons, whether underway at sea or moored in port. Wind gusts of up to 175 miles per hour have been noted, but recording instruments tend to disintegrate at such high velocities and some gusts may exceed even this maximum figure. A sailing vessel cannot hope to outrun a typhoon because heavy swells spreading outward from the center of the storm reduce the ship's speed. Moreover, the storm itself may also curve around in such a way that in trying to run away from it a ship may sail into greater danger.[5]

It is therefore not surprising that many opium ships and junks were lost in typhoons over the years. A British commentator in the 1830s said that

> At uncertain times of the year, but chiefly during the prevalence of the north-east monsoon, the most tremendous typhoons prevail, setting at utter defiance the skills and exertions of man: at one moment blowing directly astern, driving the ship with headlong violence before it, with the sea rising in mountainous waves over the taffrail; the next shifting ahead, taking everything aback, and impelling her with equal violence in the opposite direction. Very few vessels have been able to outlive this weather: they are either buried stern foremost, immediately, or if they survive the shock, they have to combat with the waves, without a stick or piece of canvas left standing. The large Chinese junks are frequently out in this weather, and almost invariably founder.[6]

Sudden, violent shifts of wind are characteristic of a typhoon. The usually understated *China Pilot* warned mariners venturing into Chinese waters that "among the islands, and near the coast, these tempests generally commence between N.W. and North, then veer suddenly to N.E. and East, frequently blowing with inconceivable fury, and raising the sea in turbulent pyramids, which impinge violently against each other."[7]

Nineteenth-century maritime reports are studded with accounts of big ships that came to grief in the South China Sea as a result of typhoons. It was so difficult for a small vessel to survive a typhoon that there are not many accounts of such adventures. Here is one of them:

> Sir Gordon Bremer, the commander-in-chief of a British military expedition sent to China during the first Opium War, and Captain Charles Elliot, the British Superintendent of Trade, were nearly lost when HM cutter *Louisa* was wrecked by a typhoon in 1841. *Louisa* carried a crew of about 21 men and was bringing Bremer and Elliot from Canton to HM *Wellesley* at Hong Kong. The typhoon came up so suddenly that the little cutter, anchored near the shore, had to slip her cable (that is, leave her anchor in the water) to get underway quickly and make for open water. To reduce wind pressure on the vessel, which was being driven towards a heavy surf beating on the rocky shore only 60 yards away, the crew cut away the mizzenmast but then some of the mainmast sails blew out, reducing the cutter's maneuverability.
>
> As the cutter tried to avoid the breakers, two men — the Second Master and the seaman at the tiller — were washed

overboard and lost. The typhoon was so powerful that the cutter was blown all the way down the Canton estuary to the Ladrone islands near its mouth. The vessel's prospects were very poor at that point but before being blown out to sea the captain managed to sail the cutter up a narrow river along the estuary. There the ship ran aground, filled instantly and broke up quickly. Miraculously all the 23 men still aboard her, including Bremer and Elliot, survived.[8]

In an August 1848 typhoon at Hong Kong and Macao, five ships were driven on shore and six others were dismasted.[9] During the same storm, the American opium clipper *Antelope* was making a passage from Shanghai to Hong Kong and was knocked down into the trough of the sea (that is, into the hollow between two wave crests). She had to cut her masts away to survive and her captain reported to the owners, "If the Antelope had not been one of the best vessels afloat she must have gone to Davy Jones' locker [that is, she would have been lost]."[10] The mate of the opium clipper *Gazelle* logged these entries on September 13, 1849:

> At noon, strong gale at North. Bar. [barometer] 29.50. 4 p.m., hard gale; blew away sails from yards. 10 p.m., blowing a hurricane, lost fore topmast. Vessel buried in the sea; cut away mainmast but could not get at lee rigging from being under water; wreck of mainmast got under stern, carried away rudder and stove in part of stern frame. Shipping large quantities of water through the cabins; everything nearly washed off the deck including compass. Pumped and bailed ship, trying to keep water down, 6 ft. in hold. Barometer fallen to 27.[11]

In June 1856 the ship *Smyrna* was thrown on her beam ends about 120 nautical miles southeast of Hong Kong; the crew was obliged to cut away the mizzenmast and jettison part of the cargo to right her.[12] During a September 1856 typhoon, while off the island of Mindoro in the Philippines the ship *Rockliffe* was hit by a great bolt of lightning, which struck the main topmast: "Mr. Joseph West, the chief officer, and John Elliot, a seaman, were aloft on the main top gallant-yard at the time of the accident, but were never seen afterwards."[13]

Off Swatow, about 200 miles northeast of Hong Kong, the lovely 115-foot-long opium clipper *Anonyma*, which was initially built in 1839 as a fast private yacht with sharply raked masts and a huge sail area and which was acquired by Jardine Matheson in 1842, was dragged ashore by a September 1858 typhoon and turned bottom-up in the surf. Another

Opium clipper *Anonyma* (private collection)

opium vessel, the brig *Gazelle*, sank at her mooring with her topmasts barely above water; only her captain and two seamen were saved. HMS *Fury* later tried to salvage Gazelle, but she was so deeply embedded in mud and sand that this proved to be impossible. *Fury* did, however, recover $80,000 worth of specie from the wreck.[14] A third ship, *Pantaloon*, probably also in the opium trade, was driven onto the rocks and was later stripped and gutted by the Chinese.[15]

There was not much even the most cautious and most experienced captain could do about typhoons. Meteorology was in its infancy, and sailing directions were vague. A standard work of 1782 could only advise, "In November, it is best for ships to come the *inner passage* between the Paracels and the Coast of Cochin China ... instead of running out to sea."[16] By the mid–nineteenth century, mariners were being instructed to avoid "the one position in which a ship may enter a revolving storm which is attended with the utmost danger, that is directly in its path. In this case the wind will not shift, as it would from either side of the line of progress, but continue in its first direction until the focus be passed, when it would *suddenly* shift to exactly the opposite point, a change which a seaman would dread."[17]

The *China Pilot* warned that

> Typhoons are dangerous tempests, which occur in the northern part of the China Sea, near Formosa, the Bashi Islands, the north

end of Luzon [as well as in neighboring waters]. These typhoons are liable to happen in both monsoons.... Many vessels have been driven from the Great Ladrone [an island southwest of Hong Kong] to the Mandarin's Cap [an islet about halfway between Hong Kong and Hainan, a distance of about 80 nautical miles], and even to the Tarya islands near Hainan [a distance of about 180 nautical miles] during Typhoons.[18]

When a captain had the bad luck to find himself directly in the path of a typhoon, he could only hope for the best. This was certainly the case with Captain Charles Low of the tea clipper *Houqua*, who ran into a typhoon on 15 January 1848 off the Indonesian island of Buru. As the storm mounted in fury, Captain Low, who was on deck and holding on to *Houqua*'s pin rail, could see a solid wall of spindrift (i.e., spray swept from the tops of waves by a violent wind and driven continuously along the surface of the sea) 20 to 30 feet high, bearing down on his ship. The spindrift struck *Houqua*'s side heavily:

> The ship stood against it for about ten minutes, when she was hove down on her beam ends. I tried to gain the weather rail and I caught at it with my right hand, but the rail being wet and slippery, and the ship going over so quickly, my feet slipped from under me and I fell into the sea to leeward, without touching the ship. I rose to see the mizzen rigging just before me, but a big sea came over me and I went down where it was dark. I never expected to see the ship again ... but my eyes were open and I saw a line before me and caught it and hauled myself up till my head struck the pin rail around the mizzen-mast before my feet struck the deck.

Lying on her side in the water, *Houqua* was on the verge of foundering, but Low and his crew managed to cut away the two masts. As they went over the side the ship slowly righted herself. During the next four days Low and the seamen made emergency repairs. On the fifth day Low obtained a few tools and cooking utensils from a passing brig, *Lady Margaret*, and next day he managed to buy (at vastly inflated prices, he complained) a spar and some ropes from *Lady Amherst*, another passing ship. These he used to jury-rig a mast (that is, make temporary repairs) on his own vessel. Finally under way once more, *Houqua* then sailed another 3500 miles and arrived at her destination, Hong Kong, on 11 March 1848 — "having made the passage from New York in one hundred and thirty-one days, sixty days under jury rig." When Low returned to New

York, he received from a consortium of insurance companies an expensive eight-day chronometer in recognition of his achievement in saving ship, cargo and crew.[19] *Houqua* herself (under another and less fortunate captain) was lost at sea in August 1864 after sailing from Yokohama, Japan.

Good seamanship and good luck also saved the opium clipper *Sin Tauka* in 1861. After running opium between Formosa and Amoy, she sailed for Shanghai laden with rice but ran into a typhoon off the Chusan Islands. Her anonymous Australian captain ordered the crew to creep under the quarter boat, which had been lashed bottom-up on the deck, while he, the mate and the gunner all stood by with axes, ready if necessary to cut away the standing rigging so that the masts would topple overboard. These three men had lashings around their waists and without them would certainly have been blown overboard.

As it was, with one mighty roar the spanker (that is, the big fore-and-aft sail at the stern of the boat) was shredded by the wind, and everything was carried off the ship's deck. During a brief lull in the storm at 3:00 A.M., the men on *Sin Tauka* could see two nearby ships that were also in distress. One turned out to be the British ship *Malakoff*, which foundered; the other was an unidentified dismasted vessel lying to leeward that managed to pick up only a few of *Malakoff*'s crew.

"Death still hovered round us," remembered the Australian skipper. "It continued to blow a hurricane all day, the gusts being too severe to show any canvas." That night the typhoon abated somewhat, and *Sin Tauka* managed to set a close-reefed topsail. The ship had been blown so far off course, however, that she suddenly found herself among rocks. Her captain thought, "It's all up with us, but, if we must die, let us see what we can do first." He therefore started bellowing orders at his frightened crew: "Hand in the chains! Set the courses! Out all reefs! Up jib, bear a hand and make all the sail you can, sir! Cut the gaskets.... Down with your tacks and aft sheets! Run your topsails up; none of your yahooing here; run away with them. Jump, you beggars!" By Herculean efforts the crew managed to get the ship away from the rocks, but it was a close call: *Sin Tauka*'s bowsprit cleared the perpendicular face of Shung Rock by only one yard and as spray from a wave running off the rock fell directly onto the ship's deck.[20]

Monsoons

Derived from the Arabic word *mausim* (that is, season), monsoons are seasonal phenomena that bring strong winds and heavy rains to India, the Indian Ocean, Southeast Asia and much of the Chinese coast. They are caused by the differences in temperature between land and sea, the land being warmer in summer and the sea in winter. The monsoon predictably blows from the northeast (i.e., from China toward India) during the winter months (October to March) and then from the southwest (i.e., from India toward China) during the spring and summer months (April to September).[21]

This is clear enough, but taking full advantage of the monsoons was never an easy task. Nineteenth-century sailing directions stressed that "making a passage from one part of the Indian Ocean to another is a somewhat complicated problem" and that the fastest tracks for ships to follow "are entirely governed by the monsoons, which thus require to be well understood before a certainty can be arrived at respecting the best track to follow."[22] East Indiamen always tried to use the southwest monsoon when sailing from India to China. The Honourable Company's ships *Diana* and *Castle Huntley* would leave Bombay in July and arrive at Macao or Lintin in September.[23] Average passages from Calcutta to Macao for East Indiamen ranged from a low of 64 days to a high of 81 days, and passages from Macao to Calcutta varied from 64 to 100 days, depending on the state of weather (e.g., the presence or absence of a helpful monsoon).[24]

One of the best examples of the difference between knowing and not knowing about what course to take during the monsoons was provided by Commander P. J. Blake, the captain of HMS *Larne*, who sailed from Macao in May 1839 bound for Singapore, Penang and Madras. He found that as a result of long practice in their calling the captains of opium clippers had "a tolerably perfect knowledge as to the best method of effecting the passage up and down the China Sea, between Singapore and Macao in either Monsoon." After comparing notes in Singapore with an experienced captain of an opium clipper, Blake saw that he had, in his own words, "thrown away at least eight or nine days" in the passage to Singapore simply because he did not know the best course to take. Blake found that although the opium clipper captain had left Macao ten days later than *Larne*, he had reached Singapore *on the same day*.

Thanks to what he learned from opium skippers, Blake could offer better sailing directions for other mariners. Here is an example of his advice:

> In beating *against*, or running *with* the strength of the Monsoon *up or down* the China Sea, ships should always pass to leeward of the Paracels [an island group 300 miles east of Vietnam], as well as of the Pratas [islands about 175 miles southeast of Hong Kong], should they be near them, on account of the invariable set of the current to leeward. An exception may be made in beating up against the N.E. Monsoon, after reaching near Lat. 14°N., as there is an extent of sea room, and a ship must get well eastward towards the coast of Luzon before she can fetch Macao.... On leaving Macao to proceed down the China Sea *against* the S.W. Monsoon, it is advisable to make the best of your way southward for the Macclesfield bank [a shallow area lying between Luzon and Vietnam], keeping in from 113°30' to 116°30' E., and taking every advantage of the least veering of the wind.[25]

Hazards to Navigation

When out of sight of land, officers could find their way from one port to another by using celestial navigation to fix their ship's position on a chart, using a two-dimensional global grid system. This system was (and still is) based on two sets of imaginary lines. One set, running north-south, provides the *longitude* scale; the other set, running round the world from east to west, gives the *latitude* scale. Lines of longitude, also known as meridians, are measured east and west with reference to the Prime Meridian, which passes through Greenwich Observatory in the United Kingdom. Lines of latitude, also called parallels, are measured north and south of the equator. Both meridians and parallels are divided into 60 minutes, which are in turn subdivided into tenths of a minute. Only parallels, however, can be used to determine distance on a nautical chart, one minute of latitude being equal to one nautical mile, which is 6,080 feet or 1.852 statute miles in length.

A compass card showed the man at the helm in which direction his ship was headed.[26] A measuring device trailed behind the ship, known as a log, would give an approximate indication of the distance run each day. The officers of an opium clipper could fix their latitude by using a sextant, which measured the vertical angles, relative to themselves, of certain celestial bodies (the sun, moon, observable planets or major stars). To determine his longitude, an officer used a chronometer (a marine clock that maintained its accuracy despite the motions and temperature variations encountered at sea) to keep track of Greenwich Mean Time. An example of a position fixed in the waters discussed in this book is lat. 17°50'N. and long. 118°0'E. This is about 75 nautical miles west of the northern portion of the Philippine island of Luzon and is where the Parsee ship *Rustomjee Cowasjee*, bound for Canton during the northeast monsoon, found herself at noon on 1 September 1844 when she ran into a typhoon.

Parts of Southeast Asian and Chinese waters were not well charted in the early decades of the nineteenth century. An Englishman familiar with the opium trade reported, "The Chinese seas have a very bad name among navigators, partly owning to the shores being but imperfectly laid down in charts; to the existence of numerous currents...; and the fact that some unfortunate vessel or other [is] constantly stumbling upon some unknown reef or shallow sounding."[27]

Some of the more reliable charts were those produced by James Horsburgh, the hydrographer of the East India Company, and a seaman today could still use Horsburg's 1823 charts of the China Sea to navigate to and from the Canton estuary.[28] The captains of East Indiamen and opium clippers helped to fill in the blanks on the charts, but some uncertainty persisted into the early years of the twentieth century. An Admiralty chart of 1882, updated to 1913, warned mariners who were navigating the Formosa Strait between the mainland of China and the island of Formosa that the shallow soundings and overfalls (i.e., breaking waves caused by wind or current over an irregular bottom or by currents meeting) there showed that "it appears probable that there may be less water on the Formosa Bank than the Chart shows. Vessels must therefore approach with caution." This was good advice because one sounding on the Bank revealed a depth of only four fathoms (24 feet), but the exact location of this shallow was marked "position doubtful."

Nineteenth-century nautical charts were big and showed so much water relative to landforms that the fine print on them identifying ports, estuaries and other features near the shore would be illegible if they were reduced in size to fit into a book like this. Ships' officers, however, also used nautical handbooks, known as *pilots*, that contained smaller charts. One of these charts, taken from J. W. Norie's *Complete East India Pilot* (1847) and showing the approaches to Canton in 1840, has been further reduced in size and is reproduced here.

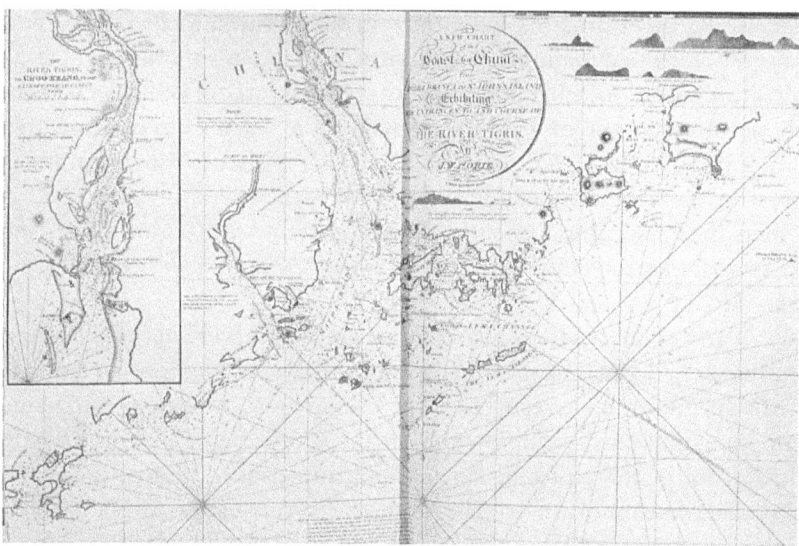

J. W. Norie, "A new chart of the Coast of China from Pedra Branca to St. John's Island exhibiting the entrances to and the course of the River Tigris" (1840). (Royal Geographical Society)

In these tropical seas, a high degree of caution was essential. Even well-charted hazards could still kill ships. For example, one danger in the approaches to Canton itself was Four-feet Rock, a small, sharp, needle-shaped rock that had only four feet of water on it at low tide.[29] Masters of ships in Far Eastern waters were counseled to leave nothing to chance. They were told to "get their Long-boats out as soon as the weather will admit, and keep the Lead constantly going ... as Coral Banks are generally of small extent, a Ship may have no warning from the deep-sea-lead." Captains were also urged to keep a man at the masthead "to attend to the color of the water by which shoals or rocks will be distinguishable from an elevation."[30] The *Indian Ocean Pilot* stressed that

> the observant seaman will keep his eyes open to every unusual appearance in the sea — such as partial ripplings, and, when out of reach of rivers, all discolored water, whether white, brown, or green, flocks of birds, or shoals of fish, as they may possibly be indications of some change in the nature or depth of the bottom; and in all such cases a deep-sea cast of the lead should be obtained.[31]

Sailors also had to make sure they knew what it was they were seeing because it was easy to make mistakes. In the open sea, waves could break against the hull of a capsized ship, a floating clump of trees or some man-made object that had gone adrift, such as an iron buoy. Any one of these might be reported erroneously as a rock, reef or shoal. Even the carcass of a whale, stripped of its blubber but still bobbing in the ocean, could cause a similar alarm. In such a case, as Herman Melville said in *Moby Dick*, "with trembling fingers is set down in the log —*shoals, rocks and breakers hereabouts: beware!* And for years afterwards, perhaps, ships shun the place."[32]

The scattered islands and reefs of a vast area about 500 miles long and 200 miles wide (now known collectively as the Spratly Islands) lie roughly halfway between Palawan Island in the Philippines and the southern coast of Vietnam. These shallow waters were extremely hazardous to navigation in the days of the opium clippers and are still known as the Dangerous Ground. The British, however, did all they could to make navigation safer. From 1863 to 1867 the survey vessel HMS *Rifleman* charted many far-flung rocks, shoals and islands both along the main sailing routes between Singapore and China (these routes either hugged the coast of Vietnam or crossed the Macclesfield Bank) and the routes of the Palawan Passage, which followed the Palawan and Luzon coastlines of the Philippines.

Among the many hazards identified by *Rifleman* on the main routes was Julia Shoal, which the ship *Christopher Lawson* had struck with such great force that the stern-post was dragged entirely out of her. On the Palawan Passage routes, mariners were advised to steer well clear of the Central London Reef—"a coral patch awash ... in every respect a most dangerous reef [that] lies directly in the path of vessels working up or down the China sea." Northwest of Brunei, the Luconia Shoals also lay in wait for the unwary. These were "a mass of coral reefs and shoals, amongst which no vessel should venture.... No directions can be given that will enable vessels to pass safely through these reefs and shoals."[33] Other ship-killing reefs, such as Fiery Cross and Flora Temple, commemorated vessels of these names, which had been wrecked upon them.[34]

Currents, eddies, tides, fog and the limits of nineteenth-century navigation itself posed still other dangers. The *China Pilot* warned that "The strength of the current on the eastern coast of China increases with the freshness and duration of the monsoon, varying from one to as much as 3 or even 4 knots per hour; and this requires to be especially guarded against when hove-to off a port or running for one in thick weather."[35]

Commander P. J. Blake of HMS *Larne* reported that during the northeast monsoon the current in the South China Sea between Vietnam and the southern Philippines could displace a ship by as much as 60 miles in 24 hours.[36] This was later confirmed by HMS *Encounter*, which in 1883 experienced, halfway between Hong Kong and Luzon, a current setting 51 miles in 24 hours (i.e., the current was running at more than two nautical miles per hour and in one day carried the ship 51 miles off her intended course).[37]

If a sailing ship was becalmed or was ghosting along under light airs, the strong currents at the approaches to or within the Strait of Malacca could drag her into shallows or rocky bays from which it was impossible to escape. A British captain reported that "the current sets very strong around the islands to the westward. I was, upon one occasion, obliged to set all studding sails in a light breeze to prevent being dragged by the current through the rocky islets and Pulo Brasse [an island], where there are rocks said to be under water."[38]

The Strait of Malacca is about 50 miles long and varies from 20 to 3 miles in width. *The China Sea Directory* warned against rocky ledges (the Middle Rocks) and shoal areas, adding that before lighthouses were built at the eastern and western entrances in 1851, "Owing to the many dangers which lie at both entrances of the strait, its navigation was formerly attended with much difficulty and anxiety."[39] Indeed, this strait is still considered one of the most difficult navigational passages in the world. Many ships have come to grief there over the years. The sharp, heavily-canvassed clipper *Sovereign of the Seas*, for example, was wrecked on Pyramid Shoal in 1859 during a voyage from Hamburg to China.[40] A modern (1992) British Admiralty chart of the eastern part of the Indian Ocean still shows unconfirmed shallows off the Butang islands near the northern entrance of the strait and the U.S. Defense Mapping Agency's *Sailing Directions* still warns mariners using the Strait of Malacca that "the shifting bottom sands make the exact location of these shallow areas unpredictable.... Most of the shoals are unmarked and there are few navigational aids or landmarks for accurately fixing a ship's position."[41] Oil tankers must be especially careful here because they can draw more than 50 feet of water and need a flood tide to pass over some of these shallows safely.[42]

For opium clippers there was also a unique hazard along the east coast of China from Hong Kong to Amoy. The narrow channels between the small islands were full of whirling eddies known as *chow-chow water*. These eddies were caused by the confluence of conflicting currents and were so violent that a sailing ship caught in them would become unmanageable.⁴³

Tides could not be ignored, either. There were strong tidal flows running at about three knots along some inshore areas in the Strait of Malacca and along the coast of Vietnam as well.⁴⁴ Although the tides themselves were not remarkably high (they ranged from seven feet at Namoa to 20 feet at Amoy), they had to be taken into account when navigating in restricted waters where there was little sea-room. With this in mind the *China Pilot* cautioned mariners that in the Chusan archipelago and the Yangtze estuaries, "great care and attention to the tides is necessary ... unless precautions are taken [a ship] will be set among the small islets of this rugged archipelago."⁴⁵ As if to underscore this warning, in about 1856 the merchant brig *Mariners Hope* struck and spent 12 hours among the Chusan Islands, perched on what became known as Mariner Reef.⁴⁶

Another natural hazard was fog, which was prevalent along the China coast during the southwest monsoon and could be so thick that from the wheel of a ship only her bowsprit could be seen. This could make piloting (i.e., navigating along the coast by using visible reference points ashore) extraordinarily dangerous. Astronomical navigation had its limits, too.

When the captain of an opium clipper was out of sight of land, he could fix his position to within one to five nautical miles by using a sextant and chronometer, provided that he could clearly see the sun, moon, planets or stars. But under less favorable atmospheric conditions a position accurate to only 10 nautical miles was more likely. An error of this magnitude was enough to put a ship into grave jeopardy. Charles Low, the American captain who saved the clipper *Houqua* when she was knocked down on her beam ends in Indonesian waters, later sailed another clipper, *N. B. Palmer*, directly onto a shoal in the Java Sea, when the ship was making eight knots and, ironically, just after Low had pricked (i.e., marked) his supposedly safe position on the chart.⁴⁷

Navigational instruments themselves were far from perfect. For example, when closing (nearing) the coast of northern California where he was soon to be shipwrecked, Captain Faucon of the opium clipper *Frolic* could not trust his two chronometers because they gave him longitude positions that differed by 16 miles.⁴⁸

When the sky was too overcast for astronomical observations, the captain of an opium clipper had to rely on dead reckoning (DR) instead.

8. Typhoons, Monsoons and Hazards to Navigation

This involved estimating a ship's position by keeping track of both the course steered (indicated by the compass) and the distance run (measured by the log), with corrections for currents and leeway (the sideways drift of a ship). Accurate DR depended on a judicious combination of helm, log, lead and lookout. The penalty for serious mistakes was shipwreck: HMS *Challenger* was lost on the coast of South America in the mid–nineteenth century because she had not obtained a celestial observation for her latitude for two days and her DR latitude was 34 miles in error.[49]

Notes

1. Conrad, *Typhoon*, p. 15.
2. Conrad, *Typhoon*, pp. 40, 74.
3. Brown, *Seaman's Narrative*, p. 7.
4. Chin, *Cyclone*, p. 7.
5. See Morgan and Valencia, *Atlas*, p. 16; and Watts, "Meteorology," pp. 320–322.
6. Downing, *Fan-Qui*, pp. 5–6.
7. *China Pilot*, p. 5.
8. After Mackenzie, *Narrative*, pp. 215–236.
9. *China Pilot*, p. 7.
10. Lubbock, *China Clippers*, pp. 8–9.
11. Lubbock, *Opium Clippers*, pp. 347–348.
12. HongKong Shipping List, 23 June 1856.
13. HongKong Shipping List, 29 September 1856.
14. Lubbock, *Opium Clippers*, pp. 347–348.
15. Lubbock, *Opium Clippers*, pp. 347–348.
16. Dalrymple, *Memoir*, pp. 17–18.
17. Findlay, *Directory*, p. 68. Emphasis in original.
18. *China Pilot*, pp. 3–5.
19. Low, *Recollections*, pp. 67–77.
20. These references are from "Sin Tauka," *Jottings*, pp. 19–20.
21. The monsoon weather pattern was well known to Marco Polo, who said in his *Travels* that "it takes a full year to complete the voyage [from China to India], setting out in winter and returning in summer. For only two winds blow in these seas, one that wafts them out and one that brings them back; and the former blows in winter, the latter in summer."
22. Findlay, *Directory*, p. 154.
23. Wise, *Analysis*, pp. 33–34.
24. Raper, *Practice of Navigation*, pp. 592–593.
25. Rosser, *Short Notes*, pp. 47–49. Emphasis in original.
26. A traditional compass card was divided into 32 points, e.g., NEbN (northeast-by-north), rather than into the 360 degrees used today.

27. Downing, *Fan-Qui*, p. 5.

28. Readers who like reading charts or maps may wish to trace out four of the routes recommended by Horsburgh:

For passages from the Strait of Malacca to Canton

The first track ran north along the west coast of Luzon and then turned northwest across the China Sea toward the Canton estuary. Horsburg noted on his 1823 chart that *Bridgewater*, an East Indiaman that later was dismasted in a typhoon of 1830 but managed to get to Madras, India, under jury-rigged masts, "left Singapore 6th Nov.r 1819 Arrived at Macao lst Dec.r Supposed the best Route in October and Nov.r Probably also in Dec.r and Jan.y."

The second track began by heading north, hugging the coast of Vietnam. It later turned northeast to skirt the east coast of Hainan and continued northeast to the Canton estuary. Horsburg said that this was the "Best Route Towards China for Leaky or Crazy [sic] Ships During the Strength of the S.W. Monsoon."

For passages from Canton to the Strait of Malacca

The third track ran southwest from the Canton estuary, passed between Hainan and the Paracel Islands and then paralleled the Vietnamese coast. Horsburg warned mariners: "Best Route From China in the Early part, and in the strength of the N.E. Monsoon — Be Guarded, when Blowing strong against a S. Westerly Current, particularly if Pelo Sapata [a small island off the central coast of Vietnam] is to be Passed Outside in the Night as Several Ships have been set [moved by the current] 40 miles to the W.S.W. and nearly Lost off that Island or on the Catwicks [other small islands off the coast of Vietnam]."

The fourth route ran due south from the Canton estuary and crossed the Macclesfield Bank. It then turned southwest toward the coast of Vietnam. Horsburg's advice was that this was the "Best Route from China Late in the Season in March and April Through the Strait of Gaspar Towards Europe." Later maps (e.g., in 1882) advised mariners to sail between the Macclesfield Bank and the Paracels rather than crossing over the shallow bank itself.

29. *China Pilot*, p. 29.
30. Dalrymple, *Memoir*, pp. 18–19.
31. Imray, *Indian Ocean Pilot*, p. 659. Emphasis in original.
32. Melville, *Moby Dick*, p. 301. Emphasis in original.
33. Rosser, *Short Notes*, p. 84.
34. Rosser, *Short Notes*, pp. 76–90.
35. *China Pilot*, p. 10.
36. Rosser, *Short Notes*, p. 47.
37. Admiralty chart, *China Sea — Northern Portion — Eastern Sheet*, 1881 surveys updated to 1917.
38. Cited by Findlay, *Directory*, p. 184.
39. *China Sea Directory*, pp. 241–246.
40. McKay, *Some Famous Sailing Ships*, p. 369.
41. Cited by Morgan and Valencia, *Atlas*, p. 80.
42. International Chamber of Shipping, *Malacca/Singapore Straits*.
43. *China Pilot*, p. 66.
44. Morgan and Valencia, *Atlas*, p. 80.

45. *China Pilot*, p. 12.
46. *China Pilot*, p. 177.
47. Low, *Recollections*, p. 130.
48. Layton, *Frolic*, pp. 138–140.
49. Cited by Hewson, *Practice of Navigation*, p. 251.

9

The Twilight of the Opium Trade

The India-China opium trade continued well into the early years of the twentieth century, but to modern eyes most of the romance had gone out of it by the end of the 1850s. The rakish opium clipper was replaced by the early steamers, which, being independent of wind and tide, were more reliable, cheaper to insure and offered lower freight rates. Moreover, the dramatic tea races from China to London by the big tea clippers caught public attention in the West. The financial incentives of the opium trade also dwindled as the Chinese began to produce opium themselves and as the antiopium lobby in Britain and the United States grew in strength.

The Coming of the Steamers

By 1828 steamboats were a common sight at Calcutta. They towed sailing ships to and from the Sandheads (the mouth of the Hooghly River) and carried mail and passengers as well.[1] The 127-foot steam tug *Forbes* is said to have been the first steamboat seen in China. Built in Calcutta in 1830 and powered by 120 horsepower engines, she towed the bark *Jamesina*, loaded with 840 chests of Bengal opium, from Calcutta to Singapore. Although *Jamesina* carried extra coal for this epic voyage, the tow from Singapore to Canton had to be cut short, and the bark proceeded to China under sail alone.²

In 1835 Jardine Matheson bought a small schooner built by Alexander Hall of Aberdeen, which was to be powered by 26-horsepower engines. Christened *Jardine*, this little vessel sailed to Lintin with her engines and paddle wheels stored in her hold. She was shown to the Chinese Admiral of the Bogue and even took his own war junk in tow, but this display of British maritime power did not please the local authorities. A vicegeral edict subsequently ordered that "the 'Smokeship' should spread her sails and begone.'" *Jardine* then was sent to Singapore and was advertised for sale as "the greatest steamship of all time" and ideally suited for the Singapore-Malacca run. However, during a picnic arranged to show what she could do, her engine room caught fire, and any potential buyers quickly lost interest. In the end her engines were removed and she sailed back to Lintin to become a coaster in the opium trade.³

Long sea voyages were still the preserve of the sailing ship, even though in 1837 the two-masted paddle steamer *Sirius* had been the first vessel to cross the Atlantic under sustained sea power. *Sirius* was a portent of things to come. Her paddle wheels, powered by side-lever engines of 320 horsepower, were each 24 feet in diameter, revolved 15 times a minute and gave her a top speed of about nine knots. She had one significant new feature: surface condensers, which fed her boilers with distilled fresh water rather than with sea water. This allowed her to keep moving ahead under steam power at all times (boilers using salt water had to be shut down occasionally so that salt concentrations could be blown out). As a backup against engine failure she also carried three square sails on her foremast and a fore-and-aft sail on her mainmast.⁴

When in 1839 Henry Wise, the captain of the East Indiaman *Edinburgh* and himself an early steam-power enthusiast, analyzed 100 voyages of the Honourable Company's sailing ships, he had to acknowledge that steamships were still slower than clippers. "My nautical readers will be well aware," he wrote, "that during fair winds, a fast ship under canvas, will compete in speed with most steam-vessels." Captain Wise therefore limited himself to recommending steam power only as an auxiliary aid to sail on long voyages.⁵ The day of the fast long-distance steamer was about to dawn, but as late as 1853 the extreme clipper *Sovereign of the Seas* could still beat the Cunard paddle steamer *Canada* by several hours in a race across the Atlantic.⁶

The heyday of opium clippers themselves was from the 1830s to the

Paddle steamer at Macao (private collection)

early 1850s. Even during this period, however, the writing was on the wall. Early in 1847 Captain Faucon of the opium clipper *Frolic* told his employers, Augustine Heard and Co., that the steamer *Sir Charles Forbes* was about to sail from Bombay with 400 chests of Malwa opium. "She is a new boat," Faucon wrote, "and her owners are desirous of selling her in China."[7] Later that same year, the Parsee firm of B. and A. Hormujee foresaw that steamers would soon be traveling regularly from Bombay to China and wished to learn whether there was any prejudice "amongst the Chinese for opium transmitted by a steamer instead of a sailing vessel" and whether shipment by steamer might in some way affect the quality of the opium itself.[8] The answer was that it would not.

In 1848 John Heard (Augustine Heard's nephew) was still hoping that clippers could compete with steamers. He calculated that 45,000 chests were being sent to China every year and that the steamers could carry only 17,000 of them. If true, this would have left 28,000 chests for the clippers. Heard therefore suggested to the Hindu firm of Kessressung Khooshalchund (hereafter, K. K.) that it help him finance a new clipper of 450 tons. K. K. turned him down flat, stating,

> You will observe the advantage of the China Clippers has entirely been reaped by the frequent running of steamers to your port [Canton] with opium and other cargo which, I fear, may probably tend to render the voyage of the "Frolic" to China most miserable.... It is no use now adays [sic] to have any interest in

the Ships and with this in view I have declined a share in the new American Clipper to which you crave my attention.[9]

K. K.'s figures show that shipping opium by steamer was appreciably cheaper than shipping it by sail:

Vessel	Shipping Costs per $500 Chest of Malwa Opium (c. 1847 and in U.S. dollars)		
	Freight	Insurance	Total
Steamer	$12.22	$5.00	$17.22
Opium clipper	$6.00	$12.50	$18.50
Price difference per chest in favor of the steamer:			$1.28

Because insurance was a fixed cost (for a steamer, it was 1 percent of the value of a chest of opium, but for the more vulnerable clipper it was 2.5 percent), a steamer needed only to lower its freight rates slightly to increase its already appreciable price advantage of $1.28 per chest.[10] Assuming a cargo of 1,000 chests, a merchant house could save $1,280 per voyage by using steam rather than sail. The days of the opium clippers were obviously drawing to a close. Even Heard himself eventually had to agree. "Steam is every day making such revolutions in trade," he conceded, "that I am not certain but that we are better off without [a new clipper], and am rather glad K. K. backed out."[11]

By 1850 *Lady Mary Wood*, a small paddle wheel steamer, was making scheduled trips between Hong Kong and Shanghai, carrying not only passengers but opium as well, consigned to the Peninsular and Oriental (P&O) Line's agent there. This traffic proved so profitable that before long five P&O steamers were carrying opium along this route and, later, directly from India itself.[12]

In 1852 the steamer *Ganges* left Bombay laden with 2500 chests of opium — the largest quantity ever carried until then in a single ship.[13] The China Merchants Steam Navigation Company, established in Bombay about 1857, began carrying cargo in *Bombay Castle*, a little bark-rigged steamer of 823 tons that was built in London in 1857 and that was trading at Hong Kong the next year. This company also ran the brig-rigged *United States* (1459 tons, built in 1858) and *John Bright*, a 1192-ton clipper-form, bark-rigged iron steamer owned by Parsees, which once carried a full cargo from Bombay to Hong Kong against the monsoon in only 22 days.[14]

By the end of the 1850s, fast racing steamers were replacing clippers on the long run from India to China because they needed only 15 to 20 days for their passage. From that time on the clippers were increasingly relegated to the China coastal trade alone, picking up opium at or near Hong Kong and carrying it north to ports along the coast.[15] Always quick to take advantage of any new technology, Jardine Matheson soon augmented its sailing fleet by adding the steamers *Reiver*, *Chevy Chase*, *Lancefield* and *Fiery Cross*.[16] In 1860 one of its competitors, Dent and Co., could boast that its own SS *Ly-ee-Moon* was the fastest opium steamer afloat, with a top speed of 17 knots.[17]

On the vast inland waterways of China the steamer was virtually unchallenged. Early in 1861 the steamer *Yang-Tsze*, owned by Dent but then steaming under American colors, arrived at Nanking and made her way up the Yangtze River to establish Dent's offices at the new treaty ports being opened there in the wake of the second Opium War. This steamer was the first foreign merchant vessel ever to arrive at Hankow [Hankou], but she was not the last.[18] In 1872 Jardine Matheson set up the China Coast Steam Navigation Company, the precursor to a bigger firm, the Indo China Steam Navigation Company, which was formed in 1881 with the aim of "running steamers on the Coast and Rivers of China to the Straits Settlements [Singapore] and Calcutta." By 1905 this firm owned 20 ships; by 1920 it was navigating the Yangtze all the way up to Chungking, 1400 miles from the sea.[19]

The Growth of the Tea Trade

There was a close symbiotic relationship between opium and tea: in fact, during the nineteenth century, Indian opium was euphemistically referred to in Canton as "tea," that is, *imported* tea.[20] Using opium to pay for tea was a common practice for Western traders. In 1856, for example, Augustine Heard and Co. included four chests of opium along with its silver dollar payments for Fujian tea.[21] Both tea and opium were eagerly sought by their respective consumers, so in addition to the names of the different kinds of Indian opium — Patna, Benares and Malwa — we can note the nineteenth-century names for famous Chinese teas — Pekoe, Souchong, Congou and Bohea (all black teas) and Gunpowder, Imperial, Hyson and Twankay (all green teas).[22]

As more Chinese tea was consumed in Britain, more opium had to be sold in China to help pay for it. In 1818 opium had officially accounted for only 10 percent of China's total imports ($1,648,500 of the $16,004,411 total), but by 1833 opium imports had increased more than seven-fold and constituted about 54 percent of all imports ($12,185,100 of the $22,304,753 total). Between 1818 and 1833 opium accounted for about 34 percent of the imports into China, and tea accounted for about 47 percent of the exports from China. The foreign trade accounts ultimately balanced because the 13 percent difference between these two figures was made up in hard cash, generally with kegs of silver dollars.[23]

The opium and tea trades grew up together and in Western Europe were virtually twins. In 1609 the East India Company first brought opium to London; in 1610 the Dutch brought the first tea to Europe. Chinese legend has it that the first person to discover the virtues of tea was the mythical emperor Shin Nong in 2737 B.C. Another account, however, says that to keep himself awake during long hours of meditation, a Buddhist monk cut off his own eyelids; tea plants sprouted where they fell to the ground. Within historical times, it is clear that in the fifth century B.C. Confucius was familiar with tea and that by A.D. 780 it was being taxed in China.

Tea, like opium, got off to a slow start in Europe. It was not until 1647 that the first East India Company teahouse opened in London, where tea in bulk was auctioned off "by candle"; that is, competitive bidding for tea shipments continued until one inch of a lighted candle had burned away. Tea by the cup was available in London coffeehouses in 1652, but the beverage was still so uncommon that in 1664 the East India Company took pride in presenting 2 pounds 2 ounces of tea to King Charles II. Regular annual shipments of tea to England began in 1684, although not everyone knew how to use it then. In 1685 the Duke of Monmouth's widow sent a pound of tea to her relatives in Scotland — who boiled it, threw the liquid away, served up the leaves as dinner vegetables and then asked themselves what Londoners found so special about this tasteless new food.

At first tea was expensive and was consumed only by the upper classes. In the seventeenth century, "Pleasure Gardens" in London popularized tea drinking, and the wives of wealthy merchants were careful to set aside fine rooms in their homes specifically for tea parties. In 1706 Thomas Twining set up shop as a tea merchant in the London Strand, and his firm is still in business today at the same location. During the early eighteenth century, the Industrial Revolution also spread the tea-drinking habit more widely. In the north of England tea was served with hot food to sustain the workers, who put in long hours under appallingly bad conditions. The demand became so great that by the end of the eighteenth century the British were consuming two pounds of tea per person per year, and London merchants were finding it hard to pay for the 4.5 million tons of tea imported from China annually.

By 1834 the East India Company's monopoly on the China trade came to an end. The tea trade boomed as other merchants began to deal in this commodity as well as in Indian opium: about 33.6 million pounds of tea were exported from China in 1834 and 44.3 million in 1835. Jardine Matheson was the dominant firm in this trade, loading 30 million pounds of tea each year for the London market.[24] As Canton, Amoy, Foochow, Ningpo and Shanghai were opened up as treaty ports along the China coast after the end of the first Opium War in 1842, the tea trade grew even further, and by 1844 over 70 million pounds of tea were being exported.[25] Like the opium trade, the tea trade was very profitable: the ship *Empress of China*—the first American ship to call at China (in 1784)—earned 30,327 American dollars, which was 25 percent of the original investment in her.[26]

Thus it was that by about 1850, Jardine Matheson and other merchant houses based in Canton were participating in both the opium and tea trades in roughly equal measure.[27] But their heavy East Indiamen, known as "tea waggons," proved to be too slow for the new market conditions because they lumbered along at only six knots. British and Americans alike had acquired a taste for the delicate, fragrant "new season's tea," and faster ships were needed to get the season's crop to London as quickly as possible. Such vessels were soon forthcoming. These were the big tea clippers, arguably the most famous, the most beautiful and the most frequently illustrated ships ever to carry cargo under sail. They dominated the China tea trade in the 1850s and 1860s until they were shouldered aside by the steamers and by the opening of the Suez Canal in 1869.

In 1845 the 750-ton *Rainbow* was launched at New York and paid for her cost two times over in just one round-trip to China.[28] Four years later the repeal of Britain's highly restrictive Navigation Laws allowed American ships to carry goods directly to Britain and between the British colonies. As a result, beginning in 1850 American clipper ships started to compete in the annual tea races to London. In that year the American clipper *Oriental* carried 1,600 tons of tea to England in only 97 days.

The sharp, heavily sparred *Witch of the Wave*, built in Portsmouth, New Hampshire, in 1851, made a record-breaking 90-day passage from China to England in 1852, carrying 19,000 chests of tea.[29]

Where tea clippers were concerned, the Americans may have taken the lead, but the British were not far behind. Jardine Matheson's *Cairngorm* logged 14 knots on her maiden passage from Aberdeen in 1853 and three years later ran from Bombay to Hong Kong in only 29 days.[30] The most famous of the great tea races was held in 1866 and was the focus of much public attention, admiration and illustrations. This contest was held between three British clippers—*Ariel* (not to be confused with the American topsail schooner by the same name), *Taeping* and *Serica*—all of which sailed from Foochow on the same evening, loaded with tea. Ninety-nine days and 15,000 miles later, all three ships dropped anchor off London's West India Docks on the same day, on the same tide and at nearly the same time: *Taeping* at 9:47 P.M., *Ariel* at 10:15 P.M. and *Serica* at 11:30 P.M.[31]

Today the only survivor of this remarkable fleet of tea clippers is *Cutty Sark*, which, as has been mentioned, was launched in 1869 and is now preserved at the National Maritime Museum in Greenwich, United Kingdom. Her spacious hull was designed for cargo carrying, not for speed, but she did take part in one tea race from China to London and made seven other voyages in the tea trade before carrying wool from Australia between 1883 and 1895. Her soaring masts and complex rigging are illustrated here.

The well-publicized races of the big tea clippers, whose captains drove their lovely "China birds" as hard as possible to get the season's crop to the London market ahead of their rivals, gradually forced the opium trade out of the limelight. Opium had always been something of an embarrassment even to its staunchest advocates. As China was opened to the West after the Opium Wars, opium was no longer the only product that could finance the tea trade. A shift in public sentiment was reflected in the great personal popularity of the Scottish businessman and yachtsman Sir Thomas Lipton (1850–1931), who was known as "the gentleman of tea" and was applauded as a philanthropist who turned his yacht *Erin* into a floating hospital during World War I. His firm's products are still in demand today. In the end, however, it was the opium trade, not the tea trade, that left the deepest marks on China itself and on its relationships with the West.

Tea clipper *Cutty Sark* (photo by the author)

The Last Days of the Opium Trade

It was only a matter of time before the Chinese realized they could grow opium at home and sell it at a lower price than imported Indian or Turkish opium. After the second Opium War ended in 1860, they began to grow poppies on a large scale, especially in Szechuan [Sichuan] and Yunnan provinces. As a result, Indian opium now faced stiff competition for the first time, not only from Chinese opium but from Persian opium as well, although to a lesser extent and only in some of the Chinese ports.[32]

Opium shipments from India, however, were still the largest single item in Chinese imports during 1875–1885 and actually showed an average annual increase of about 5,000 chests a year in this era. (The average annual imports for the decades 1865–1875 and 1885–1895 were about 77,000 and 82,000 chests, respectively.) By the end of the latter decade, however, the Indian trade went into a gradual decline. Because of their higher prices, Patna, Benares and Malwa opium were forced out of some Chinese markets entirely; in others they were sold alongside Chinese opium. Although opium consumption was definitely increasing in China, it was now Chinese opium that was being consumed. Indeed, by 1885 China was probably producing twice as much opium as it was importing, and in 1890 the cultivation of the poppy in China itself was legalized.[33]

For both commercial and public relations reasons, Jardine Matheson began to pull out of the opium business in the 1870s. Ambitious firms in India, especially David Sassoon and Sons, had cornered the market for opium. Moreover, the importing of Indian opium was being handled increasingly by Chinese merchants alone: one Chinese company would buy opium in Calcutta or Bombay; another would arrange for it to be shipped to China; a third would sell it there. And in the midst of these commercial developments, the noisy but hitherto ineffective antiopium lobby in Britain and the United States suddenly got a new lease on life.

This occurred when missionaries, evangelicals and Quakers in Britain took the lead in permanently turning public opinion against the opium trade. In 1874 the Yorkshire Quaker Edward Pease and like-minded colleagues formed a committee that became the Anglo-Oriental Society for the Suppression of the Opium Trade. The Earl of Shaftesbury was elected president of the society in 1880, and the evils of the opium trade were laid before Parliament that same year.

Prime Minister Gladstone personally believed that "this opium revenue, instead of being a sound and solid, is a slippery and dangerous, part of our Indian Revenue. India cannot be economically safe as long as she is dependent on it." He did not force this argument on the House, however, because in his view the British government could not deliver on any promise to end the trade and should therefore avoid making such a promise.[34] The House repeatedly rejected the anti-opium lobby's demands, not only in 1880 but in 1881, 1883, 1886, 1889 and 1891. Lord Shaftesbury conceded in 1885 that up to that point the lobby had made a mistake by not taking the moral high ground on this issue but had relied instead on exaggerated claims that were not borne out by the facts.[35]

The antiopium lobby might deplore on moral terms the British government's policy of "forcing opium on China," but it needed some intellectual arguments as well.[36] These came from a number of sources, most memorably from J. Spencer Hill, who held the academic title of Scholar at St. John's College in Cambridge University in the United Kingdom. His authoritative essay of 1884, *The Indo-Chinese Opium Trade*, won a prize from the University for its excellence. Perhaps of equal importance to the lobby, however, was Hill's own admission that he had begun his research with "a strong prejudice against the Anti-Opium agitators" but that his investigation of the facts and arguments on both sides of the case had forced him to the conclusion that "our connection with the traffic is wholly unjustifiable."[37]

As part of a campaign to bring public pressure to bear on Parliament, in 1891 the antiopium lobby collected and presented to the House some 2,500 petitions bearing the signatures of 205,000 concerned British subjects. The lobby demanded that a Royal Commission be set up to look into the pros and cons of the opium trade. A Royal Commission was duly established, but when its report appeared in 1895, the opponents of the opium trade were appalled.

Although the report contained about 2,500 pages of testimony from 723 witnesses, it ended up by fully endorsing the trade as it was then being carried on. It concluded that there was no widespread demand in Britain that opium production in India be halted; that to stop production in the Native States of India would interfere with the rights of the chiefs and peoples there; that the finances of the government of India were too weak to bear the cost of any prohibitive measures; and that the people of India were not willing to pay for such measures themselves.

Parliament accepted the Royal Commission's findings, and the British government was at last able to bask in this "vindication of the past actions of the Government of India ... and the views which have guided us."[38]

On the diplomatic front a good deal was going on at this time, too. In 1876 China and Great Britain had signed an opium agreement known as the Chefoo Convention, and in 1885 an additional article to the convention was agreed upon. This article was a minor victory for the Chinese because it complied with their demand that when opium was imported into China it had to be stored in bonded warehouses or in hulks and could not be sold until the tariff and an inland transportation tax known as *likin* had been paid. The Chinese were pleased that the British gave way on this latter point because until then the Chinese government had been able to get badly needed revenue only from the tariff itself: *likin* had been collected by the provincial authorities and somehow never found its way into the national treasury. This new revenue system went into operation in 1887.[39]

By the beginning of the twentieth century, conditions for ending the India-China opium trade were gradually becoming more auspicious. Opium suppression efforts were beginning to pay off for four reasons:

1. The cost of maintaining British India could increasingly be met by new methods of revenue and by investments in Indian tea and other products. During negotiations in 1904 over the status of Tibet, British officials therefore hinted to a Chinese envoy that the government of India was at last prepared to forgo its opium revenues.[40]
2. As we have seen, having lost their commanding position in the Indian opium market to David Sassoon and Sons, the British were also facing stiff competition in China itself from native-grown opium. The upshot was the British government was now more prepared to cooperate with the Chinese government in bringing the trade to a carefully orchestrated end.
3. At the same time, Chinese reformers were at work in their own country, following the lead of Zhang Zhidong, whose book *China's Only Hope* (1900) had pointed to the drug habit as one of the evils that had to be obliterated if China were to modernize.
4. Finally, the Chinese government itself was willing to use military force, if necessary, to reduce domestic production.[41]

The Official Trade Comes to an End

Opium shipments from India continued, averaging about 67,000 chests a year between 1901–1905, of which the Chinese received about 51,000 chests per year. The tide was turning, however. In 1906 an Imperial decree commanded that "within a period of 10 years the evils arising from foreign and native opium be equally and completely eradicated." For the first time since Commissioner Lin's seizure of British opium in 1839, an antiopium edict was given real teeth — in the form of specific regulations and punishments designed to stop opium production and use.[42]

The antiopium lobby was further encouraged by indications from Parliament in 1906 that it would favor ending the trade. The next year Britain and China signed an agreement reducing imports of Indian opium by 10 percent a year over a ten-year period, that is, up to 1917, provided that China also reduced its own production by the same amount.[43] This 1907 agreement called for a declining volume of imports — 61,900 chests in 1908, 56,800 in 1909, and 51,700 in 1910 — down to the point where there would be no imports at all after 1917, and the trade would officially have come to an end.[44]

At the suggestion of President Theodore Roosevelt, an International Opium Commission was established and in 1909 met in Shanghai.[45] The president of the commission was the Right Reverend Charles H. Brent, the Episcopal bishop of the Philippine Islands, who was also the head of the American delegation. Twelve other countries were on the commission: Austria-Hungary, China, France, Germany, Great Britain, Italy, Japan, the Netherlands, Persia, Portugal, Russia and Siam. Each delegation was to submit a report on opium production or use in its own country. The commission itself had no legislative powers and had to content itself with a nine-part resolution. This was its first and most important point:

> The International Opium Commission recognizes the unswerving sincerity of the Government of China in their efforts to eradicate the production and consumption of Opium throughout the Empire; the increasing body of public opinion among their own subjects by which these efforts are being supported; and the real, though unequal, progress being made in a task which is one of the greatest magnitude.

Judging from its fluent use of American English and its wealth of statistical detail, the Chinese delegation's report was almost certainly written by Bishop Brent's staff or by other American missionaries who had served in China. It shows that foreign imports of opium had declined somewhat since 1890:

Year	Average imports per year (in piculs)
1863–1870	56,226
1871–1880	68,765
1881–1890	72,012
1891–1900	58,726
1901–1908	52,809

The report warned, however, that these figures were misleading because they did not reflect the large amounts of opium that had been smuggled into China each year. To get a true picture of the situation, the report said, 20,000 piculs had to be added to the figures prior to 1887 and 5,000 piculs between 1887 and 1908. The report concluded that the decrease in demand during 1888–1906 was "attributed generally to the replacement of the foreign by the native drug."

The Chinese antiopium efforts were reportedly taking hold, however. According to the report, total opium production in China had been 584,800 piculs in 1906, but in 1908, two years after the Imperial decree of 1906, production had fallen by 37 percent to 367,250 piculs. In the same period, opium consumption in China itself had fallen by about one-third. In one of its most damning statements the report estimated that in 1906 about 27 percent of all adult Chinese males used opium and that there were then more than 13,000,000 opium smokers in China—that is, roughly 3.25 percent of a total population of 400 million people.

In 1911 yet another opium agreement was signed by Britain and China that reiterated that opium imports from India would cease entirely in 1917. This set the stage for an announcement in 1913 by the British undersecretary of state for India that henceforth his government would not sell any more opium to China if persuaded that the Chinese government was making a sincere effort to limit the illegal production of opium within China itself. Because the Chinese government of that time was weak but was in fact making efforts in this direction, as a leading historian of the opium trade puts it, "Though phrased with some care, the secretary's statement in reality meant that the Indo-Chinese opium trade had come to an end."[46]

Officially, the trade did not come to an end until 1917, the year specified by the agreement of 1907. However, getting rid of the last chests of Indian opium that had already been brought into China proved to be so difficult for bureaucratic and financial reasons that the Chinese government finally had to destroy them. From the point of view of the antiopium lobby, there was both good and bad news. The good news was that during eight days in January 1919 the remaining chests (there may have been 1276 of them) were publicly burned at Shanghai. The bad news was that not long after this dramatic gesture symbolizing the end of the official opium trade, opium cultivation sprang up again on a vast scale within China itself.

Notes

1. Sutton, *Lords of the East*, p. 126.
2. Gardiner, *Advent*, p. 31; and Keswick, *Thistle*, p. 136.
3. Keswick, *Thistle*, pp. 137–138.
4. Spratt, *Paddle Steamers*, pp. 29–30.
5. Wise, *Analysis*, pp. vii–xxi.
6. McKay, *Some Famous Sailing Ships*, pp. 194–195.
7. Layton, *Frolic*, p. 109.
8. Layton, *Frolic*, p. 109.
9. Layton, *Frolic*, p. 113.
10. These figures are from Layton, *Frolic*, p. 110.
11. Layton, *Frolic*, p. 132.
12. Owen, *British Opium Policy*, p. 199; and Matheson, *What Is the Opium Trade*, pp. 7–8.
13. Allen, *Opium Trade*, pp. 18–19.
14. Coates, *Trade*, p. 154.
15. Owen, *British Opium Policy*, p. 198.
16. Jardine Matheson, *Jardine Matheson*, p. 46.
17. Lubbock, *Opium Clippers*, p. 369.
18. Blakiston, *Five Months*, p. 15.
19. Keswick, *Thistle*, p. 142.
20. Morse, *Relations*, vol. 1, p. 179.
21. Chinese tea merchants, however, usually preferred cash to opium because they needed cash to make other purchases and because the local opium market was monopolized by four or five Cantonese firms, which forced the tea dealers to sell their opium at a steep discount. See Gardella, *Harvesting Mountains*, pp. 56 and 106.
22. *China; as it was*, p. 47.
23. Morse, *Relations*, pp. 82–93.

24. Jardine Matheson, *Jardine Matheson*, p. 13.
25. Hibbert, *Dragon*, p. 184.
26. Hao, *Commercial Revolution*, pp. 268–269.
27. After 1833 British settlers in India began to produce tea on a large scale as a plantation crop with mechanized production processes. Chinese tea, however, continued to be produced in small batches and by hand. In 1887 silk had overtaken tea as China's most important single export, and by 1888 the consumption of Indian tea in Britain had overtaken that of Chinese tea — a lead that was never to be lost. See Bramah, *Guide*, p. 18.
28. Hao, *Commercial Revolution*, pp. 268–269.
29. Cutler, *Greyhounds*, p. 23.
30. MacGregor, *Tea Clippers*, p. 63.
31. Jardine Matheson, *Jardine Matheson*, p. 43.
32. The best single discussion of the ending of the opium trade is Owen, *British Opium Policy*, p. 286 ff, which I have drawn on heavily here.
33. Williams, *History*, p. 406.
34. Anglo-Oriental Society, *Opium Traffic*, p. 30.
35. Morse, *Relations*, vol. 1, p. 551.
36. Morse, *Relations*, vol. 2, p. 539 ff.
37. Hill, *Opium Trade*, p. v.
38. Cited by Owen, *British Opium Policy*, p. 328.
39. The article negotiated in 1885 put the amount of *likin* at HK.Tls. [Haikwan taels] 80 per picul [133 lbs.] of opium. When added to the existing tariff of HK.Tls. 30 per picul, which had been set when the opium trade was first legalized in 1858, this gave the Chinese government a total revenue of HK.Tls. 110 per picul. See International Opium Commission, *Report*, vol. 2, p. 45.
40. Hao, *Commercial Revolution*, p. 137; and Hosie, *Trail*, vol. 2, p. 192.
41. Hao, *Commercial Revolution*, p. 137.
42. International Opium Commission, *Report*, vol. 2, p. 78.
43. Kuo, *Opium Suppression*, p. 1.
44. International Opium Commission, *Report*, vol. 2, p. 178.
45. The following information is drawn from the *Report* of the International Opium Commission.
46. Owen, *British Opium Policy*, p. 348.

10

Legacies of the Opium Trade

The India-China opium trade itself ended in 1917, but long before then the two Opium Wars and the "unequal" treaties ending them had left deep, long-lasting scars on China. The weaknesses China had displayed in these wars encouraged other nations to believe that they could carve up the country into their own spheres of influence. The foreign penetration of China came to a head during the Sino-Japanese war of 1937–1945, which evolved into World War II in the Far East, and it is still going on today—this time in the form of a gradual liberation of China's highly centralized economy.

The Pernicious Effects of the "Unequal" Treaties

For many generations the Chinese have denounced the agreements ending the two Opium Wars as humiliating, "unequal" treaties that were negotiated under duress and imposed on China by Western greed, Western arrogance and the force of Western arms. To understand the Chinese point of view on this matter we can review the major provisions of these treaties.

The first was the Treaty of Nanking, negotiated in 1842, which brought the first Opium War to a close and contained what to the Chinese were exceptionally onerous provisions. The chief of these was that Hong Kong had to be ceded to Britain. (Hong Kong was not restored to China for 155 years, the handover finally taking place on 1 July 1997). In addition, five "treaty ports" were opened up to British trade so that foreign commerce would no longer have to filter through the Cohong merchants in Canton but could be conducted more competitively. For the first time in its long history, China also had to recognize Britain (and, by extension, other nations as well) as its diplomatic equal. It was saddled with a huge indemnity of $21 million, a figure calculated to pay both for the opium Commissioner Lin had destroyed and for the cost of the war itself. The Chinese were also forced to agree that Europeans would supervise the collection of custom duties on goods entering their country. Finally, Western missionaries were permitted to work in the treaty ports.

The details of China's new relationships with the West were spelled out soon after the Treaty of Nanking, first in 1843 when the British negotiated two supplementary agreements with the Chinese and then in 1844 when the Americans negotiated the Treaty of Wanghia and the French the Treaty of Whampoa with them. To the xenophobic Chinese all these arrangements must have seemed bad enough, but it was the most-favored-nation policy embedded in them that was to cause the greatest humiliation. Although the Chinese themselves had used this policy for centuries when dealing with lesser states, the tables were now turned. The most-favored-nation clause provided that any privilege granted by China to any treaty signatory would automatically be granted to Britain and, by extension, to other Western states as well. By thus guaranteeing trading equality for the West, the most-favored-nation clause made it impossible for the Chinese to encourage trade or diplomatic relations selectively with one country but not the others.

The most-favored-nation clause was also the bedrock on which the policy of extraterritoriality rested. This is defined as the possession or exercise of political rights by a foreign power within a country having its own government. What extraterritoriality meant in practice was that Westerners living in China were not subject to Chinese law and could not be tried by Chinese courts.[1]

The treaties that ended the second Opium War in 1860 expanded the privileges of Westerners in China and the system of treaty ports. As mentioned earlier, after two years of defeats in the second war the Chinese had negotiated four treaties at Tientsin in 1858. These included, among other things, provisions for foreign diplomats to live and work in Peking and for Christian missionaries to evangelize anywhere in China rather than just in the treaty ports. When Chinese troops at the Taku forts fired on the Western negotiators making their way to Peking to sign these treaties, the second war was resumed and continued until 1860. In final negotiations at Peking that year China was forced to ratify the 1858 treaties and to sign new agreements with the British and French ending the second war itself. These legalized the opium trade, opened up 10 additional treaty ports and gave Westerners the right to navigate on the Yangtze and travel anywhere in China.

It is difficult to exaggerate the impact on China of these "unequal" agreements. A census of Westerners living at Macao in 1826 had counted only 76 of them: 45 British, 19 Americans, 4 Dutch, 2 Swedes, 2 Swiss and 4 Spaniards.[2] Thirteen years later, on the eve of the first Opium War, *The Chinese Repository*, an English-language journal published in Canton, estimated that the foreign presence there was still tiny: only 158 British, 62 Parsees, 44 Americans, 28 Portuguese and a handful of other nationalities. After the end of the second Opium War in 1860, however, a Chinese writer would marvel at the sudden convergence of Westerners on China, and by 1864 a former governor of Kwangtung would predict, accurately, that China was then facing a change greater than any in hundreds of years.[3] The Middle Kingdom had at last been opened up to the West. The foreign penetration of China that began with the Opium Wars has continued into our own times and will have impacts in the twenty-first century as well.

"Old Buddha"

Together with the Taiping rebellion and other popular uprisings, the defeats of the Opium Wars gravely weakened the moral authority and thus the political legitimacy of the Qing dynasty. The dynasty's repeated failures to defend China against the foreigners or to keep the domestic peace gradually proved to traditionalists that the Mandate of Heaven, that is, the approval of the cosmic order, was passing from Qing hands. Ironically, however, it was probably these setbacks that persuaded a charming, intelligent and ambitious ex-concubine that she must hold on to political power at all costs. This was Empress Dowager Tzu-hsi [Ci Xi].

Her personal name was Yehonala but in ceremonial terms she was variously referred to as the Orchid, the Imperial Yi Concubine or the

Empress of the Western Palace. In her later years she was known to those who both feared and admired her simply as "Old Buddha." Between the early 1860s and her death in 1908, this physically frail but politically formidable lady dominated the Chinese court in Peking. She prevented non-Manchus from getting key government posts. She refused to overhaul China's archaic examination system, which continued to require mastery of the classics for entry into the ranks of the scholar-officials who administered China on a day-to-day basis. She opposed any major reforms of the Chinese army, navy or other institutions, even though modest and sensible proposals were put forward to her by patriotic Chinese officials during the "Self-strengthening Movement" of 1861–1895.

Old Buddha also squandered scarce public funds on flamboyant palaces for herself: she had the Summer Palace, which had been burned by the British and French at the end of the second Opium War, rebuilt with the funds originally intended for the modernization of the Chinese navy. She feared the West and did her best to keep it at bay. At one point she told the Chinese: "My anger is about to strike [the Westerners] and exterminate them without mercy. I command all my subjects to hunt them down like wild beasts."[4]

Old Buddha was autocratic and murderous during her long reign. She ordered her eunuchs to kill the Pearl Concubine, who once had been the emperor's favorite, by pushing her down into a deep well outside the Imperial palace. The eunuchs immediately carried out this order, and the concubine was drowned. Yet in her personal life Old Buddha was a person of more moderate habits. After the day's hectic business was over she enjoyed a soothing pipe of opium, but she never became an addict.[5]

Given her own fondness for opium, it may seem surprising that she acquiesced in the Chinese government's efforts in the early twentieth century to end the trade, but she understood that the trade had corrupted and weakened China, laying it ever more open to the foreign influences she hated and feared. At the turn of the century Old Buddha was still part of the glue that held the rickety Qing dynasty together. After her death in 1908, the dynasty tottered along for a few more years, but its formal demise (in 1912) was a foregone conclusion.

Foreign Penetration of China

During the Opium Wars, China's moral and cultural values were challenged for the first time — not by the unlettered barbarians of the past who were overawed by Chinese culture but by highly trained Westerners who not only possessed better technology and military discipline but who were also convinced that their own culture was superior to China's in all respects. The story of China since the Opium Wars has been — and still is — the story of its efforts to come to terms with foreign influences.

In addition to being a cultural shock, the Western penetration of China after the Opium Wars had adverse economic impacts as well. Under the terms of the treaties the balance of trade was extremely one-sided. China could neither stop the influx of European goods nor set duties on them to earn government revenue. It could not force the Europeans to buy Chinese goods. This imbalance in foreign trade resulted in a flow of silver out of China, which made the country poorer, reduced the financial capabilities of the government and contributed to frequent financial crises and inflation.[6]

The treaty ports themselves had a profound and to Chinese traditionalists a very negative impact on their way of life. Through these ports flowed the goods, services and ideologies of the West — brought into China, consciously or unconsciously, by waves of foreign administrators, military and naval officers, business executives, traders, teachers and missionaries.

In the long run, the most important imports were not Western *things* but Western *ideas*. The Judeo-Christian beliefs of the West had a corrosive impact on Confucian values and on the Qing dynasty itself. On both personal and philosophic levels, most Westerners considered the individual more important than the family, the clan, the firm or even the government itself. In the nineteenth century Western philosophic and political concepts began to circulate freely in Canton and other parts of southern China that had long wanted to throw off the Manchu yoke. These radical notions, embedded in such documents as the American Declaration of Independence (1776) and the French Declaration of the Rights of Man (1789), were that all people have "certain inalienable rights" to life, liberty, property, personal security, freedom of speech and freedom of the press and that "men are born free and remain free and equal in rights." Quintessentially Western ideas such as representative democracy struck at the heart of the Qing's legitimacy, which was based not on the will of the people but on the Mandate of Heaven.

Many of China's late-nineteenth- and early-twentieth-century revolutionaries came from the south, where these heretical ideas were current. Sun Yat-sen (1866–1924), who in 1911 became the first president of post-Manchu China, was educated in Hawaii and Hong Kong and had lived overseas; most of his followers were young Chinese intellectuals who had been educated in Europe or the United States. These men were strongly influenced by the ideals of Western constitutional democracy. Indeed, one of Sun Yat-sen's four basic demands was that China must be a republic with a president and parliament elected by the whole nation.[7] However, Sun and his followers also felt that Western political structures could not be imported intact but would have to be adjusted to fit Chinese realities.

At the level of day-to-day life in the treaty ports the Westerners were much in evidence. They took over most of the administration of Shanghai during the days of the Foreign Inspectorate there (1850–1854). At all the treaty ports they enjoyed a privileged, protected position. Victorian imperialism and its attendant belief in the innate superiority of the "white race" were coming into full bloom at this time and it must have encouraged some of the less refined Westerners to lord it over the local Chinese, politically, financially and socially. Some parks in Shanghai had signs in them warning that "No dogs or Chinese are allowed."

The humiliation felt by proud mandarins and commoners alike can be easily imagined. Indeed, echoes of it could still be heard in 1949, when in a famous speech in Tiananmen Square in Peking proclaiming the founding of the People's Republic of China under the leadership of the Chinese Communist Party, Chairman Mao Tse-tung [Mao Zedong] promised: "Our country will never again be an insulted nation. The Chinese people have stood up!"[8]

After the fall of the Qing dynasty in 1912, reformers were quick to recognize that if China wanted to survive as an independent state it had to modernize and modernize quickly. This required huge amounts of capital, which were not available in China itself. The only solution was foreign loans, but as one Sinologist has pointed out, "the acceptance of capital from abroad led at once, every time, to further political capitulations."[9]

China's weaknesses encouraged other countries to pursue expansionist policies that further reduced the writ of successive Chinese governments. The greatest aggressiveness was demonstrated by Japan. Unlike China itself, which had remained locked into its traditional culture thanks in part to the reactionary policies of Old Buddha, Japan had modernized rapidly during the Meiji era, which began in 1867. After about 1871 Japan embarked on an imperialist campaign to surround itself with a belt of subjugated states, which were to constitute a "Greater Japanese Empire" and were to be ruled from Tokyo. In 1885 Japan declared that Korea, which had hitherto been a protectorate of China alone, was now a joint sphere of interest of China and Japan. In 1894 a Sino-Japanese war broke out over Korea; because China still did not have modern weapons or effective military forces, it lost the war and had to sign a peace treaty on harsh terms, which led to both Korea's and Taiwan's becoming Japanese colonies.

Continued Chinese weakness invited further Japanese aggression. During World War I, Japan drove the Germans out of China but did not willingly return the liberated area to the Chinese. In 1928 Japan landed its own troops at Shanghai to support a Chinese political figure who was pro-Japanese. In 1931 Japan invaded Manchuria, and in 1937 it provoked an incident that sparked the Sino-Japanese war, soon to become part of World War II, which continued until the final defeat of Japan by Allied forces in 1945.

During the nineteenth century, not only Japan but the Western nations, too, wanted to profit from China's weakness. France coveted the region of Southeast Asia later known as French Indochina (now Vietnam, Laos and Cambodia). It took over Cochin China in 1862, Cambodia in 1864, Tongking in 1874 and Annam in 1883. Up to that time these territories, although ruled by local dynasties, had been under a nominal if loose Chinese suzerainty. France's acquisitions led to a war with China in 1884, which China predictably lost and which left France with all its new possessions.

Russia, for its part, had its own eyes on Manchuria. Clashes between Russia and China over eastern Siberia ended in 1858, with China ceding part of northern Manchuria and leasing the important transshipment point of Port Arthur to Russia. A more dramatic foreign intervention was still to come. This occurred in 1900 after a militant Chinese movement tried to drive the foreigners out of China.

Known to the West as the "Boxers" (an abbreviation of their Chinese name, which was variously translated as the "Society of Righteous Fists" or "the Boxers of Honesty and Concord"), this movement had the tacit support of Old Buddha. For 55 days the Boxers laid siege to the foreign legations in Peking, where about 900 foreigners of 11 different nationalities and about 3,000 Chinese Christians had fled for safety. Sixty-seven foreigners were killed, and many more were wounded before the siege was lifted. The Boxers were finally defeated by the landing of a large foreign expeditionary force, which captured Peking, looted some of the Imperial palaces and forced Old Buddha to flee from the capital.[10] In the peace treaty that ended the Boxer Uprising, these Western nations forced China to pay huge war indemnities and to grant them further concessions.

The Opium Wars Today

The Opium Wars have been mentioned frequently in Chinese propaganda statements ever since the Chinese Communist Party came to power in 1949. These conflicts have been cited on many occasions to establish the legitimacy of the party itself. The basic arguments have been that the party has ended more than 100 years of imperialist domination, exploitation and humiliation by foreign powers; that the party has made China strong, rich and respected; and that without the party there would be political and economic instability in China itself.

A good example of such a statement is an authoritative article, "The Opium War," that appeared in the party's *History of Modern China* (1976). One of the article's key assertions is that the first war "marked both the beginning of modern Chinese history and the start of the Chinese people's bourgeois-democratic revolution against imperialism and feudalism."[11] Other excerpts showing the importance of the first Opium War can be found in Appendix IV.

Such statements continued in the 1980s and 1990s. In 1980, for example, the third edition of Israel Epstein's *From Opium War to Liberation* was published with the Chinese Communist Party's tacit blessing. Epstein, a longtime apologist for the party, listed four negative results of the first Opium War, all of which were allegedly the fault of the aggressive Westerners:

1. The legal importation of opium into China continued until 1917.
2. Extraterritoriality for foreign nationals in China lasted *de jure* until 1942 but in practice Chinese law was never applied to foreigners until the Chinese Communist Party came to power in 1949.
3. Foreign administrative concessions served as springboards for further foreign expansion and aggression.
4. The partial tax exemptions granted to Chinese merchants who were handling foreign goods helped subject China's economy to imperialism.[12]

In the mid–1990s a writer in China's *Democracy and Law Journal* rebuked any of his readers who might have been guilty of the sin of buying *foreign tea* rather than Chinese tea. He stressed that "since the Opium War, Western culture has knocked on our door many times. The Chinese people put up act after act of heroic and tenacious battle against foreign guns, foreign cannons and resistance to foreign products [such as Indian tea] and foreign garbage [such as Indian opium]."[13] In a widely publicized ceremony in July 1997 commemorating the first Opium War, immaculately uniformed Chinese police stood guard while illegal heroin was publicly burnt in Humen, southern China.

The Opium Wars also came up frequently in the negotiations between the Chinese and the British that culminated in Hong Kong's reversion to China on 1 July 1997. The Chinese even made a big-budget film, *The Opium War*, to highlight this important event. The movie, designed to be a milestone in the Chinese publicity campaign surrounding the return of Hong Kong, featured both Chinese and British actors. It was directed by 73-year-old Xie Jin, China's elder statesman of film, and was viewed by the Chinese foreign minister and other Chinese dignitaries, a fact that indicated the party's endorsement of the film as being ideologically sound.[14]

Even after the return of Hong Kong, the first Opium War continued to be a useful arrow in China's public relations quiver. In 1998, for example, a press officer at the Chinese embassy in London told the author that the Chinese people "will never forget the Opium War" because it "marked the start of 100 years of humiliation"; that it "showed the delinquency of the Qing dynasty"; and that the war has "a special meaning for the Chinese people."[15]

A Summing Up

The most important legacy of the India-China opium trade was not, in the end, the wealth it produced for Western traders or the damage it did to the health of Chinese opium smokers. Instead, the real legacy was *the revolutionary Western ideas it* introduced into a tradition-bound China by the Opium Wars. As these ideas gradually spread among literate and politically ambitious Chinese, they had more far-reaching effects than opium itself. They contributed, directly or indirectly, to the fall of the Qing dynasty in 1911, to the establishment of a Chinese

Republic from 1912 to 1948 and to the eventual triumph of the Chinese Communist Party in 1949.[16]

Even now their work in China may not yet be done. Since the late 1970s another Western idea has been penetrating the fabric of Chinese life. This is the concept of an economic liberalization gradually leading to a more market-driven economy, in place of the overstaffed, inefficient, ideologically based enterprises so prevalent in China since 1949. This liberalization involves pruning the big state-owned industries, recapitalizing the technically bankrupt banking system and chipping away at the "iron rice bowl" (i.e., China's cradle-to-grave social welfare benefits).

Judging from the collapse of the former Soviet Union, however, one consequence of moving away from a centrally planned economy toward a free market economy is that there will no longer be any justification for a single political party wielding dictatorial power. If there is relative prosperity in China, a growing middle class may put pressure on the party to share political power by allowing other parties to compete with it. If, on the other hand, mass unemployment increases because state-run enterprises are cut back or because the economy goes into recession, jobless men and women may demand social security benefits that the party simply cannot provide.

A word of caution is in order here: the parallels between the former Soviet Union and present-day China should not be overdrawn. The Chinese Communist Party is now intent only on reforming China's economic system, not its political system, and China itself does not have the ethnic diversity that helped to splinter the Soviet Union. It still seems likely, however, that liberalizing the Chinese economy will have unforeseen and unintended results. If so, it is even conceivable that in the twenty-first century the final casualty of the India-China opium trade may turn out to be the Chinese Communist Party itself.

Notes

1. Ironically, it was an American diplomat — Caleb Cushing — who spelled out how extraterritoriality would work in practice. This clarification was necessary because a British miscreant could simply be taken to the border of Hong Kong and handed over to the British colonial authorities there. However, the Americans did not have a convenient Hong Kong. Thus Cushing had to define how the new institution was to work for them. (Private communication from Dr. Jacques M. Downs of 25 May 1998.)

2. Morse, *Chronicles*, vol. 4, pp. 128–129.
3. Cited by *Cambridge History of China*, p. 156.
4. Cited by Fraser, *Flashman*, pp. 297–298.
5. The standard reference on Tzu-hsi's life (1834–1908) is Bland and Backhouse, *Empress Dowager*.
6. Eberhard, *History*, p. 300. Some of the information in the rest of this chapter was also drawn from this source.
7. The other three demands were the expulsion of the Manchus, the restoration of Chinese rule and the equalization of land rights. See Franke, *Chinese Revolution*, p. 64.
8. Cited by Epstein, *From Opium War*.
9. Eberhard, *History*, p. 317.
10. The belief that the Empress Dowager was supporting the Boxers was widespread at the time. Mary Hooker, an American woman who kept a diary during the siege of the legations, recorded on 29 June 1900 that

> the Emperor and his party for progress were completely snowed under in 1898 by the Empress-Dowager and her old Manchu Conservatives, who, lacking the desire to accept anything modern — even diplomatic relations of the most simple kind — decided, in a childlike and unreasoning rage, that everything foreign must be swept down into the sea, and it really looks now as if the first steps of her policy may be realized.

As the siege of the legations wore on, prospects for the foreigners grew so dim that Mrs. Hooker wrote in her diary on 16 July: "I have in my pocket a small pistol loaded with several cartridges, to use if the worst happens. A Belgian secretary stole it from the armoury for me —'in case you need it, mademoiselle.'" Fortunately, Mrs. Hooker did not have to commit suicide. On 15 August an international expeditionary force consisting of American, English, French, Russian and Indian troops fought its way into Peking and saved both the foreigners and the Chinese who had sought shelter in the legations. (See Hooker, *Behind the Scenes*, pp. 12, 127–128, 171–180.)

11. "The Opium War" in *History of Modern China*, p. 1.
12. Epstein, *From Opium War*, p. 19. The earlier editions of his book were published in 1956 and 1964, suggesting party approval over a long period of time.
13. Cited by Steven Mufson, *International Herald Tribune*, 20 May 1996.
14. Scarlet Cheng, "Opiate of the People," a review of the film *The Opium War* in *Far Eastern Economic Review*, June 26, 1997, p. 54.
15. Private telephone conversation with a press officer at the Chinese embassy in London on 24 March 1998.
16. Like all other communist parties in the world, the Chinese Communist Party has its intellectual roots in the dialectical materialist theory of history put forward by the nineteenth-century theoretician Karl Marx and

his colleague Frederick Engels and as elaborated by Vladimir Ilyich Lenin. Mao Zedong, however, understood that conditions in China were fundamentally different from those in Western Europe and that Marxism-Leninism had to be adapted to Chinese realities. So although Marxism-Leninism taught that revolution had to begin in the cities and had to rely on the industrial proletariat, Mao saw that in China the revolution would have to begin in the countryside and rely on the peasants.

Appendix I: A Modern Recipe for "Country Captain"

This is a good main course for two hungry or three well-fed people. Because individual tastes vary so much, the quantities of most of the ingredients needed are left to the cook's discretion. A fiery "Country Captain," however, will be closer to its historical roots than a bland one.

Ingredients

One plump medium-sized chicken (cut into serving pieces with skin removed; use the skin and carcass to make chicken stock — see below)

Flour

Salt

Freshly ground black pepper

Butter

Vegetable oil

Diced onions

Green peppers (cut up)

A pinch of cayenne pepper

A generous amount of curry powder

Garlic

Thyme

A touch of sugar

Juice of 1 lemon

Stewed tomatoes, fresh or canned

Raisins or dried currants

Toasted almonds (slivered)

Mango chutney

Rice (preferably Basmati rice cooked in chicken stock)

Cooking Method

In a plastic or paper bag shake the flour, salt and black pepper together until thoroughly mixed. Add the chicken pieces, and shake until coated. Using butter and a little oil to keep the butter from burning, brown the chicken in a frying pan. At the same time, in a bigger frying pan or heavy pot cook in butter and oil the onions, green peppers, garlic, curry powder, cayenne and thyme. When the onions are golden brown and the peppers soft, add the lemon juice, stewed tomatoes and, after a few minutes, the chicken pieces, raisins or currants and the slivered almonds. Add some water, cover the pan or pot, and cook for about 45 minutes or until the chicken is tender. Adjust the seasoning (add a bit of sugar if you wish), and serve with Basmati rice and mango chutney.

Appendix II: *Falcon* and Her Crew

This account was written in the latter half of the nineteenth century by an officer who served aboard Jardine Matheson's flagship, Falcon. *It first appeared in the* Yachtsman, *a British magazine, and was quoted by Basil Lubbock in* China Clippers, *pp. 15–22, from which these excerpts are taken. It is interesting to note that there is no mention here of opium, which was* Falcon's *chief cargo.*

The Ship

With a bow round and full above the waterline, she was as sharp as a wedge in her entrance below. Her midship sections gave her a long flat floor, whence commenced a clean run aft, that, with her form of entrance, minimised resistance and displacement to a marvellous degree. Her breadth of beam over this long floor enabled her to stand up under a more than ordinary press of canvas, while it afforded quarters for a small battery of guns, including a long brass piece amidships and some pivot and swivels over bows, counter and quarter, that made her a wholesome terror to the swarming fleets of pirates, which then infested the Hok-keen Coasts.

In all cases of bad weather, the heaviest of these were run in and well secured; indeed, there were times and occasions when the whole armament was dismounted and put under hatches, so that nothing should encumber the spacious white flush deck beyond the neat coils of running gear placed in tubs made for the occasion.

The *Falcon* was a full-rigged ship, heavily but beautifully masted, as to rake and proportion. Her yards and spars were of dimensions equal to a ship of, perhaps, twice the size in actual carrying power in the ordinary Mercantile Marine. These were beautifully fashioned and finished — not in the tapered and pointed style affected by traders within the tropics, nor of the dilettanti in the summer seas at home, but in a style that savoured rather of massive strength and utility. There was no skysail or moonsail or flagstaff extensions. Our masts seldom went more than a few inches beyond the rigging that supported them.

In summer-like weather we sent up topgallant and royal masts in one, but during the strength of the monsoons and in all passages to the northward — and we sometimes went very far north — short topgallant masts were fidded [i.e., they were attached to the lower masts by means of a bar of wood or iron known as a fid]. We trusted more to spread than to hoist; and in going free the show of canvas upon our square yards, further extended by lengthy stunsail booms — in the rigging out of which our topmen had few compeers — would leave an observer in no doubt of the immense pressure under which the comparatively slight and beautiful fabric trembled and vibrated in its headlong career.

I hesitate to touch upon the secondary furnishings and fittings of the *Falcon*, but I remember that they were unusually elegant and substantial and costly; that where metal was employed it was mostly of copper or brass, even to the belaying pins; and that toprails, stanchions, skylights and coamings were of mahogany, whilst the accommodation below for the officers and crew was extravagantly luxurious.

It will better become me to speak of her higher and greater qualities, qualities which made her an object of pride and real affection, as of the tenderest care, of her crew, officers and men. She was easy, handy and smart in every evolution. She swam like a duck and steered like a fish. She was fast, yet dry; lively, yet stiff. Sensitive and responsive to every yard of canvas that could be judiciously spread, as to every touch of the braces, tacks and sheets, and to every spoke of the wheel.

It was in the *Falcon* that I learnt to comprehend and to adopt a singular belief that prevails among seamen; and it was in her, and by her, that I was first touched by that strange sympathy which is created by a favourite ship upon the minds of an appreciative crew. If the *Falcon* had been a living thing that sympathy could scarcely have been greater. She would resent every neglect in her handling, and rebel at once against any over-pressure or any tampering with her trim, so that our common expressions — expressions that could have no meaning to a landsman — that she was complaining or sulking or huffed or offended seemed to us to be rightfully applied.

One felt proud to watch her dealing with opposing forces so persistently and so gallantly. We had been afloat in her for upwards of three years with few losses and fewer changes than could have been expected in so large a crew; and, having watched and studied her pretty ways for so long a period, we had acquired readiness and skill in her management, and had learned to look upon her as a thing to be loved and petted. "She can do everything but speak," was a common remark among the crew.

The Officers

The officers were for the most part the younger sons of good families at home, who had to use every effort and wait long to fill a vacant appointment, which was very difficult to obtain, as applicants had to undergo the severest tests of fitness, both mental and physical. Some acquaintance with nautical astronomy and the physical sciences, with a taste for Eastern languages and a tongue and a turn for Eastern colloquials; approved physique, steadiness and courage; reliability of temper, with the higher moral gifts of coolness and patience under trial and provocation — all these were essentials. And it may be remarked that among the officers were many sons of clergymen, who, after a period of active service afloat, would retire to succeed ultimately to their fathers' livings or to practice at the bar, not a few finding their way into Parliament.

The Men

Our spars from deck to truck were, or had been, modelled by rough and ready artists, in the persons of our carpenter and his mates, who had sometimes more than they could do to supply our frequent losses. Famous among us as he was — and as he deserved to be — our carpenter yielded to the superior art of our sailmaker. Much as they did to enhance each others' merits, the sailmaker bore the palm. No academician ever draped a classic figure with more consummate taste and art than that with which our sailmaker draped the *Falcon*. Nothing in still life could be more picturesque than the *Falcon*'s sails, which, unfurled at anchor or in a calm or other condition of repose, fell in full, heavy graceful folds from her yards and booms. Nothing could convey so strikingly the triumph of art, when the same sails were filled and trimmed — full and by — in the first case presenting a cloud of swelling segments, pressing forward as if in spirited and living rivalry; in the second case held like boards by sheet, tack, brace and bowline, the rounded luff and foot leaving no rift twixt spar and canvas; in both cases gladdening and satisfying a seaman's heart and eye.

At daylight every morning there was a general resetting of sails, a repointing of yards, and a "freshening of the nip" in every sheave. Many watchful eyes and ready hands were on the alert, upon these and similar occasions, to make the slightest change of wind, whether in force or in direction, available to add a knot to the coming day's work.

Long have I lingered in my description of the carpenter and sailmaker. I cannot honestly proceed further without a word of praise of another deserving petty officer, the boatswain, who, with a couple of mates and four quartermasters, had come out from England in the *Falcon*.

The boatswain had been a foreman rigger in one of the great commercial docks at home, where his daily practice for many years had familiarised him with the every description of craft of every possible rig, and with fittings and refittings to suit almost every taste. He was a master of his craft and was as intelligent as he was expert. His leading peculiarity was his faculty of teaching and communicating to others not only the mode, but the philosophy and spirit and beauty of his own gifts, so that the three years we had spent together in the *Falcon* had made us all riggers.

All able seamen, by the mere use of the term, profess to be competent to "hand, reef and steer and heave the lead"; but there wasn't a seaman on board the *Falcon*, who couldn't — besides these requisites — turn in a dead-eye, gammon a bow-sprit, fish a broken spar, rig a purchase of any given power, knot, point, splice, parcel and serve, spinning his own yarn or lines, of such length and dimensions as could be adapted to the power of our winch and rope-walk. With such a crew the state of our rigging, stays, backstays, standing and running gear and fittings may be accepted as most perfect and complete. As instance of the capacity of the *Falcon*'s crew, I may state that we have stretched, cut and fitted a set of coir lower rigging on our own decks at sea; and at sea we have placed it over the naked lower mastheads, and set it up, one mast at a time, completing the whole work in three days. And at sea we have constructed a raft of spare spars, and transferred to it our guns, stores, and much of our ballast. And to the raft so loaded, we have hove down the ship and repaired and cleaned the copper bottom from the keel to bends in two days. Our crew was a large one, I must admit, sufficient in number to make three strong watches, either of which could reef the three topsails together. But I would remind my nautical reader that no number — no mere number — of unskilled or undisciplined men could have been trusted to perform tasks as onerous as those I have described.

If I am asked why such feats should have been performed at all, or even attempted, I may say that the *Falcon* was always at sea; that her cruising grounds were over a long extent of coast that, in those days, swarmed with pirates; that it afforded no place of shelter where strangers could safely enter; that the whole coast was *terra incognita*, except to the lawless, rapacious natives and to the few like ourselves who had spent many years in its navigation in all weathers.

Appendix III: *Antelope* and Her Crew

This was written by a seaman who served aboard the opium clipper Antelope. The following account has been drawn from quotations used by Basil Lubbock in his China Clippers, pp. 25–33, whose source was "an American book of voyages ... long forgotten and out of print."

The Ship

There was just then [about 1844] lying in the River Hooghly one of the prettiest little craft that was ever in the opium business. She was called the *Antelope*, and had only come out from Boston six months before. With her low, black hull, tall rakish masts, and square yards, she was a regular beauty, just such a vessel as it does an old tar's heart good to set eyes on — though, for the matter of comfort, keep me out of them, for what with their scrubbing and scouring in port and their carrying on sail at sea to make a good passage and half drowning the crew, there's very little peace aboard them...

The vessel was well armed, having two guns on a side besides a Long Tom amidships. Boarding pikes were arranged in great plenty on a rack around the main mast, and the large arms chest on the quarter-deck was well supplied with pistols and cutlasses. We were fully prepared for a brush with the rascally Chinese, and determined not to be put out of our course by one or two mandarin boats…

If ever a vessel had canvas piled on her it was the *Antelope*. Our topsails were fully large enough for a vessel of double her tonnage. We carried about all the flying kites that a vessel of her rig has room for. Skysails, royal studding sails, jib-o-jib, staysails, alow and aloft, and even water sails, and saveralls to fit beneath the foot of the topsails.

Captain and Crew

[*Antelope*] steered like a top, but our nervous skipper, who was not for a moment day or night at rest, but ever driving the vessel … [which] could not deviate a quarter of a point off her course, or while we were in the wind the royals could not lift in the least, before he was upon the helmsman, cursing and swearing like a trooper, and making as much fuss as though she had yawed a point each way.

Our crew consisted of seventeen men, all stout able fellows. There were no boys to handle the light sails, and it was sometimes neck-breaking work to shin up the tall royal mast when skysails were to be furled or royal studd'nsail gear rove. We had but little to do on board: to mend a few sails and steer the vessel was the sum total of our duty. On board these ships the men are wanted mainly to work ship expeditiously and to defend her against the attacks of the Chinese officers, whose duty, but ill fulfilled, it was to prevent the smuggling of opium into the country.

Appendix IV: Excerpts from "The Opium War"

The article from which these excerpts are taken was written by members of the history departments of Futan University and Shanghai Teachers' University. Appearing in the History of Modern China *(Peking, 1976), it was an authoritative account of Chinese policy at that time.*

The Opium War of 1840–42, in which the Chinese people fought against British aggression, marked both the beginning of modern Chinese history and the start of the Chinese people's bourgeois-democratic revolution against imperialism and feudalism. The Chinese people's great leader Chairman Mao pointed out in 1939: "The history of China's transformation into a semi-colony and colony in collusion with Chinese feudalism is at the same time a history of the struggle against imperialism and its lackeys." (from p. 1)

The Treaty of Nanking was the first unequal treaty the British aggressors imposed upon China, and the first of the fetters which the foreign invaders laid on the Chinese people. It marked the beginning of the impairment of China's sovereignty, the forcing open of its markets, and its transition from a feudal society to a semi-colonial and colonial society. From that time on, imperialism and feudalism in collaboration intensified their enslavement and exploitation of the Chinese people while the great Chinese people waged a brave, protracted struggle against their domestic and foreign enemies. (from pp. 96–97)

China's defeat in the Opium War and the conclusion of the Treaty of Nanking had enormous consequences, as from then on China had lost its independence and significant changes occurred within its society.... Chairman Mao has pointed out: "Foreign capitalism played an important part in the disintegration of China's social economy; on the one hand, it undermined the foundations of her self-sufficient natural economy and wrecked the handicraft industries both in the cities and in the peasants" homes, and on the other, it hastened the growth of a commodity economy in town and country" (from pp. 110–111).

Appendix V: Selected Wade-Giles/ Hanyu Pinyin Equivalents

Wade-Giles   *Hanyu Pinyin*

People

Ch'ien Lung (Emperor) .... Qianlong
Confucius (philosopher and teacher) .... Kong Fuzi
Howqua (Cohong merchant; also spelled Houqua) ..... Wu Bingjian
Lin Tse-hsü (Imperial Commissioner) .... Lin Zexu
Mao Tse-tung (Chairman of the Chinese
    Communist Party) .... Mao Zedong
Tzu-hsi (Dowager Empress) .... Ci Xi

Places

Amoy (also spelled Hsia-men) .... Xiamen
Canton .... Guangzhou
Chinkiang .... Jinjiang
Chuenpi (also spelled Chuenpee, Ch'uan-pi) .... Chuanbi
Chusan .... Zhoushan

Chapu	Zhapu
Foochow	Fuzhou
Fukien	Fujian
Hankow	Hankou
Hong Kong	Xianggang
Kwangtung	Guangdong
Lintin	Lingding
Nanking	Nanjing
Ningpo	Ningbo
Peiho (also spelled Pei-ho)	Hai
Peking	Beijing
Szechuan	Sichuan
Taku	Dagu
Tientsin	Tianjin
Whampoa	Huangpu
Wusung (also spelled Woosung)	Wusong

Miscellaneous

Ch'ing (dynasty)	Qing
Cohong (group of merchants; also spelled kung hang, kung hong)	gonghang
hong (merchant)	hang
feng-shui (influence of natural surroundings on people and buildings)	fengshui

Bibliography

Aberigh-Mackay, G. R. *The Chiefs of Central India.* 2 vols. Calcutta: Thacket and Spink, 1878.
Alexander, Major-General R. *The Rise and Progress of British Opium Smuggling.* London: Seeley, Jackson and Halliday, 1856.
Allen, Nathan. *The Opium Trade.* 2d ed. Lowell, Mass., 1853.
Anderson, Lindsay. *A Cruise in an Opium Clipper.* London: George Allen & Unwin, 1935.
_____. *Among Typhoons and Pirate Craft.* London: Chapman and Hall, 1892.
Anglo-Oriental Society for the Suppression of the Opium Trade. *The Opium Traffic Between India and China.* London: Dyer, 1880.
Arlington, L. C., and Lewisohn, William. *In Search of Old Peking.* New York: Oxford University Press, 1987.
Beeching, Jack. *The Chinese Opium Wars.* London: Hutchinson, 1975.
Bernard, W. D. *Narrative of the Voyages and Services of the Nemesis, from 1840 to 1843.* 2 vols. London: Colburn, 1844.
Bingham, Commander J. Elliot, RN. *Narrative of the Expedition to China.* 2 vols. London: Colburn, 1843.
Blackburn, Graham. *The Illustrated Dictionary of Nautical Terms.* Newton Abbot (Devon): David & Charles, 1982.
Blakiston, Thomas W. *Five Months on the Yang-Tsze.* London: Murray, 1862.
Bland, J.O.P., and Backhouse, E. *China Under the Empress Dowager.* London: Heinemann, 1910.
Booth, Martin. *Opium: A History.* London: Simon and Schuster, 1996.
Bowen, Frank C. *America Sails the Seas: The History and Romance of America on the High Seas from the 15th to the 19th Century.* New York: McBride, 1938.

Bramah, Edward. *Guide to the Bramah Tea & Coffee Museum*. London: privately published, no date.
Brown, Edward. *A Seaman's Narrative of His Adventures During a Captivity Among Chinese Pirates*. London: Westerton, 1861.
Campbell, George F. *China Tea Clippers*. London: Adlard Coles, 1985.
Canton Register, a shipping newsletter printed in Canton from about 1837 to 1841.
"Canton Trade and the Opium War," in *Cambridge History of China*, vol. 10, pp. 155–173. Cambridge: Cambridge University Press, 1985.
Chapelle, Howard Irving. *The Baltimore Clipper: Its Origin and Development*. New York: Dover, 1988.
———. *The Search for Speed Under Sail 1700–1855*. London: Allen & Unwin, 1968.
———. *The History of the American Sailing Navy: The Ships and Their Development*. New York: Norton, 1949.
———. *The History of American Sailing Ships*. London: Putnam, 1936.
Ch'en, Jerome. *China and the West: Society and Culture 1815–1937*. Bloomington: Indiana University Press, 1979.
Cheong, W. E. *Mandarins and Merchants: Jardine Matheson & Co., a China Agency of the Early Nineteenth Century*. Scandinavian Institute of Asian Studies Monograph Series No. 26, London: Curzon, 1979.
Chin, P. C. *The Life History of a Tropical Cyclone*. Hong Kong: Royal Observatory, 1977.
China; as it was, and as it now is: with a Glance and the Tea and Opium Trades. Author anonymous. London: Cradock, 1842.
China Pilot. 2d ed. London: Hydrographic Office, 1858.
The China Sea Directory. Vol. 1, London: Hydrographic Office, 1867.
The China Sea Directory. Supplement. London: Hydrographic Office, 1876.
The Chinese Repository [an English-language periodical published in Canton from 1832–1851].
Clark, Arthur H. *The Clipper Ship Era*. New York: Putnam, 1911.
Clemens, Samuel L. [Mark Twain]. *Life on the Mississippi*. New York: Penguin, 1986.
Coates, W. H. *The Old "Country Trade" of the East Indies*. London: Imray, Laurie, Norie & Wilson, 1911.
———. *The Good Old Days of Shipping*. Bombay: Times of India Press, 1900.
Collis, Maurice. *Foreign Mud*. London: Faber and Faber, 1964.
Conrad, Joseph. *The Nigger of the "Narcissus," Typhoon, Falk and Other Stories*. London: Dent, 1974.
Cooper, Arthur (trans.) *Li Po and Tu Fu*. Harmondsworth: Penguin, 1973.
Cordingly, David, and Falconer, John. *Pirates: Fact & Fiction*. London: Collins & Brown, 1992.
Country Life Book of Nautical Terms Under Sail. London: Trewin Copplestone, 1978.
Crisis in the Opium Traffic: Being an Account of the Proceedings of the Chinese Government to Suppress That Trade. Canton, 1839.

Cumberlege, Claude. *Master Mariner*. London: Davies, 1936.
Cutler, Carl C. *Greyhounds of the Sea: The Story of the American Clipper Ship*. Northants, Wellingborough, 1930.
Dalrymple, Alexander. *Memoir Concerning the Pirates of the Coast of China; Supplement to the Memoir; and Memoir Concerning the Passages to and from China, June 1782*. London: Ballantine, 1806.
Dana, Richard Henry, Jr. *Two Years Before the Mast*. New York: Harper, 1840.
_____. *The Seaman's Friend*. London: Moxon, 1863.
Danton, George H. *The Culture Contacts of the United States and China*. New York: Columbia University Press, 1931.
Davis, George. *Recollections of a Sea Wanderer's Life*. New York: Kellog, 1887.
Davis, John Francis. *Sketches of China*. 2 vols. London: Knight, 1841.
_____. *The Chinese: A General Description of China and Its Inhabitants*. 3 vols. London: Knight, 1844.
_____. *China During the War and Since the Peace*.
2 vols. London: Longman, Brown, Green and Longmans, 1852.
_____. *China*. 2 vols. London: Murray, 1857.
De Quincey, Thomas. *Confessions of an English Opium Eater, 1822*. Oxford: Woodstock, 1989.
Downing, C. Toogood. *The Fan-Qui in China in 1836-7*. 3 vols. London: Henry Colburn, 1838.
Downs, Jacques M. "Fair Game: Exploitive Role-Myths and the American Opium Trade." In *Pacific Historical Review* (May 1972).
_____. *The Golden Ghetto: The American Commercial Community at Canton and the Shaping of American China Policy, 1784-1844*. Bethlehem: Lehigh University Press, 1997.
Dudden, Arthur Power. *The American Pacific: From the Old China Trade to the Present*. New York: Oxford University Press, 1992.
East India Company. *Collections of the Board of the East India Company*. Vol. 59, 1799-1800.
Eberhard, Wolfram. *A History of China*. 4th ed. Berkeley: University of California Press, 1977.
Edwards, J. Passmore. *The Triple Curse: The Evils of the Opium Traffic on India, China and England*. London: Judd, Glass, 1858.
Eitel, Ernest J. *Feng-Shui*. Singapore: Brash, 1985.
Epstein, Israel. *From Opium War to Liberation*. 3d ed. Hong Kong: Joint Publishing Co., 1980.
Excerpts from Three Classical Chinese Novels. Beijing, China: Panda, 1984.
Fairbank, John King. *Trade and Diplomacy on the China Coast*. 2 vols. Cambridge: Harvard University Press, 1953.
Falconer's Marine Dictionary. London: Cadell and Davies, 1830.
Fay, Peter Ward. *The Opium War, 1840-1842*. Chapel Hill: University of North Carolina Press, 1975.
Finch, Roger. "Descriptive notes" in facsimile edition of E. W. Cooke's *Shipping and Craft*. London: Masthead, 1970.
Fincham, John. *A History of Naval Architecture*. London: Whittaker, 1851.

Findlay, Alexander George. *A Directory for the Navigation of the Indian Ocean.* 4th ed. London: Laurie, 1882.
Forbes, Robert Bennet. *Personal Reminiscences.* 3d ed. Boston: Little, Brown, 1892.
_____. *Remarks on China and the China Trade.* Boston: Dickinson, 1844.
Fox, Grace. *British Admirals and Chinese Pirates.* London: Kegan Paul, Trench, Trubner, 1940.
Franke, Wolfgang. *A Century of Chinese Revolution, 1851-1949.* Columbia: University of South Carolina Press, 1980.
Fraser, George MacDonald. *Flashman and the Dragon.* London: HarperCollins, 1994.
The Friend of China: The Organ of the Anglo-Oriental Society for the Suppression of the Opium Trade. London: King, 1875.
Fry, William Stone. *Facts and Evidence Relating to the Opium Trade with China.* London: Pelham Richardson, 1840.
Fung Yu-lan. *A Short History of Chinese Philosophy.* New York: Macmillan, 1948.
Gardella, Robert. *Harvesting Mountains: Fujian and the China Tea Trade 1757–1937.* Berkeley: University of California Press, 1994.
Gardiner, Robert (ed.). *Sail's Last Century: The Merchant Sailing Ship 1830–1930.* London: Conway, 1993.
_____. *The Advent of Steam: The Merchant Steamship Before 1900.* London: Conway, 1993.
Gibson, James R. *Otter Skins, Boston Ships, and China Goods: The Maritime Fur Trade of the Northwest Coast, 1785–1841.* Montreal: McGill-Queen's University Press, 1992.
Gill, Claude S. *The Old Wooden Walls.* London: Foyle, 1930.
Gillmer, Thomas C., and Johnson, Bruce. *Introduction to Naval Architecture.* Annapolis: Naval Institute Press, 1982.
Glasspoole, Richard (Owen Rutter, ed.). *Mr. Glasspoole and the China Pirates.* Golden Cockrell Press, 1935.
Graham, Alexander. *The Right, Obligation, and Interest of the Government of Great Britain to Require Redress from the Government of China for the Late Forced Surrender of British-Owned Opium at Canton.* Glasgow: Stuart, 1840.
Greenberg, Michael. *British Trade and the Opening of China 1800–1842.* Cambridge: Cambridge University Press, 1951.
Greenhill, Basil. *The Merchant Schooners.* London: Conway, 1988.
Hao, Yen-p'ing. *The Commercial Revolution in Nineteenth-Century China.* Berkeley: University of California Press, 1986.
Hehir, Patrick. *Opium: Its Physical, Moral and Social Effects.* London: Balliere, Tindall & Cox, 1894.
Hewson, Cdr. J.B. *A History of the Practice of Navigation.* Glasgow: Brown, Son and Ferguson, 1951.
Hibbert, Christopher. *The Dragon Wakes: China and the West, 1793–1911.* Middlesex: Penguin, 1984.
Hill, J. Spencer. *The Indo-Chinese Opium Trade.* London: Frowde, 1884.
Hobsbawm, Eric. *The Age of Capital.* London: Weidenfeld & Nicholson, 1996.
_____. *The Age of Revolution, 1789–1848.* London: Weidenfeld & Nicholson, 1962.

Holt, Edgar Crawshaw. *The Opium Wars in China*. London: Putnam, 1964.
HongKong [sic] Shipping List, various nineteenth-century dates.
Hooker, Mary. *Behind the Scenes in Peking*. Hong Kong: Oxford University Press, 1987.
Horsburgh, James. *The India Directory*. 7th ed. 2 vols. London: Allen, 1855.
Hosie, Alexander. *On the Trail of the Opium Poppy: A Narrative of Travel in the Chief Opium-Growing Provinces of China*. 2 vols. London: George, Philip, 1914.
Hsu, Immanuel Chung Yueh. *The Rise of Modern China*. Oxford: Oxford University Press, 1970.
Hunter, William C. *Bits of Old China*. London: Kegan, Paul, Trench, 1885.
H. W. C. [Hunter, William C.] *The "Fan Kwae" at Canton*. London: Kegan, Paul, 1882.
"The Impact of Western Power and Wealth 1860–95." In *The Cambridge History of China*. Vol. 11 (1800–1911). p. 156.
Imray, James F. *Indian Ocean Pilot*. London: Imray, 1886.
Inglis, Brian. *The Opium War*. London: Hodder & Stoughton, 1976.
International Chamber of Shipping. Oil Companies International Marine Forum. *Malacca/Singapore Straits: Guide to Planned Passages for Deep Draught Vessels*. Revised ed. London: Witherby, 1981.
International Opium Commission. *Report of the Proceedings and Report of the Delegations*. 2 vols. Shanghai, 1909.
Jackson, Stanley. *The Sassoons: Portrait of a Dynasty*. London: Heinemann, 1989.
Jardine, William. Private Letter Book. Jardine Matheson archives.
Jardine Matheson & Company. *Jardine, Matheson & Company: An Historical Sketch*. Hong Kong: Jardine Matheson, 1960.
Jardine Matheson Archives, unpublished documents held by the Cambridge University Library, Cambridge, United Kingdom.
Jardine Matheson Holdings Limited, *Group Profile, 1997 Annual Report* and *1997 Annual Results Presentation*.
Jeffereys, Julius. *The British Army in India*. London: Longmans, 1858.
Johnson, Robert Erwin. *Far China Station: The U.S. Navy in Asian Waters, 1800–1898*. Annapolis: Naval Institute Press, 1979.
Keay, John. *The Honourable Company: A History of the East India Company*. London: HarperCollins, 1991.
Kennedy, Admiral Sir William. *Hurrah for the Life of a Sailor*. London: Blackwood, 1900.
Kerr, Phyllis Forbes (ed.). *Letters from China: The Canton-Boston Correspondence of Robert Bennet Forbes, 1838–1840*. Mystic Seaport: Mystic, Conn., 1996.
Keswick, Maggie (ed.). *The Thistle and the Jade: A Celebration of 150 Years of Jardine, Matheson & Co*. London: Octopus, 1982.
Kuo Tze-hsiung. "Opium Suppression in China." In *Information Bulletin*. Nanking: Council of International Affairs, vol. 1. no. 9, August 1, 1936.
Lay, G. Tradescent. *The Chinese As They Are*. Albany: Jones, 1843.
Layton, Thomas N. *The Voyage of the 'Frolic': New England Merchants and the Opium Trade*. Stanford: Stanford University Press, 1997.

Leavenworth, Charles S. *The Arrow War with China.* London: Sampson, Low, Marston, 1901.
Li Ruzhen. "Flowers in the Mirror," in *Excerpts from Three Classical Chinese Novels*, trans. by Yang Xianyi and Gladys Yang. Beijing: Panda, 1984.
Lindsay, H. Hamilton. *Is the War with China a Just One?* London: Ridgway, 1840.
_____ and Gützlaff, Rev. Karl. *A Voyage to the Northern Ports of China.* London: Fellowes, 1833.
London, Jack. *The Sea-Wolf and Other Stories.* London: Penguin, 1989.
Low, Captain Charles P. *Some Recollections Commanding the Clipper Ships "Houqua," "Jacob Bell," "Samuel Russell," and "N.B. Palmer,"* in *The China Trade, 1847–1873.* Boston: Ellis, 1905.
Lubbock, Basil. *The Opium Clippers.* Glasgow: Brown, Son and Ferguson, 1933.
_____. *The China Clippers.* 4th ed. Glasgow: James Brown, 1919.
MacGregor, David R. *The Tea Clippers: Their History and Development, 1833–1875.* London: Conway, 1984.
_____. *Square Rigged Sailing Ships.* Watford, Herts.: Argus, 1977.
_____. *Fast Sailing Ships: Their Design and Construction, 1775–1875.* Lymington: Nautical, 1973.
Mackenzie, Keith Stewart. *Narrative of the Second Campaign in China.* London: Bentley, 1842.
Martin, R. Montgomery. *Opium in China, Extracted from China; Political, Commercial, and Social.* 2 vols. London: Madden, 1847.
Matheson, Donald. *What Is the Opium Trade?* Edinburgh: Constable, 1857.
Matheson, James. *The Present Position and Prospects of the British Trade with China.* London: no publisher given, 1836.
_____. Private Letter Book. Jardine Matheson archives.
May, Ernest R., and Fairbank, John K. (eds.). *America's China Trade in Historical Perspective: The Chinese and American Performance.* Cambridge: Harvard University Press, 1986.
McKay, Richard C. *Some Famous Sailing Ships and Their Builder, Donald McKay.* New York: Putnam, 1928.
Mellersh, Admiral Arthur, unpublished correspondence held by the National Maritime Museum, Greenwich, United Kingdom.
Melville, Herman. *Moby Dick.* New York: New American Library, 1961.
Milburn, William. *Oriental Commerce.* London: Kingsbury, Parbury, and Allen, 1825.
Miyazaki, Ichisada (Conrad Schirokauer, trans.). *China's Examination Hell: The Civil Service Examinations of Imperial China.* New Haven: Yale University Press, 1981.
Morgan, Joseph R., and Valencia, Mark J. *Atlas for Marine Policy in Southeast Asian Seas.* Berkley: University of California Press, 1983.
Morison, Samuel Eliot. *The Maritime History of Massachusetts.* Boston: Houghton Mifflin, 1941.
Morrison, Hedda. *A Photographer in Old Peking.* Hong Kong: Oxford University Press, 1985.
Morrison, John Robert. *A Chinese Commercial Guide.* Canton: Albion Press, 1834.

Morse, Hosea Ballou. *The Chronicles of the East India Company Trading to China, 1635–1834. 5 vols.* Oxford: Clarendon Press, 1926.
_____. *The International Relations of the Chinese Empire*. 2 vols. London: Longmans, Green, 1910.
_____. *The Trade and Administrative Structure of the Chinese Empire*. London: Longmans, Green, 1908.
Murray, Lieut. Alexander. *Doings in China*. London: Bentley, 1843.
Murray, Dian H. *Pirates of the South China Coast, 1790–1810*. Stanford: Stanford University Press, 1987.
Notices Concerning China and the Port of Canton, Malacca: Mission Press, 1823.
Nye, Gideon. *The Morning of My Life in China*. Canton, 1973.
The Opium Revenue of India. London: Allen, 1857.
The Opium War. Peking: Foreign Language Press, 1976.
"The Opium War" in *The History of Modern China*. Peking: 1976.
Ouchterlony, John. *The Chinese War: An Account of All the Operations of the British Forces from the Commencement to the Treaty of Nanking*. London: Saunders and Otley, 1844.
Owen, David Edward. *British Opium Policy in China and India*. New Haven: Yale University Press, 1934.
Paasch, H. *Illustrated Marine Encyclopedia*. Antwerp, 1890.
Peggs, James. *A Voice from China and India, Relative to the Evils of the Cultivation and Smuggling of Opium*. London: Harvey and Darton, 1846.
Perry, Frederick. *Fair Winds and Foul: A Narrative of Daily Life Aboard an American Clipper Ship*. London: Hopkinson, 1925.
Phipps, John. *A Practical Treatise on the China and Eastern Trade*. London: Allen, 1836.
Polo, Marco. *The Travels*. Ronald Latham (trans.). Harmondsworth: Penguin, 1958.
Raper, Henry. *The Practice of Navigation and Nautical Astronomy*. 3rd ed. London: Bate, 1849.
Rosser, W. H. *Short Notes on the Winds, Weather, & Currents, Together with General Sailing Directions and Remarks on Making Passages; To Accompany Charts of the China Sea, Indian Archipelago & Western Pacific*. London: Imray, 1868.
Rupture with China, and Its Causes ... in a letter to Lord Palmerston, Secretary Foreign Affairs, By a Resident in China. London: Sherwood, Gilbert & Piper, 1840.
Seidmann, Gertrud. "Opium." *Journal of the British Royal Society for the encouragement of Arts, Manufactures & Commerce* (November/December 1997).
Shen Fu. *Six Records of a Floating Life*. London: Penguin, 1983.
Ship *Thames*, unpublished Log held by the National Maritime Museum, Greenwich, United Kingdom.
"Sin Tauka" (pseud.), F. C. Jarrett (ed.). *Jottings from the Log of a New South Welshman, or, Six Years in the Opium Trade*. Sidney: Gibbs, Shallard, 1867.
Sirr, Henry Charles. *China and the Chinese*. 2 vols. London: Orr, 1849.
Smyth, Admiral W. H. *The Sailor's Word-Book*. London: Blackie, 1876.

Some Pros and Cons of the Opium Question; with a Few Suggestions Regarding British Claims on China. London: Smith, Elder. 1840.

Souza, George Bryan. *The Survival of Empire: Portuguese Trade and Society in China and the South China Sea 1630–1754.* Cambridge: Cambridge University Press, 1986.

Spence, Jonathan D. *The Search for Modern China.* London: Hutchinson, 1990.

Spratt, H. Philip. *Transatlantic Paddle Steamers.* 2nd ed. Glasgow: Brown, Son and Ferguson, 1980.

Stelle, Charles Clarkson. *Americans and the China Opium Trade in the Nineteenth Century.* New York: Arno Press, 1981.

Sutton, Jean. *Lords of the East: The East India Company and Its Ships.* London: Conway Maritime Press, 1981.

Svensson, Sam. *Sails Through the Centuries.* London: Macmillan, 1965.

Tan Chung. *China and the Brave New World: A Study of the Origins of the Opium War (1840–42).* New Delhi: Allied Publishers, 1978.

Taylor, W. Cooke. *A Popular History of British India, Commercial Intercourse with China, and the Insular Possessions of England in the Eastern Seas.* London: Madden, 1842.

Thompson, Joseph. *Considerations Respecting the Trade with China.* London: Allen, 1835.

Tuchman, Barbara W. *Sand Against the Wind: Stillwell and the American Experience in China, 1922–1945.* London: Futura, 1981.

Turner, F. S. *British Opium Policy and Its Results to India and China.* London: Sampson, Low, Marston, Searle and Rivington, 1876.

Turner, J. A. *Kwang Tung or Five Years in South China.* Oxford: Oxford University Press, 1982.

Twain, Mark. *Life on the Mississippi.* New York: Viking Penguin, 1984.

Underhill, Harold A. *Deep-Water Sail.* Glasgow: Brown, Son and Ferguson, 1963.

_____. *Masting and Rigging: The Clipper Ship and Ocean Carrier.* Glasgow: Brown, Son and Ferguson, 1946.

United States Department of Health, Education and Welfare. "Opium in China," in *Perspectives on the History of Psychoactive Substance Use.* Washington: USDHEW, 1978, pp. 134–140.

Van Ours, Jan C. *The Price Elasticity of Hard Drugs: The Case of Opium in the Dutch East Indies, 1923–1938.* Rotterdam: Erasmus University, 1995.

Villiers, Alan. *Monsoon Seas: The Story of the Indian Ocean.* New York: McGraw-Hill, 1952.

_____. *Voyaging with the Wind: An Introduction to Sailing Large Square-Rigged Ships.* London: Her Majesty's Stationery Office, 1975.

Wakeman, Frederic. "The Canton Trade in the Opium War." In *The Cambridge History of China.* (1976), Vol. 10, Part I, pp. 163–212.

Waley, Arthur David. *The Opium War through Chinese Eyes.* London: Allen & Unwin, 1958.

Watts, Alan. "The Meteorology of Heavy Weather." In Coles, K. Adlard, and Bruce, Peter. *Heavy Weather Sailing.* 4th ed. London: Adlard Coles Nautical, 1991.

Waung, W. S. K. *The Controversy: Opium and Sino-British Relations, 1858–1887.* Hong Kong: Lung Men Press, 1977.

White, Walter. *China Station 1859–1864: The Reminiscences of Walter White.* Greenwich: National Maritime Museum Monographs and Reports No. 3, 1972.

_____. *A Sailor-Boy's Log Book: From Portsmouth to the Peiho.* London: Chapman and Hall, 1862.

Wilkinson, George. *Sketches of Chinese Customs & Manners, in 1811–12.* Bath: Brown, 1814.

Williams, S. Wells. *A Chinese Commercial Guide.* 4th ed. Canton: Office of the Chinese Repository, 1856.

_____. *A History of China.* London: Sampson, Low, Marston, 1897.

_____. *The Middle Kingdom.* 2 vols. New York: Wiley, 1879.

Williamson, Captain A. R. *Eastern Traders: Some Men and Ships of Jardine, Matheson & Company.* London: privately printed, 1975.

Wiltshire, Tia. *Hong Kong—Last Prize of Empire.* Hong Kong: Form Asia, c. 1990.

Winius, George D., and Vink, Marcus P. M. *The Merchant-Warrior Pacified: The VOC (The Dutch East India Company) and Its Changing Political Economy in India.* New Delhi: Oxford University Press, 1994.

Winton, John. *Hurrah for the Life of a Sailor! Life on the Lower-deck of the Victorian Navy.* London: Michael Joseph, 1977.

Wise, Henry. *An Analysis of One Hundred Voyages To and From India [and] China.* London: Norie and Allen, 1839.

Worcester, G. R. G. *Sail and Sweep in China.* London: Her Majesty's Stationary Office, 1966.

Yung Lun-Yen (Charles F. Neumann, trans.). *History of the Pirates Who Infested the China Sea, from 1807 to 1810.* London: Oriental Translation Fund, 1831.

Index

Alert 11, 16, 82
Alligator 142
America 9
Amsterdam 78–79
Anderson, Lindsay 21, 23, 34, 90–91, 144–145
Anglona 84–85
Ann McKim 84
Anonyma 154, 155
Antelope 12, 154, 88–89, 205–206
Antiopium lobby (Chinese) 100
Antiopium lobby (Western) 178–183
Ariel (American opium clipper) 12, 85
Ariel (British tea clipper) 176
Arrow 100, 105
Augustine Heard and Co. 85, 89–90, 171, 172, 173
Ayacucho 82

Balclutha 12
Black Joke 140
Blake, Commander P.J. 158–159, 162–163
Blonde 113
Bombay Castle 172
Boxer Rebellion 191–192
Bremer, Sir Gordon 153–154
Brent, Right Reverend Charles H. 181, 182
Brown, Edward 142–144
Buckinghamshire 134

Cairngorm 176
Canada 170
Canton 141
Canton Register 9
Castle Huntley 158
Challenger 165
Chang Paou 135–136, 137
Charles W. Morgan 11
Chefoo Convention 180
Chevy Chase 173
China Coast Steam Navigation Company 173
China Merchants Steam Navigation Company 172
China Pilot 153, 155–156, 162, 164
The China Sea Directory 163
Chinese Communist Party 29, 190, 192, 194, 195
The Chinese Repository 142, 187
Ching Ah-'ling 143
Ching-Chi-ling 132
Ching Shih 135, 136, 137
Ching Yih 134–135
Ching Yih Saou 135
Chiu Appo 141
Christopher Lawson 162

Index

Citizen 13
Clifton, Captain William 85–86
Clive 88
Cohong 48–49, 186
Colonel Young 92, 138
Columbine 141
Comanjee Hormusjee 92
Complete East India Pilot 160–161
Confucius, teachings of 43–44, 45, 48, 49, 53, 174
Conrad, Joseph 11, 12, 15, 151–152
Convention of Chuenpi 116, 123
Coromandel 142
"country" ships 75–77
Cowasjee and Co. 85
cumsha 6
Cutty Sark 11–12, 176, 177

Dalrymple, Alexander 132
Dana, Richard Henry 11, 14, 16, 19, 82, 83, 89
Dansborg 13
Davis, George 140–141
Dent and Co. 85, 91, 93, 105, 173
de Quincey, Thomas 26, 33
Dhaulle 84, 85
Diana 158
Don Manuel 13
Downing, Toogood 83, 91–92, 95–96
Dumaresq, Captain Philip 89

Eagle 23–24, 95
Eamont 21, 23, 34, 90-91, 144–145
East India Company 35–37, 49, 51, 52, 75, 78, 80, 81, 88, 132, 134, 158, 160, 173, 174, 175
East Indiamen 24, 76, 78–81, 92, 175
Edinburgh 170
Elliot, Captain Charles 99, 113, 116, 117–118, 153–154
Empress of China 175
Encounter 163
Entan 84
Ewan 12
examinations, civil service 42–48, 53, 188
extraterritoriality 186, 192, 194

Fairy 81, 92, 138–139
Falcon 87–88, 199–203

Faucon, Captain Edward Horatio 89, 90, 164, 171
Fiery Cross 173
Forbes 169
Forbes, Captain Robert Bennet 7, 18, 23, 85, 89, 116
Frolic 12, 13, 17, 89–90, 164, 171
Funter, Robert 132–133
Fury 141, 155

Ganges 172
Gazelle 12, 13, 140–141, 154, 155
General Quiroga 13
Glasspoole, Richard 134, 136
Governor Findlay 93
Gützlaff, The Reverend Karl 7, 92

Harriet 94
Hay, Commander C. Dalrymple 141
Heard, John 171
Hellas 139
Hill, J. Spencer 179
Hormujee, B. and A. and Co. 171
Horsburgh, James 160, 166
Houqua 156–157, 164
Hunter, William C. 77, 93

Indian Ocean Pilot 161
Indo China Steam Navigation Company 173
Innes, James 7
International Opium Commission 181–182

Jamesina 23, 169–170
Japanese aggression against China 190–191
Jardine 170
Jardine, Andrew 20
Jardine, William 87, 138
Jardine Matheson 1, 3, 4, 17, 24, 81, 84, 85, 87, 92, 93, 94, 100, 104, 138, 145, 154, 170, 173, 175, 176, 178, 199
John Bright 172
junks 88, 89, 93, 95–96, 109–110, 120, 133–134, 135, 143, 144, 145, 147, 153

Kennedy, Midshipman William 125–126
Khooshalchund, Kessressung 171–172

Index

Kim-quan-seng 144
Koxinga 132
Kwan, Admiral 110–111, 124
Kwo Pow Tai 137

Lady Grant 12
Lady Mary Wood 172
Lancefield 173
Lanrick 84
Larne 158, 162
lascars 13
laudanum 26
Leebow 132–133
Letitia 13
likin 180, 184
Lin Tse-hsü, Commissioner 6, 28, 47, 54, 99–100, 104, 107, 108, 110, 121, 181, 186
Lintin 23
Lipton, Sir Thomas 176
London, Jack 11, 14
lorcha 10, 100, 143
Louisa 10, 153–154
Low, Captain Charles 156–157, 164
Lubbock, Basil 3, 4, 12, 13, 199, 205
Ly-ee-Moon 173

MacKay, Captain 138
Malakoff 157
Mandate of Heaven 42, 187
Mao Tse-tung 190, 196, 207, 208
Mariners Hope 164
Marquis of Ely 134
Martin, Montgomery 84
Matheson, Donald 1
Matheson, Hugh 88
Matheson, James 27, 28, 81, 139–140
Mellersh, Arthur 142
Melville, Herman 11, 13, 162
Moby Dick 11, 13, 162
monsoons 158–159
most-favored-nation policy 186

navigation, hazards to and limits of 159–165
N.B. Palmer 164
Nemesis 111, 112, 114, 123
Norie, J.W 160–161

Ohio 133

"Old Buddha" 187–188, 190, 192, 195
Olyphant and Co. 7
Omega 93
opium: addiction 26–28, 33–34, 51–52, 182; British policy 6–7; Chinese ships involved in the trade 94–96; clippers 81–91; coasters 92–94; complicity of Chinese officials 93–94; end of the trade 178–183; financing the trade 23, 39, 50–51, 115, 172, 173–174, 178; legality or illegality of the trade 5–7; medicinal uses 24, 26, 34–35, 39–40; overview of the trade 1; physical and chemical properties 31–33; production in China 178, 182, 183; production in India 36–39, 178; receiving ships 91–92; role in Opium Wars 101–103; Royal Commission on the opium trade 179–180; smoking opium 40–42
Opium Wars 1, 5, 7, 28, 42, 47, 50, 81, 88, 96, 99–128, 142–143, 175, 176, 178, 186–187, 188, 189, 192–193, 207–208
Oriental 175

Pantaloon 155
Pearl (brig) 116
Pearl (cutter) 145–146
Peking Convention 106
Peninsular and Oriental (P&O) Line 172
Pequod 13
Phlegethon 141
Pilgrim 11, 12, 14, 82
pirates 93, 95, 109, 131–148
Punch 144
Pylades 139

Qing Dynasty 45, 46, 106–107, 125, 187, 188, 189, 190, 193

Rainbow 175
Red Rover 85–87, 88
Rees, Captain J. 138
Reiver 173
Rifleman 162
Rockliffe 154
Roosevelt, Theodore 181

Rose 92–94
La Rose 13
Russell and Co. 23, 24, 85, 87
Rustomjee Cowasjee 76, 160
Rustomjee, D & M & Co. 140

Sailing Directions 131, 163
Sailing Directions for the Coast of China 142
Salamander 83
Sassoon, David and Sons 178, 180
Serica 176
Shaftesbury, Earl of 178, 179
Shap-'ng-tsai 141–142
Shillaber, John 138
ships and crews 8–16, 75–96
Shunloi 143
Silver currencies 16–18, 20
"Sin Tauka" 145–147, 157
Sin Tauka 145, 157
Sir Charles Forbes 171
Sirius 170
Smyrna 154
Sovereign of the Seas 163, 170
Spider 12
steamers 169–193
stink-pots 110, 134, 143
Summer Palace 106, 127–128, 188
Sun Yat Sen 189–190
sycee silver 17, 115
Sylph (American brig) 84
Sylph (Indian bark) 88

Taeping 176
Taiping Rebellion 6, 125, 129, 187
Tay 135

tea trade 28, 87, 173–178, 183
Thames 79–80
Tientsin, treaties negotiated at 105–106, 126, 186–187
Time 84
Torrington 83
Treaty of Nanking 104, 105, 106, 114, 116–117, 124–125, 185–186, 207, 208
treaty ports 1, 28, 186, 187, 189, 190
Troughton 137–138
Turner, John 135
Twain, Mark 15–16, 17
Two Years Before the Mast 11, 84–84, 89
Typhoon 19, 151
typhoons 21, 151–158
Tzu-hsi *see* "Old Buddha"

"unequal" treaties 185–187, 207–208
United States 172

Vindex 83
Volage 120

Wellesley 121, 123, 153
Western ideas, impact of 189–190, 193–194, 195–196
Westerners, Chinese dislike of 42, 48–50, 53, 54–55
Wetmore and Co 7
White, Walter 127
Wild Dayrell 91
Wise, Captain Henry 170
Witch of the Wave 176

Yang-Tsze 173